Understanding SAP ERP Integration

A Guide to SAP TERP10 Certification

Viswa Viswanathan

Robert Szymanski

Infivista Inc.

PUBLISHED BY INFIVISTA INC.

ISBN-10: 194177301X

ISBN-13: 978-1-941773-01-7

First printing, June 2015

Contents

List of Figures

List of Tables

Preface

We wrote this book as an aid to students who are attending a TERP10 certification academy.

As certified instructors of the SAP TERP10 course, we have taught the course numerous times. In our judgment, most students find the course to be hard mainly because of their unfamiliarity with common business processes. The very comprehensive official course material from SAP is, understandably, written for an audience that is much more familiar with common business processes. The official course material focuses on the SAP way of addressing business processes.

When students without a reasonable understanding of common business processes attend a TERP10 academy, they face a lot of difficulty in understanding the course material. They find it very difficult to associate anything concrete with many of the common terms used – like *Sales Order*, *Transfer Requirement* and so on. As a result, students end up believing that they need to memorize lots of material in order to pass the certification examination. Given the vast amount of ground that the TERP10 course covers, passing by memorizing is not an option at all for anyone. Even if it were possible to pass by relying on rote memory, is that a desirable outcome?

Most instructors know that once we have a common-sense understanding of business processes and can provide concrete real-life associations for the terms used, then we can logically figure out answers to most questions without having to rely solely on memory.

We wrote this book to fill this need.

This book does not aim to replace the official course material; instead it is a complement to it. Ideally a student will read the relevant portion of the book **before** reading the corresponding portion of the official course material or before attending a related lecture. Armed with a solid understanding of the underlying business scenario and being familiar with the key terms, the students will get a lot out of the official material or the lecture.

We have used portions of this book in our own sessions and found them to be extremely useful. We hope that instructors and students who use this book have similar experiences.

The Big Picture

This book covers the core business processes and their realization within SAP. The book also emphasizes the integration of these business processes. We use the term *business process* very broadly to mean common organizational processes in businesses, governments and non-profit organizations. Although the sheer volume of material covered appears daunting, pure common sense can help us to navigate it quite easily. Much of the complexity actually arises from terminology.

You will encounter numerous terms, but as long as you can clearly associate the terms with common-sense business activities, you will progress smoothly through the material. In this chapter we provide a bird's-eye view of some of the important business processes and the associated SAP terms.

Study Strategy

The SAP course material (henceforth SAPCM) seems daunting just in terms of volume. Although very informative, you will probably not find the material to be self-contained. We have therefore created this book to help you navigate each unit of SAPCM. In this book, you will find different kinds of supporting material for each unit of the SAPCM. In this section we suggest a sequence of activities that will help you to best absorb each unit.

Figure 1 shows the suggested study strategy.

The following sections provide a whirlwind tour of some common business processes in manufacturing organizations. Along the way, we introduce some terms that we will encounter in later chapters as we delve deeper into these business processes. Be sure to memorize these terms and to connect them with real world business situations. Try to gain a com-

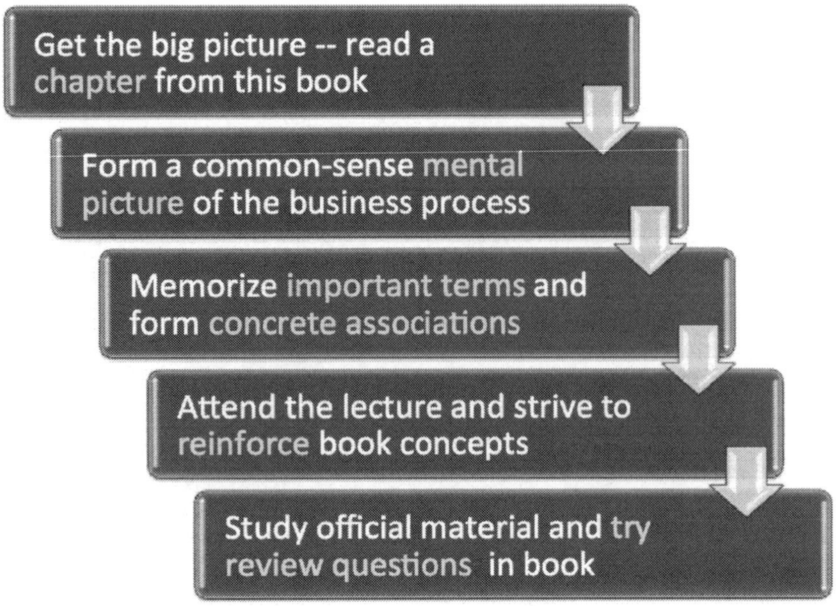

Figure 1: Study strategy for each chapter

mon sense understanding of what each term represents. As we introduce each term, we highlight it in the right margin.

Setting the stage

Manufacturing organizations purchase raw materials and convert them into finished products for sale. Such organizations need to plan carefully for materials to ensure that material availability meshes properly with production plans. Otherwise they may realize they are short of some of the required materials just as they are about to begin a production shift. That could be disastrous.

They cannot just play safe and have huge quantities of materials either – because that would mean holding a lot of inventory and incurring working capital costs. The material can also get spoiled or even go to waste if they decide to discontinue making some products. You can see how proper material planning plays a big role in profitability. With very stiff competition among companies, even a 2-3% increase in costs can hurt.

Importance of Material Planning

We consider a trivial example to unveil some of the main issues involved in *Material Planning*.

TablesRUs (TRUS) produces and sells study tables. TRUS

buys the legs and the top as raw materials, assembles them into tables and then paints them to ready them for sale. TRUS makes only one kind of table.

Sno	Material	Quantity	Units
1	Legs	4	nos
2	Top	1	no
3	Primer	2	liters
4	Paint	2	liters

Table 1: BOM for a TRUS study table

To make one table, they need:

- Four legs
- One top
- 2 liters of primer
- 2 liters of paint

We see a very simple list above because of our simplifying assumptions. The list would be more complex in more realistic situations.

Business organizations use the term *Bill of Materials* – or just *BOM* for short – to refer to such lists. Table 1 shows the BOM for a TRUS study table.

Bill of Materials or BOM

Manufacturing organizations deal with *raw materials* and *finished goods*. They use raw materials to make finished goods. SAP uses the generic term *material* to refer to raw materials and finished goods (as well as *trading goods*, which we will shortly encounter).

As Table 1 shows, a BOM for a material mentions the raw materials and the quantity of each one needed to manufacture or *assemble* the material. Materials that we make by putting together – or *assembling* – other materials are referred to as *assemblies*.

BOMs play an important role in determining how much of each material a company should buy (or make) while taking into account the production plans, current inventory, anticipated deliveries, how much time suppliers need to deliver the materials, and many other such factors. When companies deal with thousands of materials, the task becomes large and complex. Enterprise systems like SAP help companies to efficiently manage this complexity.

Sno	Material	Quantity	Units
1	B	3	nos
2	C	1	nos

Table 2: BOM for material A

Let us consider another example: to make one unit of a material A, we need 3 units of material B and one unit of material C.

However, in this example, material B itself is an *assembly*; to make one unit of material B we might require 2 units of material D and 5 units of material E. Let us assume that materials C and D and E are *atomic* and not assemblies – that is, we do not need to assemble any other parts to make materials C, D or E.

Sno	Material	Quantity	Units
1	D	2	nos
2	E	5	nos

Table 3: BOM for material B

The above example shows a *multi-level* BOM, that is, one in which materials that form a part of a BOM for one material could themselves be assemblies – and therefore have their own BOMs.

SAP uses the term BOM to mean exactly how we have used it here. However, BOM is a generic term used in industry and is not SAP specific.

The first set of review questions in this chapter appears below. You can find suggested answers to all the questions in this chapter starting from page 211.

> **Review 1:** Look around you and select an object. Make up a BOM for it.

> **Review 2:** If TRUS has to make 50 tables and already has 100 legs, 12 tops, 60 liters of primer and 80 liters of paint in inventory, how much of each material would it need to buy or *procure*?

> **Review 3:** Refer to tables 2 and 3. If we have to make 10 pieces of material A and have no stock of materials B, C, D and E, how much of each of these materials would we need to *procure*?

BOMs help in *material planning*. Let us also understand an important SAP-specific term that often goes along with BOMs – *Routing*.

Whereas a BOM specifies the materials and their quantities needed to make a product, a *Routing* specifies the operations to be carried out to make a finished product or assembly. Table 4 shows the routing for the study table.

Purchasing lead time

TRUS buys table legs and the tops from vendor Country Lumber, and primer and paint from vendor Village Depot. While purchasing these materials from vendors, let us suppose that the vendors cannot supply the materials immediately and

Table 4: Routing for TRUS table

Operation number	Description	Materials needed	Work center	Standard time
10	Fix legs to table	Top and 4 legs	Assembly area	20 minutes
20	Sand and apply primer	Primer	Finishing area	15 minutes
30	Paint	Paint	Finishing area	15 minutes
40	Dry	None	Finishing area	2 hours

that there is a delay between ordering these and their arrival at the factory. We refer to this delay as *Purchasing lead time.*

Lot size

Companies also do not usually buy items in arbitrary quantities. Instead they buy most materials in multiples of certain quantities called the *lot size*, which could differ from material to material. For example, it might be the case that TRUS has a lot size of 100 for legs. In this case, if the company needed 360 legs, it would buy four lots of 100 each. This represents an example of *fixed lot size.*

Table 5 shows the lead times and lot sizes for the materials that TRUS uses.

Table 5: Lead times and lot sizes for TRUS raw materials

Material	Vendor	Purchasing Lead time	Lot size
Legs	Country Lumber	1 month	100 nos
Tops	Country Lumber	2 months	25 nos
Primer	Village Depot	2 weeks	100 liters
Paint	Village Depot	3 weeks	50 liters

TRUS buys raw materials from these vendors regularly. To do so, TRUS places *Purchase Orders* with these vendors. Let us suppose that TRUS prints and sends out *Purchase Orders* by regular mail. Since TRUS does business regularly with several vendors, it might might be beneficial for them to be able to pull up vendor information on demand. Also assuming that TRUS uses a computerized system to generate the *Purchase Orders*, the program can pull relevant information about a vendor automatically. Some items of information that companies might store about their vendors include (among many others) Vendor name and Vendor address. Of course, companies need to maintain such information for all the vendors they do business with. Obviously the same situation applies to customers as well – companies maintain information about all their registered customers – same with materials and lots of other things.

Information Systems professionals refer to such information as *Master Records*. The master record for a specific vendor would thus be a *Vendor Master Record* for that particular vendor.

We refer to the collection of all vendor information as the *Vendor Master*. If a company does business with 1,000 vendors, then its Vendor Master would contain 1,000 *Vendor Master Records*, one for each vendor.

Vendor no	Vendor name	Vendor address	email	...	...	...
1	Country Lumber	100 Main st, ...	...	...	...	...
2	Village Depot	150 South Orange Ave, ...	...	...	...	...
3	Ace Hardware	95 Brooklyn street, ...	...	...	...	...
...	...	...	...	...	...	...

Table 6: Vendor Master containing Vendor Master Records, one per vendor

Similarly, companies maintain *Customer Masters* with *Customer Master Records* and *Material Masters* with *Material Master Records* and so on.

To generate a *Purchase Order*, TRUS would obviously need information about the materials that it wants to order. You can easily see that some of this information would come from the *Material Master Records* of the corresponding materials.

Thus far, we have talked about two different *types* of materials that TRUS deals with – the table that TRUS sells is a *Finished Good* while the materials that TRUS uses to make the table are *Raw Materials*. Sometimes companies do not manufacture any of the products that they sell – they simply buy from vendors and sell them to end customers without any additional processing. Amazon.com's book and digital media business is an example. WalMart would be another. Sometimes companies do both – that is, they make and sell some materials and also simply resell others. SAP refers to materials that a company simply buys and sells without further processing – that is, material that a company *trades* in – as *Trading Goods*.

Suppose TRUS, in addition to manufacturing and selling tables, also sold chairs, but did not manufacture them. Instead TRUS just buys chairs from another manufacturer and simply resells them (at a profit). In this case, we should not treat chairs as finished goods; these chairs represent *Trading Goods*.

The Material Master contains information for all three types of materials raw materials, finished goods and trading goods, one Material Master Record per individual material. If a company deals with 500 raw materials, 25 finished goods and 4 trading goods, its Material Master would contain 529 Material Master Records.

Incidentally, the BOM and routing for our finished product are also considered master data.

Review 4: Answer the following:

1. What information does a BOM contain?
2. What information does a routing contain?
3. What is purchasing lead time?
4. What is lot size?
5. How many different lot sizes have been mentioned in this document? What are they?
6. What is the name of the document that indicates to a vendor what materials and in what quantities we want to buy them?
7. Where is information about a particular material stored?
8. What is the name given to the entity that keeps information about all materials?
9. What contains information about a particular vendor?
10. What is the name given to the entity that keeps information about all vendors?
11. To store information about the vendors mentioned in Table 5, how many vendor master records would we need? Explain.
12. To store information about the materials mentioned in Table 1 as well as information about a TRUS table itself, how many material master records would we need? Explain
13. What *type* of material is a TRUS table?
14. What *type* of material is paint in the context of TRUS?
15. List the different types of materials discussed in this chapter.
16. What is a Trading Good?

Armed with this basic information about TRUS we can readily imagine the following business processes that would be absolutely essential for it to operate:

- purchasing raw materials (procurement cycle)
- producing finished products (manufacturing execution)
- selling finished products (sales order processing)

Would these processes alone suffice? Think of what else the company would need to do in order to function.

However, looking closer, we can see that, in addition to the above processes, TRUS also needs to perform various other activities. For example:

- **Sales and Operations Planning – SOP**: How much of finished goods should the company produce in various time periods – next week, the following week, and so on. TRUS will need to base this on several things:
  - forecasted demand for its products
  - finished goods already in stock
  - production capacity constraints
  - ...
- **Materials Requirement Planning – MRP**: Once TRUS has a *SOP*, it needs to then translate that into raw material requirements and prepare a plan for how much of each material to buy at specific times. In more complex situations companies may buy raw materials and create intermediate products or *sub-assemblies* that they then incorporate into their final products. In such cases, they would also need to plan when to make these *sub-assemblies* as well, and determine the timing and quantities of raw material purchases accordingly. When companies deal with many raw materials and finished products, all this can become too complex to track manually. Furthermore, these processes happen continuously with prior plans being changed often to accommodate changes in the environment.

Suppose for example, that TRUS needs to produce 140 study tables on March 31, and has nothing in stock – no raw materials and no finished goods. How much raw materials would they need to purchase and by when should the purchase orders be sent out to the vendors? Assume for simplicity that all of the tables will be made in one day and that we are concerned with planning for just that one day of production.

Review 5: Answer the following:

1. How many tables are to be made on March 31?
2. How many legs are needed?
3. How many tops are needed?
4. How many liters of primer are needed?
5. How many liters of paint are needed?
6. At the latest, when should they purchase order for legs go out?
7. How many legs should they order?
8. At the latest when should the purchase order for tops go out?
9. How many tops should they order?
10. At the latest when should the purchase order for primer go out?
11. How many liters of primer should we order?
12. At the latest when should the purchase order for paint go out?

Given a *BOM* for a material M – which could be a finished good or a subassembly – the process of finding out how much of various other materials we need for producing a certain quantity of M is called *BOM Explosion*. This might look trivial, but when we have complex BOMs with several levels of nesting and numerous materials, *BOM Explosion* can be tedious. Automating it can increase efficiency. When we consider that companies often make many finished goods, with several of them having at least some common raw materials and subassemblies, you can see how useful automated *BOM explosion* can be for *Materials Requirement Planning* or *MRP*.

BOM Explosion

Review 6: Answer the following. Try to give concrete examples wherever possible:

1. What is BOM explosion?
2. What is MRP? Don't just expand the acronym. Instead give a concrete example of your own.
3. In the TRUS case, what information should be considered when determining when a purchase order should be sent out?
4. What information determines the quantity of an item to be ordered?
5. In the TRUS case, all materials needed to produce a table are purchased from outside and therefore MRP only has to pro-

duce purchase documents. Suppose some of the parts to assemble a final table are themselves assembled in our own factory using raw materials procured from outside, what other considerations enter the MRP process?

So what is this book about?

Thus far, we have looked at some obvious business processes in a simple manufacturing company. In a real-life situation, companies obviously have to do more:

- At the very least, companies are required by law to do **Financial Accounting**.
- To operate efficiently, we can imagine that companies will also perform **Management Accounting** to make good decisions based on accounting information.
- Most companies, especially manufacturing and trading companies deal with materials and have to handle **Inventory and warehouse management** and **Procurement**.
- Any company with a reasonable number of employees has to also perform **Human Resources Management**.
- A company with manufacturing facilities certainly has to perform **Plant Maintenance** or **Enterprise Asset Management** . This will encompass both routine **Preventive Maintenance** to reduce the risk of mechanical breakdowns (like oil changes for cars), as well as **Breakdown Maintenance** when things do go wrong.
- In addition, companies often execute projects – like constructing new manufacturing facilities, conducting sales conferences, building new information systems and so on. Companies therefore need to do **Project Management** as well.

The business world generally classifies processes directly related to the production and sale of the end products of a business as *Main Value Chain* activities, and classifies other processes as *Supporting Value Chain* activities.

Figure 2 lists the main and supporting value chain processes we have discussed thus far.

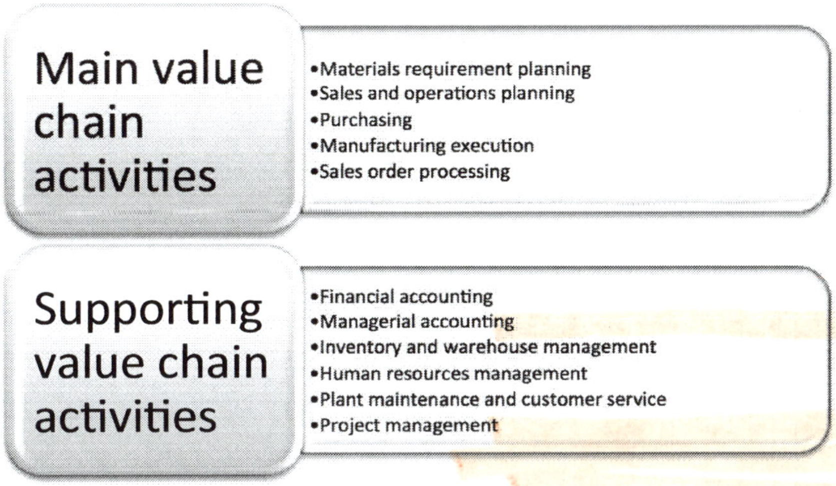

Figure 2: Main and supporting value chain business processes

This course addresses how SAP models each of the above business processes and highlights their inter-linkages.

To benefit from the course or to pass the SAP TERP10 certification examination, you need to *clearly understand* the above business processes and their inter-linkages. Rather than just seeing each process and term we cover as something abstract that you need to memorize, you should be able to relate everything we talk about to concrete real-world occurrences.

This book covers a lot of ground and gets down to fairly minute details about many things. It might seem complex, but grasping everything well only requires you to attach a common-sense meaning to the numerous terms that you will encounter. This chapter has already introduced many terms and will introduce some more before we are done.

As a solid first step you should master the exact meaning of the terms and be able to recall their meanings as soon as you see them. With that kind of mastery, you will be able to handle the course and the SAP certification examination quite easily. Most crucially, you will understand much more of what goes on in the organization that you already work

for, or will soon work for.

Key process flows

After that overview of the course topics, let us turn our attention to some key process flows in SAP. You will grasp the upcoming chapters much better once you have this broad picture.

In this section, we want to show you a common theme that underlies many business processes in SAP. Before we look at that common theme, let us look at a concrete process. We start with *Sales Order Processing* – also called as the *Order to Cash* Process.

The *Order to Cash process* covers all the steps involved in customers ordering products from a company, the company fulfilling the order and the customer paying for the products.

The formal process starts when a customer places a concrete *Sales Order* with the company. However, in a business-to-business (B2B) situation some steps will usually precede the formal step of placing a *Sales Order*. The unit that covers the *Sales Order* or *Order to Cash* process in detail will discuss many possible preliminary steps. We discuss one of them in this chapter.

A customer could initiate the process with a *Sales Inquiry*. Through a *Sales Inquiry*, a prospective customer merely seeks some information about the products, pricing and availability, with no contractual obligation involved. After getting the information, the customer could decide not to buy and that will end the process.

Alternately, the customer might proceed to place a *Sales Order* – which is a legally binding document. The company will start the process of shipping the product and the customer will be bound to pay for the shipped products. Note the key difference between a *Sales Inquiry* and a *Sales Order*. As we mentioned earlier, instead of with a *Sales Inquiry*, the overall *Order to Cash* process might begin in other ways as well. For example a prospective buyer might send a *RFQ – Request for Quotation*. We will cover those in a later chapter.

Once the company receives a *Sales Order* from the customer, it will need to start the process of *fulfilling* the order. That is, the sales department has to give the green signal to initiate the process of picking the materials from the warehouse and shipping them out to the customer.

Although the Sales department might receive the *Sales Order*, other departments will take care of many of the subsequent steps.

The finished goods stock from which the company will fulfill the order might be located in a warehouse in some other part of the country or even elsewhere around the globe. Therefore someone in the warehouse will need to see that they have a new delivery to fulfill and initiate the steps to *pick* the materials from the warehouse shelves. The sales department, after verifying that everything about the *Sales Order* is correct, initiates the shipping process by creating a document called the *Outbound Delivery*. This document authorizes the subsequent steps to take place.

In large companies, picking an item out of a warehouse shelf might not be as trivial an operation as it sounds. The warehouse could be huge – the size of several football fields – and so someone with a forklift, or a robot, will need to go to the correct location and pick out the material. In large warehouses, picking materials each time an order comes in could be woefully inefficient and hence warehouse operators will need to optimize the whole process. For example, they might accumulate orders for a while and then determine an optimal routing through the warehouse to pick out the materials while expending as little energy as possible in the process (and incurring as little wear and tear on the equipment as possible). Given all of these intricacies in warehouse operations, companies typically use complex software to manage warehouse operations. SAP also supports warehouse operations. Thus the picking step involves an integration between the *Sales Order Processing* system and the *Warehouse Management* system.

Once the warehouse completes the operation of taking a material off the shelves – *picking* – the material can then be formally removed from the company's stock. Suppose the company had 1000 laptops of a certain model in stock for sale and some customer ordered 90 of these. Once the 90 units are allocated to the customer sales order, the company now has only 910 units in stock. Which department tracks this?

Warehouse management is only concerned with the warehouse logistics of efficiently putting materials away and retrieving them.

Inventory Management is the entity that tracks the quantities of various materials in stock at various storage locations.

Thus we see that in fulfilling a *Sales Order*, we also have an interaction between *Warehouse Management* and *Inventory Management*.

The step of reducing the inventory once the warehouse operation is completed is called *Posting of Goods Issue*. At this step, the company allocates the picked materials to the concerned sales order and records the fact that it now has fewer units of the concerned material in stock. The company does not own these materials anymore. Who owns them?

At this point, the customer who ordered the items owns the material and therefore owes the company some money.

To initiate the process of receiving payment, the company sends an *Invoice* to the customer for payment. This step shows an interface between the sales process and *Financial Accounting*.

Eventually, the customer sends a payment and the company's Accounting department will *post* the payment to the customer's account. This completes the process.

Figure 3 shows the major steps in the *Order to Cash* process.

Enterprise Systems strive to provide smooth integration across departmental boundaries. Individual steps of business processes must, of necessity, be initiated within some module of the enterprise system. However, completing a step in all but the most trivial business processes involve interfacing with one or more other modules of the enterprise system.

Figure 4 shows the *Order to Cash* process with additional details about the module in which each step might be initiated and the other key modules with which each step might interface

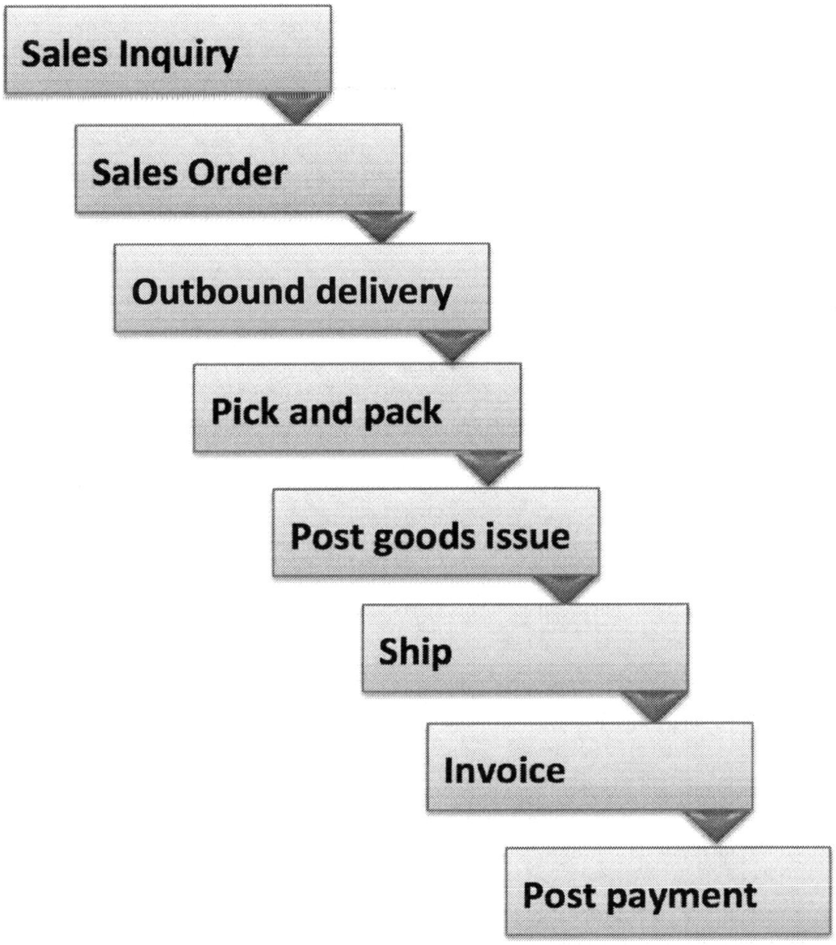

Figure 3: The Order to Cash process

<table>
<tr><th>Step</th><th>Initiated in SAP module</th><th>Possible interfaces</th></tr>
<tr><td>Sales Inquiry</td><td rowspan="7">Sales and distribution</td><td rowspan="2">Inventory, procurement, production</td></tr>
<tr><td>Sales Order</td></tr>
<tr><td>Outbound Delivery</td><td></td></tr>
<tr><td>Pick and Pack</td><td>Warehouse</td></tr>
<tr><td>Post goods issue</td><td>Inventory</td></tr>
<tr><td>Ship</td><td>Transportation</td></tr>
<tr><td>Invoice</td><td>Financial accounting</td></tr>
<tr><td>Post payment</td><td>Financial Accounting</td><td></td></tr>
</table>

Figure 4: The Order to Cash process showing more details

Generic process structure in SAP

Several SAP business process share a common structure and you might find it useful to understand this basic structure.

Many important processes begin with a preliminary step to initiate the process – like *Sales Inquiry* in the *Order to Cash* process.

This preliminary step is usually tentative, with no firm requirement for further action. For example, a customer could initiate a *Sales Inquiry*, but then not follow it up with a *Sales Order*. However, once the *Sales Order* is created, then the process goes forward.

Figure 5 shows the generic structure of many important processes in SAP, and shows how the Order to Cash process maps to that generic structure.

Figure 6 shows a similar mapping for other business processes, with *Order to Cash* included for reference. Later chapters go into further details on these processes, but we briefly describe each one below.

We see that each business process that Figure 6 covers has a preliminary step to initiate the process – *Sales Inquiry*, *Purchase Requisition*, *Planned Order*, *Transfer Request* and *Maintenance No-*

Figure 5: SAP generic process structure and its mapping to the Order to Cash process

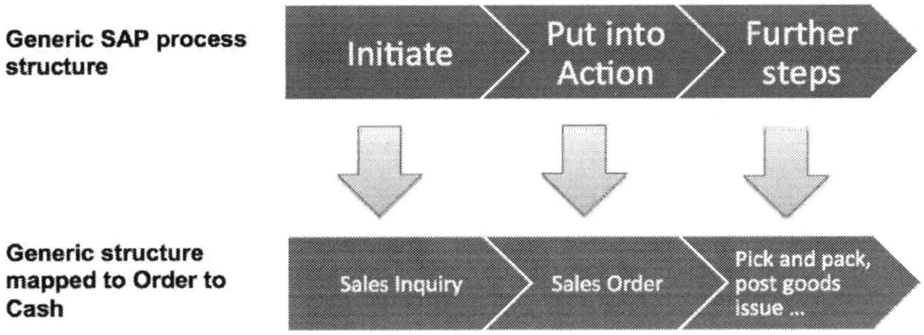

Figure 6: SAP generic process structure and its mapping to several key processes

	Initiate	Put into action	Further steps
Order to cash	Sales Inquiry	Sales Order	Outbound delivery, Pick and pack, Post goods issue, Ship, Invoice, Post customer payment
Purchasing	Purchase requisition	Purchase order	Goods receipt, Invoice verification, Payment
Manufacturing	Planned order	Production order	Goods issue, Confirmation, Goods receipt, Order settlement
Warehouse	Transfer request	Transfer order	Confirmation
Plant maintenance	Maintenance notification	Maintenance order	Goods issue, Confirmation, Settlement

tification. All of these represent preliminary steps with no guarantee that the process will actually be executed to completion. The formal step occurs when these informal steps result in a corresponding ***Order*** – *Sales Order, Purchase Order, Production Order, Transfer Order* or *Maintenance Order*.

The subsequent steps differ from process to process.

Not all the steps in the above process template occur all the time. It is entirely possible that the process stops with the informal step itself – an *Order* might never be created. For example, a *Sales Inquiry* might never get converted into a *Sales Order*; a *Purchase Requisition* might not be converted into a *Purchase Order*.

The informal step is not mandatory. For example, it is possible for the *Order to Cash* process to start with the creation of a *Sales Order* directly and for the *Purchasing* process to begin with the creation of a *Purchase Order*.

We now provide a thumbnail description of each of the above processes. Be sure to see the commonsense nature of these processes and to memorize the steps and the documents in each one. That will significantly ease the process for you of integrating more intricate details in later chapters.

Figure 7 shows the steps in the *Procure to Pay* business process and re-emphasizes their mapping to our generic process template.

Figure 7: Outline of the Procure to Pay process

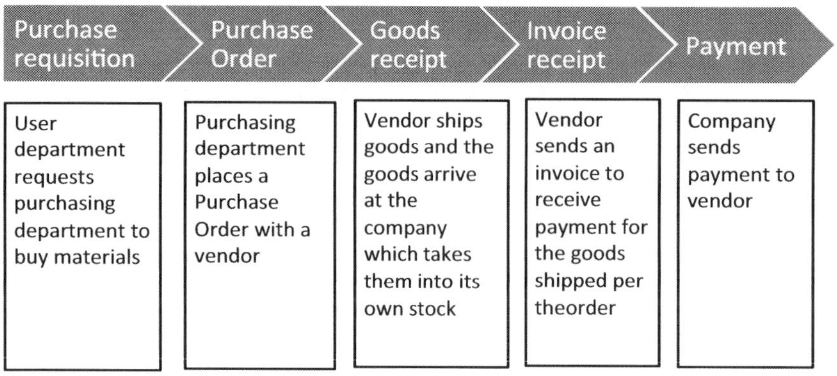

The *Purchasing* or *Procure to Pay* business process starts with some department requesting the purchasing department to buy some materials. The department needing the materials does this by creating a *Purchase Requisition*. Assuming that this requisition progresses further, the purchasing department might create a *Purchase Order* and send it to a vendor. You will see the details of vendor selection as well as other options for initiating the purchasing process in the corresponding course unit.

After receiving the *Purchase Order*, the vendor eventually ships the ordered materials and these materials show up at our company's warehouse. Thus far, the materials do not belong to our company and we execute the step of *Goods Receipt* to formally receive the goods into our possession. Naturally this increases our stock of the materials received. We might sometimes have additional steps – like quality inspection – before we take in the goods. We will cover these aspects later in the book.

The vendor will then send an *invoice* for the materials shipped. The *Invoice Receipt* step covers the process of verifying the invoice – after all we have to make sure that the invoice is for materials that we have actually ordered and received.

Finally our company sends out a *Payment* to the vendor, thereby completing the process.

Figure 8 briefly describes the steps in the *Manufacturing* business process.

The *Manufacturing* business process begins with the creation of a *Planned Order* – just a plan and not yet anything that causes any action. *Planned Orders* can be created manually, but are usually automatically generated by the material requirements planning, or *MRP*, process.

Once the company decides to go ahead and actually execute the *Planned Order*, it creates a *Production Order* that authorizes actual manufacturing work.

Once the *Production Order* is *released* – and not before that – the manufacturing department can go ahead and issue the materials needed for the *Production Order* via the step, *Goods Issue*.

Figure 8: Outline of the Manufacturing process

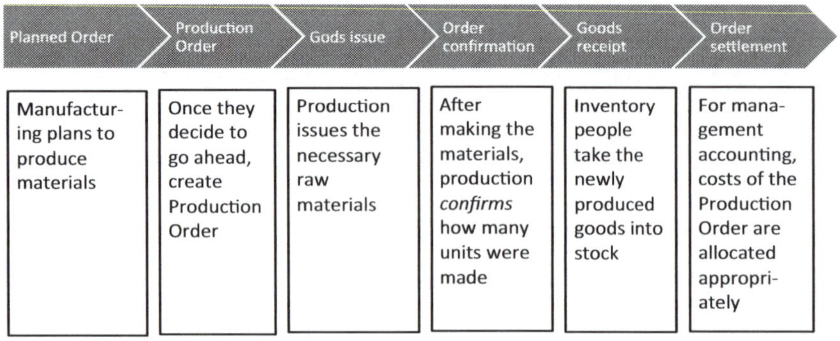

In SAP, the term *release* has a special connotation from a cost accounting viewpoint. From the viewpoint of production, a company would clearly be interested in tracking production costs. Let us suppose that a company has created a *Production Order* to produce 1000 units of some material. The company will surely want to track the production cost for this batch of 1000 units. The company should therefore accurately track all costs that go into this *Production Order*. In SAP, so-called *Cost Objects* can accumulate costs. To do this, whenever we record an expense, we can indicate the *Cost Object* to which the expense applies.

To facilitate this tracking, once the *Production Order* is *released*, SAP treats it as a *Cost Object*. This applies not just to *Production Orders*, but to all *Order* objects once they are *released* – it is at this point in time that they become *cost objects*. They are called *Order-Related Cost Objects*.

As production progresses, the manufacturing department *confirms* the number of units of the materials were produced. Why would they need to do this – did they not start out to make a specific quantity of the material anyway? Well, actual production could come out quite different from what was intended. This could be because of quality or productivity issues. For management accounting, the company will need to know the exact quantity produced. This would be needed for computing the unit cost of manufacturing, and for other purposes.

In SAP, you will come across the term *confirmation* in a few different contexts. In manufacturing it denotes the completion of manufacture of some materials. In general it *confirms* that some activity that was started has been completed and often causes other dependent activities to start.

Once manufacturing has produced the goods, the resulting materials have to go into our company's stock. Let us suppose our company had 200 tables in stock and manufacturing just completed making 50 more, we need to take those new tables into stock by executing the *Goods Receipt* step.

Although this seems to complete the manufacturing process, the process is not complete until the corresponding management accounting steps are complete. In the process of manufacturing some materials, the company has incurred some costs and these costs have to be allocated to the appropriate entities in the company. That whole process is called *Order Settlement*. You will also encounter the term *Settlement* quite a bit in SAP and it represents the step of allocating costs or revenues.

Figure 8 briefly describes the steps in the *Warehouse* logistics process. This simple figure needs no further elaboration.

Figure 9: Outline of the warehouse logistics process

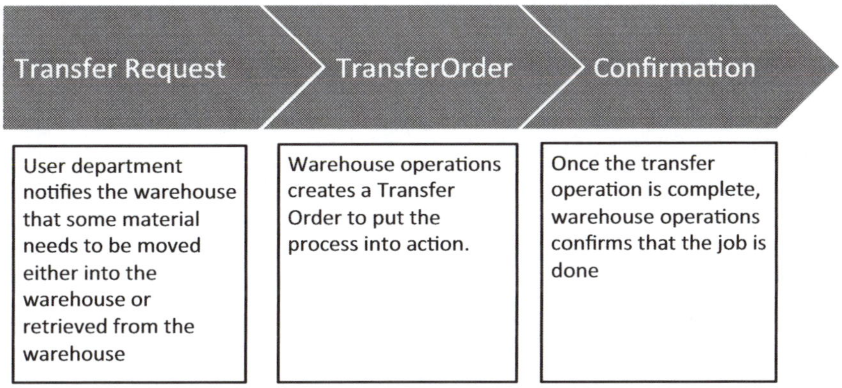

Figure 10 briefly describes the steps in the *Maintenance* process.

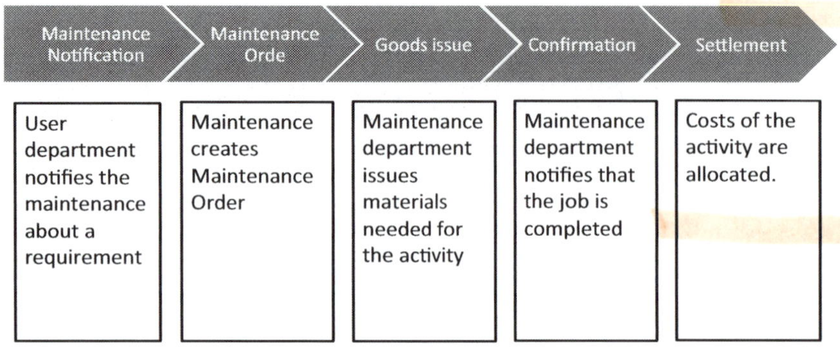

Figure 10: Outline of the Enterprise asset management process

Configuring and customizing an ERP system

SAP provides a packaged solution that a user organization can adapt to its needs. Organizations differ significantly in their internal structures and operational policies and therefore we cannot expect a packaged solution like SAP to work out of the box for its user organizations. Of course, packaged ERP solution vendors like SAP know that organizations differ in many ways and provide features that allow user organizations to *configure* the ERP system to meet their requirements. In other words, ERP products ship with built-in functionality for several different ways in which companies do business and a particular company can choose the specific variants it needs.

For example, a user organization might not want all the standard steps that SAP provides in its *Sales Order Processing* module and might choose to turn off some of the steps. People implementing SAP for a user organization expend considerable effort. The process involve extensive discussions with managers in the user organizations to clearly understand their requirements, and to configure SAP accordingly. Configuration does not involve changing any code in the system or adding new code.

Given how businesses differ significantly, organizations often have specific features or practices that none of the built-in configuration settings can capture. In these cases, user organizations have to *customize* the ERP system by adding new code for their specific functionality. *Customization* calls for significantly more time, resources and effort than *configuration*.

Given the challenges of *customization*, organizations try to avoid it as much as possible. In some situations, organizations may choose to change their business processes to suit how the SAP software operates. Although this might sound like cutting your feet to fit the shoes, the approach might not be all that bad. After all, companies that sell packaged ERP offerings do so after extensive experience with numerous client organizations and often incorporate industry best-practices in their software. In most situations, adapting to their product is likely to be a wise choice.

Of course organizations also try to gain competitive advantages in key areas by doing things differently and perhaps more efficiently than their competitors. In such situations, blindly adapting what an ERP system has to offer might not be in the best interests of a company. To summarize, companies might choose to *customize* the system in areas of their core competency where they would like to gain a strategic advantage by doing things differently. In other areas, they might just choose to go along with the features that the product has to offer.

Review 7: Explain in your own words the terms *Configuration* and *Customization*.

Review 8: Find two reasons why *Customization* might require more time and resources than *Configuration*.

Organization Levels in SAP

You already know that SAP is a packaged solution that is intended to meet the needs of many different organizations. Each organization adopts a structure to suit its own requirements. For example one organization might divide its sales function in one way and another one might do it differently.

However a packaged solution like SAP cannot possibly reflect the thousands of variations on how organizations could be structured. The SAP ERP system has its own structure. Mapping the structure of a user organization to those in the SAP system forms a key part of *configuration*.

SAP calls these basic structures as *Organization Levels* – do not confuse this with the common use of the term to represent levels in an organization's managerial reporting structure.

To properly understand SAP, you need to master the various *Organization Levels* in it.

In SAP, a *Client* represents a conglomerate company – or a company that has several subsidiary companies within it. Take for example, the pharmaceutical giant Johnson and Johnson (J&J). Although J&J is a *company* in the legal sense of the term, internally it has several *companies* as legal entities and it is thus a conglomerate consisting of many companies.

Consider Google or Microsoft. These companies have their foreign subsidiaries – for example, Google UK, Google China, Google India and so on, with each of these being legal entities in their own right, registered in the respective countries.

Most large companies are actually conglomerates made up of other companies (legal entities). SAP uses the term ***Client*** to represent such a conglomerate entity. In SAP, *Client* is the highest organizational level.

The SAP term *Client* has no relationship to our normal use of the term.

SAP calls the individual companies that exist within a *Client* as *Company codes*. Each company code is a separate legal entity.

A company code is the smallest SAP entity to support a full set of *books* – or legal financial records. We will discuss this further in a later chapter. Figure 11 illustrates these ideas.

Company codes represent *Legal entities* from the viewpoint of statutory reporting requirements and other legal considerations. Thus each company code has a *Chart of Accounts* and a *General Ledger* and can generate financial statements like the *Balance Sheet* and *Income Statement*.

Consider a conglomerate called *ERPI* with eight company codes as Figure 12 shows.

Each company code of conglomerate ERPI operates in one or

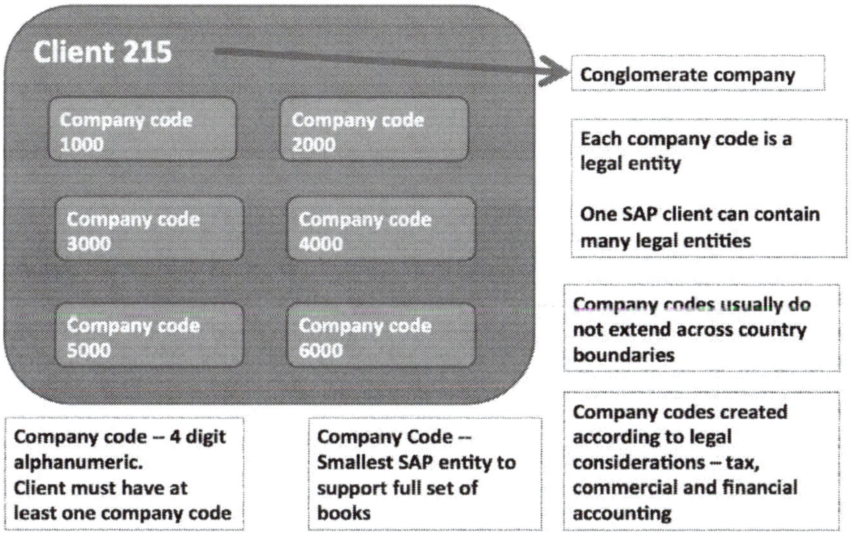

Figure 11: Client and Company Codes in SAP

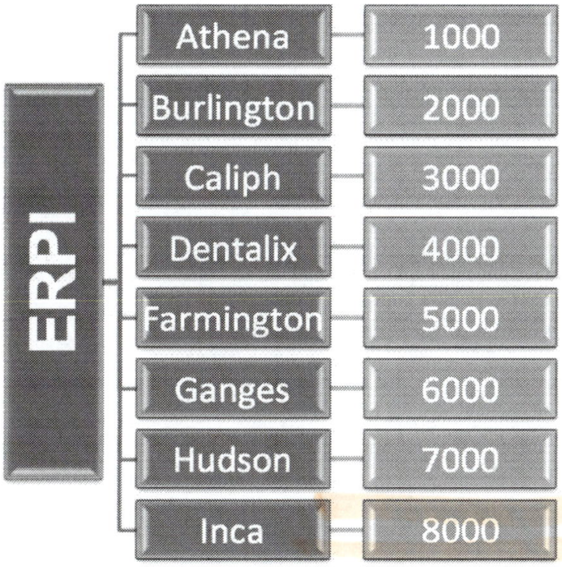

Figure 12: ERPI – A conglomerate with 8 company codes

more of the following market segments – Automotive, Pharmaceutical, Consumer Electronics and Medical Electronics.

Furthermore, large companies who do business in multiple countries often need to track the financial information for each of these segments. Since the company would create a company code for each of the countries in which it operates, there may be additional legal requirements to generate financial reports for each of these business segments. Using our ERPI example, Figure 13 shows how these business segments can span across one or several company codes. As an example, it can be seen that the Medical Electronics business segment spans across every company code, while the Automotive business segment spans across all but company codes 1000 and 8000. Should company code 2000 (Burlington) require segment reporting, ERPI would be required to generate separate financial statements for each of the four business segments.

Business segments

Company codes

	Automotive	Pharmaceutical	Consumer Electronics	Medical Electronics
1000	☐	☑	☑	☑
2000	☑	☑	☑	☑
3000	☑	☑	☐	☑
4000	☑	☐	☑	☑
5000	☑	☐	☑	☑
6000	☑	☐	☐	☑
7000	☑	☑	☑	☑
8000	☐	☐	☑	☑

Figure 13: ERPI – Four business segments across eight company codes

Each company code has individual financial reporting capabilities. However companies may often need to generate financial statements for each business segment that spans across several company codes. To facilitate such a need, SAP makes use of *business segments* to support this process. If ERPI were to generate a set of financial statements for its overall Automotive business segment, it would include the relevant financial information from company codes 2000, 3000, 4000, 5000, 6000, and 7000.

In a conglomerate scenario, different company codes often share certain activities for efficiency. For example ERPI could perform centralized purchasing for some company codes that use the same material. In such situations, the costs of shared activities need to be divided properly across the company codes that use these activities. Once again we see the need to cut across company codes.

SAP uses the organization level called *Controlling Area* to facilitate management accounting across company codes. Only those companies belonging to the same *Controlling Area* can participate in cost sharing. We will see this in greater detail in the chapter on Management Accounting.

Figure 14 shows an example of *controlling areas* and their mapping to company codes.

SAP uses four digit numbers to represent company codes as well as controlling areas. Thus a company code and a controlling area could have the same number. Do not let this confuse you. For example, company code 1000 is completely different from controlling area 1000.

Company codes 1000, 2000 and 3000 all belong to the controlling area 1000 and thus they can share some costs.

Likewise, company codes 6000, 7000 and 8000 all fall under controlling area 4000 and can share costs. Each of the company codes 4000 and 5000 has its own controlling area and therefore cannot share costs with any other company codes.

Review 9: Answer the following:

1. Name two company codes in ERPI which cannot share costs with company code 7000.
2. Name two company codes that can share costs with company code 3000.
3. Can company codes 1000 and 4000 have a common purchasing department? Why or why not?
4. Can company codes 6000 and 7000 share a power generating plant? Why or why not?

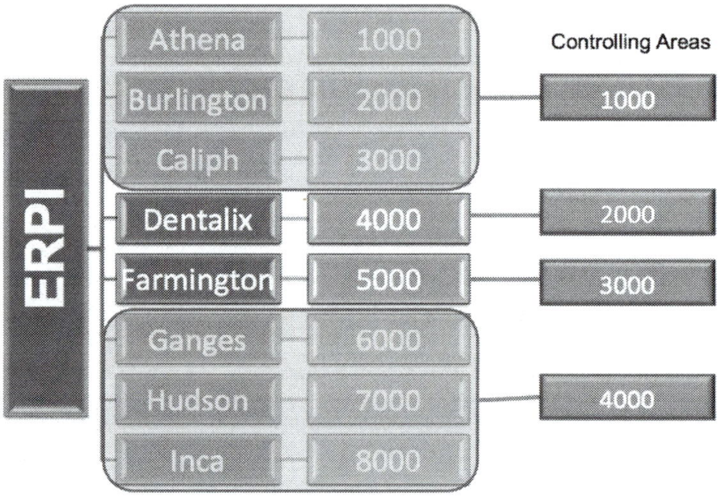

Figure 14: ERPI – Controlling areas and their mapping to company codes

Financial Accounting

Financial accounting plays a key role in enterprise systems. Much of financial accounting goes on in the background as enterprise systems like SAP carry out transactions. Nevertheless, we cannot function effectively in an enterprise system without a basic grasp of financial accounting. SAP can perform seamlessly, by making the accounting postings quietly in the background. For this to occur, we have to set it up correctly to know which accounts to update at each stage of various business transactions. Setting this up properly requires us to understand basic accounting principles. This chapter provides the necessary background in accounting for you to be able to grasp the accounting implications of various steps in the business processes that we cover. By no means should you consider this brief introduction to even remotely reflect a complete coverage of financial accounting. The chapter covers the bare minimum that you will need to grasp what we cover in SAP.

Introduction

The Financial Accounting process tracks the financial implications of business operations. Examples of business transactions with financial implications include:

- A vendor sends an invoice for products that we ordered
- We send out an invoice to a customer for products that they ordered and we shipped
- A customer makes a payment against an invoice that we sent out
- We make a payment to a vendor based on an invoice that the vendor sent
- We pay our employees

- A tax payment is coming up
- We collect sales tax from our customers
- We use some material in production
- We receive goods at our warehouse
- A machine depreciates
- Value of land owned by the business appreciates
- ...

Businesses carry out numerous such transactions as they execute their operations, and need an orderly means of keeping track of their financial implications. A simple-minded approach would involve just recording every transaction. The way we record our check transactions in a check ledger serves as a simple example of *single-entry book-keeping*. While being simple, the approach does not allow easy access to certain kinds of information that businesses need.

For example, with single-entry book-keeping:

- We cannot easily get an idea of the health of a business
- We will be hard-pressed to know much money is locked up in accounts receivable or inventories
- We will not be able to quickly find out how much money we owe others – our accounts payable.

We would need other systems outside of a *single-entry book-keeping* system to track such of things. Furthermore, the single entry system does not allow us to easily spot errors.

Because of the shortcomings of single-entry book-keeping, organizations have been using double-entry book-keeping since the medieval times. Under this system, each financial transaction is entered in two places rather than in just one place. This approach reflects the simple fact that a financial transaction always has two sides to it. For example, when we pay cash and buy an item, our cash is reduced, but in exchange we get the item, and hence, the value inherent in it. *Single-entry book-keeping* does not reflect this basic balance. *Double-entry book-keeping*, on the other hand, is designed around this fundamental balance and it also erases many of the problems with single-entry book-keeping.

The Accounting Equation and the Balance Sheet

At any point in time, a business has things of value or assets – directly as cash, or things it can sell and get cash in exchange. What might be some examples?

- Cash (direct currency, or money in the bank)
- Land
- Plant and machinery
- Raw materials and finished goods in stock
- Accounts receivable – money that people owe the business. While this might not appear to have a cash value, it actually does. After all, eventually some or all of the money owed will be paid back. Accounts receivable can indeed be sold. If you were to sell a business, the buyer of the business would inherit the accounts receivable and hence the rights to receive the payments as and when they are made.
- Investments that are held by the company

How did the business acquire all of these assets? They certainly did not materialize from thin air and the business must have paid money to acquire these assets. Where did the business get the money to buy (or otherwise get) all of these things? The business used the owners' money, and perhaps other borrowings, to fund all of these assets. For example, suppose the combined assets of a business are worth $1 million. This might be made up of, for example, cash and bank balances of $ 500,000, material stocks of $ 300,000, accounts receivable of $100,000 and investments worth $100,000. We need to account for how the business obtained assets worth $1 million. That is, how did they fund these assets? Here is one possible scenario:

- The owners started the business with an initial capital of $100,000
- The company has outstanding bank loans worth $700,000
- The company has $50,000 worth of raw materials that suppliers have supplied, but the company has yet to pay for (accounts payable)
- Over the years the company has ploughed back profits worth $150,000 into the business (accrued retained earnings)

This accounts for the $1 million in assets. The items bank loans and accounts payable are called liabilities, and the items initial capital and accrued retained earnings are together called owners' equity.

The above exemplifies the basic accounting equation:

Assets = Liabilities + Owners' equity

or, in the current context:

\$1 mn assets = \$750,000 liabilities + \$250,000 owners' equity

This just reflects the simple fact that whatever the company currently has by way of assets must have been obtained only by using the company's liabilities and owners' equity.

A company's Balance Sheet in essence depicts the basic accounting equation as it applies to the company.

However, instead of just showing the assets, liabilities and owners' equity as single numbers, the balance sheet breaks these down further as we show below.

Various kinds of assets:

- current assets
- fixed assets
- land and buildings
- raw material inventories
- finished goods inventories
- marketable investments
- accounts receivable
- ...

Various kinds of liabilities:

- short term loans
- long term loans
- accounts payable
- ...

and various kinds of owners' equity:

- preferred stock
- ordinary stock
- retained earnings
- ...

We can also think of the balance sheet as a snapshot of a company at a specific point in time – like a photograph showing the assets, liabilities and owners' equity at that instant. If the company completely stops all its operations and comes to a complete halt (performs no activities that have any financial implications), the snapshot of its assets, liabilities and owners' equity represents its balance sheet. The balance sheet depicts a static view of the company. Of course, things are always happening and the company seldom comes to a complete halt in all respects. Just like we never come to a complete stop, but people can still take an x-ray image to check on our health. A balance sheet is like an x-ray image to assess some aspects of the health of a company.

Accountants show the assets on the left hand side and the liabilities and owners' equity on the right hand side as Table 7 shows:

Table 7: Sample Balance Sheet

Assets		**Liabilities and owners' equity**	
Cash & bank	$500,000	Bank loans	$700,000
Inventories	$300,000	Accounts payable	$50,000
Accounts receivable	$100,000	Initial capital	$100,000
Investments	$100,000	Accrued retained earnings	$150,000
	$,1000,000		$1,000,000

The first set of review questions for this chapter appears below. You can find suggested answers to all the review questions in this chapter starting from page 216

Review 1: For each of the following items, indicate whether it is an Asset, Liability, Owners' Equity or none of those:

1. New shares worth $450,000 that the company issued
2. Shares worth $100,000 that this company purchases in other companies as a way of investing some of its earnings
3. $26,500 that the company is yet to pay its suppliers for goods already supplied
4. The value of goods supplied in the above item (lying in inventory and not yet used)
5. Money in a checking account maintained by the company
6. Money that the company has paid as salary to its employees in the current month

7. A power generation plant that the company maintains to supply power to one of its factories
8. Bank loans amounting to a total of $700,000 that the company has taken out to finance its business operations

Review 2: In your own words, explain the logic behind the accounting equation.

Review 3: Draw up a balance sheet from the following information about John, a kid who operates a lemonade stand:

- John borrowed $15 from his parents and put $7 from his profits back into his business
- John has equipment (glass jugs, drinking glasses, mixing spoons, etc.,) worth $10.
- John has borrowed 10 lemons from mom and will pay them back after the next weekend. These lemons cost $5.
- John has stocks of sugar worth $5
- Some of John's friends bought lemonade worth a total of $7 during the past weekend and have promised to pay him back soon.
- John has $5 in his cash box.

Review 4: For each of the following business transactions, explain whether the total of assets (and therefore liabilities and owners' equity) will have a different value at the end of the transaction than it had at the beginning. If there will be a change, explain which components on the two sides of the accounting equation change. If the total does not change, explain whether there will be any redistribution among the components within a particular side of the equation. We have given two examples:

1. **Example:** Company uses cash to buy raw materials worth $500. **Answer:** No change to total assets. Redistribution occurs only within the assets side. Cash decreases by $500 and inventory

increases (the company now has additional raw material worth $500).

2. **Example:** Company takes out a new long term loan for $100,000

   Answer: Total assets increase because the company now has $100,000 more in cash (on the left hand side of the equation). To compensate, there is now also an additional long-term liability (the new bank loan that the company now has to pay back) of $100,000 on the right hand side. The two balancing entries therefore ensure that the accounting equation balances.

3. The company receives raw material worth $50,000 and has been invoiced by the vendor in full. The company has not yet paid for this purchase.

4. The company uses $200,000 of its cash to buy back (repurchase) some of its own stock.

5. The company pays back $100,000 of its outstanding loan.

6. The company pays $50,000 to the vendor mentioned above.

7. The company places a new purchase order with a vendor to supply goods worth $35,000

8. The company sells some of its land for $1,000,000

The Income or Profit and Loss Statement

If we view the balance sheet as a snapshot of a company at some instant, the income statement summarizes the things a company did over a period of time as it moved from one state to another (or from one Balance Sheet to another). In this sense it presents a dynamic view of what a business did during a time interval – as opposed to the state of a business at some instant which the Balance Sheet shows.

For example, a company had a balance sheet on the start of January 1, 2014 and another at the end of December 31, 2014. These two are almost certain to be quite different. The income statement covering the period January 1, 2014 through December 31, 2014 will show the financial aspects of what the company did by way of operations during this period. Table 8 shows an example.

Income statements generally show the following items:

Table 8: Income or Profit and Loss statement

Sales Revenue	$200,000
Less: Cost of goods sold (cost of raw materials, labor and other things directly attributable to the products sold)	$100,000
Less: Overhead expenses (selling, general and administrative expenses)	$50,000
Less: Depreciation (to account for wear and tear of equipment, also discussed later)	$10,000
Less: Interest expenses (for bank loans)	$10,000
Interest and other income	$0
Profit before taxation (PBT)	**$30,000**
Less: Taxes (@40%)	$12,000
Profit after taxation	**$18,000**
Less: Dividends	$5,000
Retained earnings	**$13,000**

Chart of Accounts

Thus far, we have seen the structure of the balance sheet and the income statement. Within each, we have seen different broad headings under which financial accounts are aggregated. If we take a closer look, we can see that there are five different account categories:

1. **Asset accounts:** To track things of value owned by the business
2. **Liability accounts:** Track money that the business owes to outsiders
3. **Owners' equity:** Track amounts the business owes its owners
4. **Revenue accounts:** Track various incomes from business operations
5. **Expense accounts:** Track payments necessary to run the business

Under each category, we might keep several different sub headings for convenience. For example, under *asset accounts* we could keep different accounts to track the following things separately:

- Raw material inventories
- Finished goods inventories
- Bank account
- Plant and machinery
- Land
- Investments and marketable securities
- ...

Similarly, under *expense accounts*, we could have many different accounts to separately track the following:

- Payments for raw materials
- Labor charges
- Rents
- Utility charges
- ...

Each company might choose to maintain a different set of accounts in each category depending on its individual needs and how fine-grained it wants the tracking to be. For example, a company could keep just one single expense account – perhaps called *rents paid* to track all rents that it pays. A different company might keep four different expense accounts to track the rents it pays – office rents, equipment rents, executive residence rents and other rents. What a company actually uses depends on its own needs.

Can you think of three different revenue accounts that a company might keep?

A company that sells several products could keep separate revenue accounts for each product group. A company could also keep separate revenue accounts to track revenues from sale of products and sales of services.

The **Chart of Accounts** is a complete list of different accounts that a business chooses to maintain to keep track of its financial transactions.

As we already know, with double-entry book-keeping, every single transaction affects at least two of these accounts

Of course, it is important that a company chooses its accounts judiciously so that it can track finances at the level of granularity and detail that it wants to.

Each account in a *Chart of Accounts* is identified by a unique account number with each one belonging to one of the 5 account categories – asset, liability, owners' equity, revenue or expense. Table 9 shows an example of a Chart of Accounts.

A *Chart of Accounts* is simply a set of account numbers, their types and the purpose for which each account number will be used. The *Chart of Accounts* is just an empty structure and does

Account number	Account name / purpose
1000	Cash (Checking account)
1100	Debtors (accounts receivable)
1200	Stock on hand (inventories)
2000	Creditors (accounts payable)
2100	Bank overdraft
3000	Capital (Owners' equity)
3200	Accrued retained earnings
4000	Credit sales
4100	Other income
5000	Cost of goods sold
5200	Accounting fees
5300	Bank charges
5400	Rent

Table 9: Example Chart of Accounts

not have any actual financial information in it. It has no values included in it. It is merely a design for some company to use as a basis for its actual accounting.

For example many companies can use the *Chart of Accounts* in Table 9 as a basis for their accounting.

Every *Company Code* must have a *Chart of Accounts* associated with it. Several company codes within a *Client* could adopt the same *Chart of Accounts*. Each *Company Code* within a client could also adopt a different *Chart of Accounts*.

> **Review 5:** For each account mentioned in the Chart of Accounts in Table 9 , identify the category to which it belongs (asset, liability, etc). Do you see any pattern?

> **Review 6:** Find a friend and explain to them, in your own words, the concept of Chart of Accounts.

SAP provides several pre-defined charts of accounts. We can also create custom charts of accounts for our own needs. When multiple company codes share a common *Chart of Accounts*, they all have a similar accounting structure. This facilitates easy account consolidations across company codes.

General Ledger

Companies keep the details of accounting transactions in their General Ledger (G/L). The G/L is a collection of all accounts in the company along with the details of al transactions posted in these accounts.

When we said earlier that a company code must have a *Chart of Accounts*, what we meant is that the G/L of every company code must be based on a *Chart of Accounts*.

If a company chooses to base its G/L on the *Chart of Accounts* shown in Table 9, then the G/L will have all the accounts shown there and each transaction that occurred in those accounts will be listed in the G/L.

The *General ledger* is a report showing for each account (in the *Chart of Accounts* being used), the transactions that occurred for that account over a certain period of time. For example, the general ledger account for the bank account would keep track of all withdrawals from and deposits into the account. Likewise, the material stock account will keep track each instance where materials were received into stock and each instance where materials were issued from stock. The sum total of debits and credits (discussed below) in the overall general ledger must always match because of the practice of double-entry book-keeping – if not, we know that something is wrong.

Review 7: What is the relationship between the Chart of Accounts and the General Ledger?

Review 8: If two different company codes use the same Chart of Accounts for their General Ledger, does this mean that they will always have identical transactions posted for each account? Explain.

Accounting Transactions

In SAP, accounting entries mostly occur silently in the background as we carry out other business transactions like buying, selling and manufacturing. Of course this is possible only if someone has properly configured things so that SAP has enough information to determine which accounts to update for each stage of a business process. Despite accounting entries mostly being posted automatically, you still need to understand the logic.

Single vs. double-entry book-keeping: As we have seen already, in *single-entry book-keeping* we enter each transaction in only one place. In *double-entry book-keeping*, every transaction impacts at least two different accounts, and sometimes more. In *double-entry book-keeping*, every account has two sides – *debit* and *credit*. The amount of each transaction is recorded equally on the debit and credit sides of different accounts. This redundancy helps to avoid some types of errors.

For an accounting transaction worth $1,000, there will be a total debit of $1,000 entered into one or more accounts and an equal amount entered as credits into one or more other accounts. The rules for debits and credits can sometimes seem quite confusing, but they need not be. We now turn our attention to these rules.

Logic of double-entry book-keeping: Whenever there is a financial transaction, there is a shift of value from one entity to another. For example, if Adam gives Bob $1,000, then $1,000 have changed hands from Adam to Bob. Although some value has changed hands, the total value between their two accounts is still constant.

The source of confusion in accounting rules lies in our (mis)interpretation of the terms *debit* and *credit* in terms of their normal day-to-day usage. We tend to erroneously think of debit as a decrease, or as an outflow, and credit as an increase, or as an inflow.

The key to financial accounting heaven (if ever there can be such a thing), lies in banishing these evil misunderstandings. So, for now, simply forget any association of *increase* or *decrease* with the terms *debit* and *credit*.

You have to remember just a single rule for correctly understanding *debit* and *credit* accounting postings!

The original creator of the double-entry system of book-keeping quite arbitrarily decided that when an *asset increases*, we should *debit* the corresponding asset account.

You need to remember just that single rule. You can derive all the other rules from it. Consider these examples:

- Suppose we buy a machine, our fixed assets increase. So we debit the fixed asset account.
- Suppose our material stocks increase (because a vendor shipped items that we ordered), then we debit the stock account. As simple as that!

What did we mean when we said that we can infer all other rules from this one *axiom*? Let us see.

What would you do when an asset account decreases in value?

Suppose we sell a machine and therefore the fixed assets decrease. Think a bit before reading on.

Should we not do the reverse of what we did when an asset increased? Yes, of course! In this case, we credit the fixed assets account.

What about revenue and expense accounts?

Think a bit about the relationship of these to assets and liabilities. If we can figure out where these would eventually end up on the balance sheet as everything must (why?), then we can finagle the rules we already have to arrive at the posting rules for these as well.

So how does sales revenue affect the balance sheet? The answer lies in understanding the income statement. Note that the last line of the income statement says that the money left over after taking away all costs, interest, taxes and dividends is transferred to retained earnings on the balance sheet – which is part of owners' equity. It therefore behaves like a liability. Sales revenue will tend to increase this figure and expenses will tend to decrease this.

Thus revenue accounts can be treated similar to liabilities and expense accounts can be treated the opposite – that is, like assets. That is all there is to it!

Table 10 summarizes the logic of account postings.

Let us consider a few examples of manual posting of transactions:

Table 10: Accounts posting logic

Type of account	Increase/decrease	Action	Logic
Asset	Increase	Debit	Axiom
Asset	Decrease	Credit	Opposite of above
Liability / Owners' equity	Increase	Credit	Opposite of first rule because liabilities and owners' equity represent sources of funds whereas assets represent uses of funds.
Liability / owners' equity	Decrease	Debit	Opposite of above
Revenue	NA	Credit	It is a source of funds and hence behaves like a liability
Expense	NA	Debit	Opposite of above – it is a use of funds and hence behaves like an asset

1. The business owner gives the business $2,000 as capital by transferring it to the company's bank account. Which accounts are involved here? Owners' equity and Cash are the accounts affected by this. Let us look at it from two viewpoints. Consider owners' equity – it is increasing by $2,000. By our rules, it should be credited and hence cash should be debited. Alternately, look at cash. It is an asset and is increasing. So it should be debited according to the rule. So Owners' equity should be credited. Both ways of reasoning lead to the same result.

   We credit Owner's equity account for $2,000 and debit the Checking account by the same amount. Table 11 shows the entries.

	Debit	Credit
Checking account	$2,000	
Owners' equity		$2,000

Table 11: Account postings for owner giving $2,000 to the business

2. The Company buys raw materials worth $300 from a vendor, and the terms of payment are 40% up-front (from our checking account) and 60% due in 15 days. Assume that the vendor has delivered the material. Look at the state after we have paid the 40% and are yet to pay the 60%. Which accounts does this affect?

   Checking account, since we pay 40% or $120 up-front; **Material stock**, since the vendor has delivered, causing the material stock to increase; and **Accounts Payable**, since we still owe 60% or $180 to the vendor. What happened to each of these accounts?

   Cash, an asset, went down – so it (the checking account) should be credited for the $120 that it decreased by. Accounts payable, a liability went up, so it should be credited by the $180 it increased by. Material stock, an asset has gone up and hence should be debited for the entire $300. Table 12 shows the full picture.

	Debit	Credit
Checking account		$120
Accounts payable		$180
Material stock	$300	

Table 12: Account postings for material purchase in example 2

3. The company spends $1,500 on advertising.

   The affects cash (or checking account), and an expense account

	Debit	Credit
Checking account		$1,500
Advertising	$1,500	

Table 13: Account postings for $1,500 advertising expense

(advertising). The balance in the checking account went down and so we credit it. The expense account went up and so we debit it.

4. The Company sells goods worth $500. The customer pays $300 up-front and will pay the balance in 30 days. The cost of goods sold (the cost of making the goods) is $400.

   This affects cash (asset), sales revenue (revenue) and accounts receivable (asset). Cash has increased – debit. Revenue has increased – credit. Accounts receivable has increased – debit. Table 14 shows these.

   However, we are still not done here. After all, the materials the company sold were in the material stock account. After the sale, these materials are gone from there, but our earlier postings have not reflected this change.

   This part of the transaction affects the material stock account (asset) and the cost of goods sold account (expense).

   Table 15 shows this posting.

	Debit	Credit
Sales revenue		$500
Checking	$300	
Accounts receivable	$200	

Table 14: Initial account postings for material sales in example 4

	Debit	Credit
Material stock		$400
Cost of goods	$400	

Table 15: Account postings for material stock in example 4

Sub-ledgers and Reconciliation Accounts

We already know that accounts receivable and accounts payable appear on the balance sheet as assets and liabilities respectively. For external reporting, maintaining these as single accounts might suffice. But does this suffice for a company's operations?

Clearly not. Knowing, for example, that we need to collect a total of $200,000 does not do much good unless we know how much each customer (debtor) owes. Similarly, knowing that we owe a total of $175,000 to various vendors does not do much good unless we know how much we owe to specific vendors.

Companies maintain general ledger accounts for accounts receivable and accounts payable and also maintain separate ledgers (called *sub-ledgers*) for the lower level accounts (one for each vendor and one for each customer). As the company conducts business, it posts debits and credits to these sub-ledger accounts. However, since the main accounts – the accounts receivable and accounts payable G/L accounts – just accumulate these sub-ledger accounts, the system **automatically** makes postings to these accounts as well. We call these higher level accounts *reconciliation accounts*. Thus, the accounts receivable and accounts payable balance sheet accounts are two examples of *reconciliation accounts*. There could be others as well – in any situation where the company maintains sub-ledgers to track individual transaction details and maintains a summary account that automatically accumulates these sub-ledger accounts, the summary account is a reconciliation account.

Can you think of any restriction that might apply to reconciliation accounts? That is, what can one do with a normal account that one cannot do with a reconciliation account?

We highlighted the word "automatically" in the previous paragraph for a good reason. Clearly, the system cannot allow us to manually post anything to a reconciliation account. We can post to the sub-ledger accounts and the system **automatically** posts these to the reconciliation account. SAP does not allow manual posting to reconciliation accounts.

Figure 15 illustrates the concepts with an example.

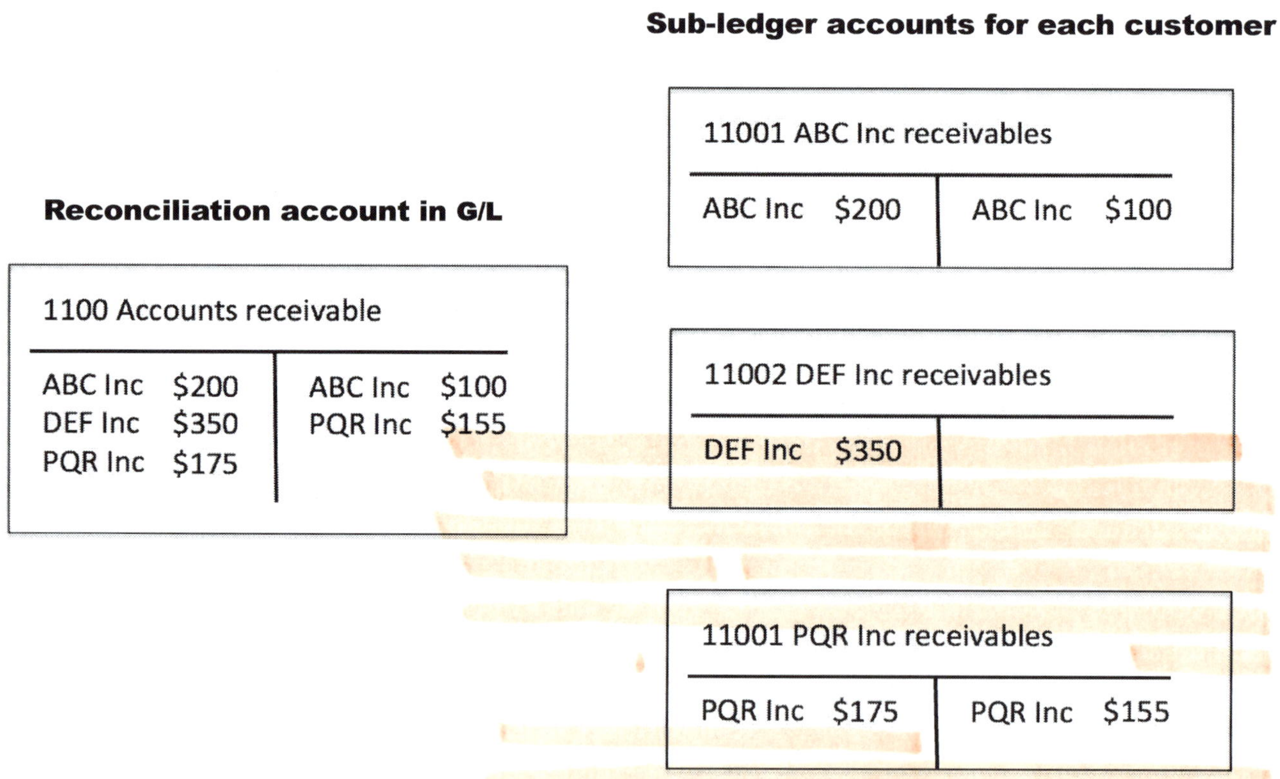

Figure 15: Reconciliation and sub-ledger accounts. The sub ledger accounts show that customer ABC Inc owed the company $200 and has already paid $100 of that. Someone posted these to ABC Inc's sub-ledger account and SAP automatically copied these over to the Accounts receivable reconciliation account in the G/L.

Depreciation

Some assets get used up within a year after being purchased, for example, raw materials from which a company makes finished products. Other assets have a long life and are used up much more gradually. For example, a machine could last 10 years.

Suppose a company bought a machine for $10,000 at the start of 2013. Let us assume that the machine would last five years. At the time of purchase the value of the machine would have been a part of the plant and machinery asset account. It would have also appeared as an asset on the balance sheet, if the company had generated a balance sheet soon after purchasing the machine.

Should the company have treated $10,000 as an expense for the 2013?

Clearly not – since that machine would be used to make products not just in 2013, but for four more years. We should consider only a part of the value of the machine as having been *used up* in 2013 and hence the company should consider only a portion of the $10,000 as an expense for 2013.

However, if we look at the actual outflow of money, the company spent $10,000 in 2013. Furthermore, in 2014, the machine will still help the company to produce materials but the company would not have paid anything at all during that year.

Accountants handle this matter through *depreciation*. They would consider the value of the machine as depleting slowly over a certain number of years and allocate only the portion applicable to a particular year as an expense for that year. In the present example, the company might consider the expense for each of the five years of the life of the machine as $2,000.

While it is very difficult to figure out exactly how much value has been used up, the government has set up rules to determine how much can be charged off as an expense each year. For example, laws could allow a company to depreciate the value of a machine over 10 years. It is possible that the machine might be used for longer than ten years, but after ten years it will no longer be treated as an asset with value.

We saw that depreciation appears as an entry in the income statement (as an expense) and affects the profits earned. Therefore, the rate at which a company depreciates impacts its financial performance (on its income statement). A large value decreases profits and a low value tends to inflate profits.

Companies can potentially use this as a way of manipulating their reported profits – hence the governmental rules.

Let us see how *straight line depreciation* (a common method) works. Under this, a company depreciates an asset in equal amounts over a time span. Suppose a company depreciates a $10,000 machine over ten years using the straight line method, then the company charges depreciation expenses of $1,000 each year. That is, the company debits $1,000 to the depreciation expense account and credits the plant and machinery asset account $1,000 each year.

In addition to the straight line depreciation method, accountants employ other methods as well. We will not go into the details.

Review 9: What is impact on profits if a company charges less depreciation than it should?

We have seen that laws govern how a company can depreciate its assets. In the example above, we depreciated a $10,000 asset over a 10 year period. The laws governing depreciation do not account for the actual lifetimes of specific assets – that would make the laws very complex and difficult to enforce. However, it is possible that an asset that a company depreciates over 10 years actually lasts 15 years. By depreciating it over 10 years the company is reporting lower profits in the first 10 years than would be possible if it could depreciate it over 15 years.

If the company uses this higher depreciation to determine the cost of manufacturing (and hence the profitability) of a product that uses this machine, then it would be underestimating the profitability in the first ten years of the life of the machine.

Accurate estimates of costs can help companies considerably in making the right decisions on pricing, among other things.

However if the company has to follow rules on depreciation, it would appear that a company cannot have an accurate estimate of its production costs. What can companies do about this?

Laws only govern external reporting and do not prevent a company from charging depreciation in whatever way it wants for internal use. Therefore a company could follow the law for depreciation as far as external reporting goes, but use a different approach to depreciation when it comes to internal decision-making.

SAP uses the concept of *depreciation areas* to achieve this. The same asset could belong to different depreciation areas with different policies.

To make things concrete, suppose an asset costs $10,000 and the law requires it to be depreciated in 10 years. However, for internal analysis the company might believe that the asset actually lasts 15 years. The company could keep two depreciation areas A and B, with A depreciating the asset over 10 years and B depreciating it over 15 years. Table 16 shows the depreciation that will be charged in each of the first five years as well as the asset's value at the end of each of the first 5 years:

	Depreciation area A (10 years)		Depreciation area B (15 years)	
Year	Deprn. for year	Asset value yr end	Deprn. for year	Asset value yr end
0		10,000		10,000
1	1,000	9,000	667	9,333
2	1,000	8,000	667	8,666
3	1,000	7,000	667	8,000
4	1,000	6,000	667	7,333
5	1,000	5,000	667	6,666

Table 16: Depreciation areas showing how the same $10,000 asset might be depreciated differently in each area.

Chapter-end review questions

You can find suggested answers to all these questions starting from page 220.

To answer questions marked with ★, you will need to have read the official SAP TERP10 course material.

1. What are reconciliation accounts?

2. What level is the G/L managed at?

3. What is the organization level corresponding to a legal entity in SAP?
4. Which is the smallest SAP entity that supports a full set of books?
5. Which organization element supports the creation of Balance Sheet and income statements that cut across company codes?
6. Which organization element is concerned with tracking of profits within a component of a company code? ★
7. Which organization element is concerned with tracking the performance of external market segments? ★
8. How many company codes can be in a client?
9. How many company codes can a business area be associated with?
10. How many business areas can a company code be associated with?
11. Where does controlling area fit into the organizational elements of SAP?
12. How many company codes can be allocated to a controlling area?
13. What restriction applies to a company code when we consider its assignment to a controlling area?
14. At what level are charts of accounts maintained?
15. How many charts of accounts can a company code use? ★
16. How many company codes within a client can use the same Chart of Accounts?
17. From where do G/L accounts get their definition? ★
18. What are the segments in a G/L master record? ★
19. Which segment of the G/L master contains general information about an account? ★
20. Which segment of the G/L master contains specific information about how a company chooses to use an account? ★

21. _______________ allows for "real-time integration" of G/L accounts with sub-ledger accounts.

22. The account for an individual vendor or customer would be found in the _______________ ledger.

23. The Accounts Receivable G/L balance sheet account used to consolidate individual customer receivables is a _______________ account.

24. The feature of the G/L that allows for postings within a document to be categorized into different areas, such as profit centers and segments is called _______________. ★

25. SAP customers can take advantage of light-weight management accounting functionality by using _______________ within FI.★

26. In SAP FI, there is a single ledger at the client level called, the _______________. ★

27. It is always possible to drill down into the line item list of an account from the balance display for a G/L account T/F? ★

28. The vendor master is defined at the following three levels: _______________, _______________ and _______________. ★

29. The reconciliation account number for Accounts Payable in the G/L is stored in the _______________ level of the vendor master. ★

30. Information about the payment terms for a vendor can be found in the _______________ level of the vendor master. ★

31. When a purchase order is created, the _______________ account is credited and the _______________ account is debited.

32. When goods are received against a PO, the _______________ account is credited and the _______________ account is debited.

33. When a vendor invoice is saved, the _______________ account is credited and the _______________ account is debited.

34. When the vendor is paid, the ________________ account is credited and the ________________ account is debited.

35. The customer master has information at the following three levels: ________________, ________________ and ________________. ★

36. The credit control master record is stored as an extension of the ________________ master record. ★

37. The two levels of the credit control master are: ________________ and ________________. ★

38. Information about the total credit limit for a customer across all credit control areas is stored in the ________________ level of the credit control master record. ★

39. When a customer payment is posted, the ________________ account is credited and the ________________ account is debited.

Management Accounting

Financial Accounting keeps track of monetary flows in an organization with the goal of external reporting according to established laws. Management Accounting also aims at tracking monetary flows, but aims to use such information for making sound managerial decisions. This chapter introduces the broad ideas involved in management accounting, and specifically explains some important SAP concepts and terms involved. Once you grasp the contents of this chapter, you will be ready for the official materials provided by SAP. Without this background you might have some unnecessary difficulties with following the lectures and using the SAP course materials.

As with prior chapters, this chapter also contains review questions which you should try and answer before proceeding. Even if you do not know an answer, you will find it useful to still try hard to provide a meaningful answer before peeking. Doing so will make it easier for you to absorb what follows.

The first review question appears below. You can find suggested answers to all the review questions in this chapter starting on page 224

> **Review 1:** Explain in your own words why the information gathered for financial accounting might not be readily usable for decision-making.

Financial Accounting vs. Management Accounting

Financial accounting aims to accurately record all the monetary flows in an organization. Being externally focused, it strives to generate compliant external reports like the balance sheet and income statement for the company as a whole.

Management Accounting provides financial and other information in a form suitable for decision-making – as opposed to producing accurate and compliant reports useful for entities outside an organization to assess its financial health.

Financial and management accounting differ in many ways.

For example, financial accounting can tell us quite precisely what the profitability of the entire company – not very surprising – because *financial accounting exists for that very purpose.* However when it comes to providing an accurate picture of the profitability at finer levels of granularity, financial accounting falls short. For example, a company would be interested in determining the profitability of each of its products, or each of its divisions or departments or at even finer levels of granularity – like the profitability of a given product in a given market, manufactured in a specific plant.

Review 2: Explain why financial accounting might not be well-equipped for the profitability computations mentioned in the previous paragraph.

A management accounting scenario

Let us consider the concrete example of a company that manufactures two products A and B. During a given month the company made 10,000 units of A and 6,000 units of B. The company manufactures both products in a single plant. The company uses some dedicated machinery for each product (machines used only for that product). However the company also has some machines that both products share.

Products A and B require different materials and have dedicated manufacturing personnel. However, the same plant supervisors and foremen oversee production operations for the two products. Likewise, a single marketing department markets both products and the same sales force sells both.

The company currently sells Product A at $10 per unit and product B at $15 per unit.

Review 3: Explain how you might go about calculating the profit margin separately for the two products. Just mention the approach – you do not have enough information to come up with a number.

Clearly, to calculate the profit margin, we need to know the revenue and all costs involved. Given the unit price and the quantity of each product we sell, we can easily compute the revenue. Big challenges lie in calculating costs. We can attribute some of the costs directly to each product.

Review 4: From the above description, which costs can we directly attribute to the individual products?

From the description, we can attribute the following costs to each product:

- Direct labor costs (personnel dedicated to each product)
- Costs related to machinery dedicated to one product or the other
- Cost of raw materials

If $5 worth of raw materials go into the making of one unit of product A, then we can directly attribute that cost to the cost of making a unit of product A. That is, we can very easily attribute some costs directly to specific products. Management accounting refers to these as *direct costs*.

Certain other costs represent resources consumed in the manufacture of a product, but contribute to both products – perhaps equally, perhaps not. For example, the costs of the foremen, supervisors, top management, marketing and sales are all applicable to both products. It might not be immediately obvious as to how they contribute to the individual product costs. These represent *indirect costs*. To calculate the profit margin for the two products, we need to know all the costs – *direct* and *indirect* – involved in making each product.

Total unit cost of A = Direct cost per unit of A + Indirect cost per unit of A

Review 5: Choose any one of the indirect costs mentioned above (costs of the foremen, supervisors, top management, marketing and sales) and explain one way by which you can allocate the cost to the two products. We cannot specify a single correct answer, but thinking about it can aid understanding.

We might have data to indicate that, on the average, each foreman spends twice the amount of time on product B than on A. One meaningful approach to allocate the costs of foremen might be to allocate a third, or 33.33%, to product A and two-thirds, or 66.67%, to product B. There could be other meaningful approaches as well and the actual situation will determine the best approach to employ.

Review 6: Identify at least one indirect cost that the above narrative has not explicitly mentioned.

Review 7: Identify at least two decisions that might be influenced by your calculation of the profit margins of the two products.

Review 8: Suppose we allocate a third of the foreman's cost to product A and two thirds to product B. If it actually turns out that the foreman actually spends an equal amount of time on both products. How would this affect our cost estimates for products A and B?

Review 9: Explain how under or over-allocating indirect costs to a particular product might affect the quality of the decisions you identified in an earlier question.

Review 10: Suppose our company uses machine X only for product A. The company produced 10,000 units of product

A during the previous year. How can we compute cost per unit of machine X per unit of product A for the previous year?

Cost Center and Profit Center

The concepts *Cost Center* and *Profit Center* play a very important role in management accounting.

- **Cost Center:** As the name indicates, a *Cost Center* is a part of an organization which incurs costs and to which costs can be allocated. For example, the accounting department of a company might be considered as a cost center. The department directly incurs costs – for example, the salaries paid to employees in the department and the cost of stationery that the department uses. Other costs although not directly incurred by the accounting department, might still be allocated to it – for example, rents paid for the office building (part of which accounting occupies).
- **Profit Center:** A part of an organization that is responsible for revenues and for costs. The paints division of a company might be a profit center. The iPod division of Apple Inc might be a profit center.

Review 11: Would it make sense to treat the accounting department of a company as a profit center? Why or why not?.

Need for cost allocation

In the foregoing, we discussed the main spirit of management accounting – whereas financial accounting deals with accounting to record transactions so that we can produce statutory reports, management accounting records transactions in a way that suits business decision-making.

Many business decisions rely on accurate cost and revenue computations for various sub-units of a business, and management accounting focuses heavily on this aspect.

We have already seen that an organization can attribute some costs directly as applicable to an entity. For example, we can attribute the salaries paid to employees in the accounting department to the costs of that department.

From the foregoing discussion, we also know that units in an organization share many costs. In such cases, we have to properly divide the costs to reflect each entity's "fair share" of the cost. Management accounting uses the term *allocation* to refer to this process.

As an organization carries on its business, it might perform thousands of transactions each day. We already know that financial accounting uses the G/L and sub-ledgers to record all financial implications of these transactions as they occur. This is all well and good for financial accounting. What about management accounting? Financial accounting can only answer those questions that it is set up to answer. The way the G/L and sub-ledgers are set up determines how monetary transactions are recorded in specific slots. Experience has shown that we need to go beyond financial accounting to answer many important questions.

Consider some of the following questions that financial accounting might not generally be set up to address :

- What was the total cost incurred by the sales department? This includes costs directly attributable to the department and those that are *allocated* to it, like electricity and rent. For example, the sales department might occupy a portion of a rented building that the company occupies. The company cannot hold the sales department responsible for the rent for the entire building. Instead, it should determine the department's fair share and allocate only that amount to the sales department. Likewise with electricity.
- What is the cost incurred by Assembly Line A during the month of December 2014? We can attribute many expenses to Line A. For example, there might be a manager whose complete salary and benefits we hold Line A responsible for. Lots of materials might be purchased specifically for Assembly Line A – for example, a special cleaning agent to clean spills. In addition, Line A might be responsible for a share of rent and electricity. Given all this, the cost of Line A comprises many costs that apply directly to it as well as several *allocated* costs.

One might say that the above calculations are not exactly rocket science. Conceptually, all this is pretty simple. However organizations incur thousands upon thousands of individual costs, many of which are shared and many of which are not.

Just putting everything in the right place and computing costs correctly can still be a gargantuan task. Doing this by hand can be next to impossible for large companies.

It would be far better to automate the process. Just as enterprise systems handle much of financial accounting in the background as business transactions occur, we want to set up the system and ensure that all of this management accounting (for example, cost allocation) also happens automatically in the background as organizations transact business.

The Management Accounting module of SAP (abbreviated as CO – short for Controlling) enables us to set up how management accounting is to be performed behind the scenes as a company conducts its business.

Review 12: We know that, in SAP, a *client* represents a conglomerate company and can have several company codes within it. Given this scenario, can management accounting cut across company code boundaries? Support your answer with examples.

Key SAP terms and concepts in Management Accounting

Management accounting in general, and SAP in particular, use specific terms. Understanding the precise meaning of these terms will take you a long way towards mastering *Enterprise Systems*.

Below, we discuss some important terms related to *Management Accounting*:

- Cost center
- Cost element
- Cost element accounting
- Settlement period
- Sender cost centers and receiver cost centers
- Primary cost element
- Secondary cost elements
- Controlling area

Cost Center

To facilitate management accounting, whenever costs are incurred, we should immediately assign that cost to some entity. Otherwise someone will have to manually perform these tasks later in management accounting. Management accounting tracks costs by assigning them to cost centers.

Roughly speaking, for management accounting purposes, a company is divided into many cost centers so that when costs occur at these cost centers, management accounting assigns the costs appropriately. As long as this process is properly configured, no one will need to go back and do this manually. For most operational transactions, we can set up the system so that applicable costs are allocated to the proper cost center.

Let us take a concrete example. Suppose there is a department called "Administration", and a cost center is created for this department so that all utility costs in the company can be tracked in this department. Let us also assume the cost center is labeled "Administration". When utility expenses are incurred, the company will want all of these costs to go directly to the "Administration" cost center.

Review 13: List three utility costs that might be assigned to the "Administration" cost center.

Review 14: Name three other possible cost centers in a typical organization. Do not take the easy path and go off the same theme as utilities and name other utilities. Try harder!

The company has set up "Administration" as a cost center to keep track of utility costs and to manage them. This cost center could also be managing other types of costs, but for purposes of our demonstration, let us keep things simple and focus only on utility costs.

As utility bills come in to the company, the costs will be directly posted to this cost center. In this way, the company can centrally manage all of the utility costs in one place and then allocate them at a later time to other responsible cost centers.

Utilities could account for a significant portion of the product cost and hence the company wants to manage this carefully. The following could all be relevant questions that management accounting would need to answer:

- How does what we spend compare with similar companies?
- If we cut down the spending on this area by 10% how much can we save?
- If we cut down the spending on this area, can we price our product more competitively?
- What amount should we budget for the next year for utilities?

Identifying something as a cost center and tracking costs enables us to focus on the costs and also to assign responsibility for managing the cost.

> **Review 15:** Having a cost center called "Administration" helps the company keep track of utility costs and manage them. Suppose a company found that it spent $1,200,000 on utilities during a specific quarter. How might this impact the profit margin that the company calculates for a particular product?

It is important to know the total cost of utilities for the company so as to manage this cost well. Many parts of the company use these utilities – for example, the cost of electricity and water might form an important part of the unit production cost of products. The company first aggregates all the costs for utilities at a cost center. It can then set up rules to reallocate the cost to other cost centers, or to manufactured products.

For accumulating costs, management accounting divides a company into many cost centers. As costs occur, they can be assigned to some cost center. For example, an employee might belong to a cost center. Whenever we pay salary to that employee, this cost automatically goes to the corresponding cost center.

We might also have several other cost centers. Cost centers can be structured hierarchically to help organize and manage where costs occur, as Figure 16 shows. The figure is just an example and does not necessarily reflect all cost centers needed in a typical company.

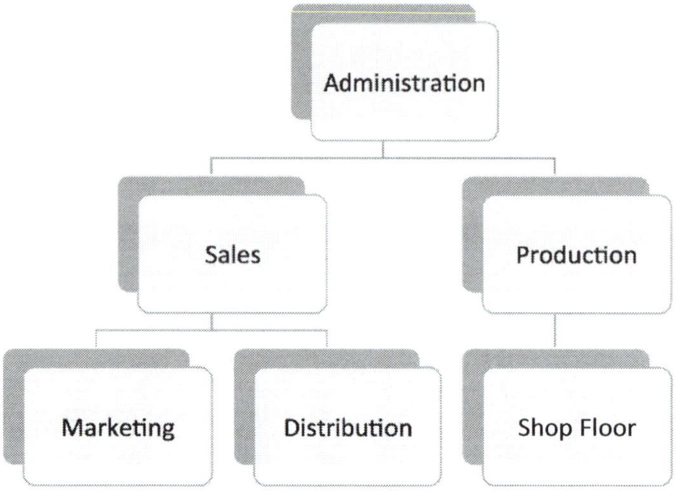

Figure 16: Possible cost center hierarchy for *Administration*

Being a hierarchy, the higher level cost centers aggregate costs from the cost centers below them. For example, the top level cost center "Administration" accumulates the costs of all the cost centers below it. Of course it is also possible that some costs – such as the utility costs described above – can be directly allocated to the "Administration" cost center. Therefore the sum of all the costs of the cost centers below "Administration" need not equal the costs accumulated in the "Administration" cost center.

Additionally, the costs in the "Sales" cost center will include the costs of the two cost centers directly below it as well as costs directly charged to it.

Cost Element

The term *cost element* is used to refer to a *category* of cost. Thus *rent payment* might be a *cost element*. For example, suppose the company pays rent of $3,000 in one transaction, that represents an occurrence of the cost element *rent payment* and can be assigned to some cost center.

Consumables purchase might be another cost element and if the company buys some consumables for use by a particular department, that is an occurrence of the cost element *consumables purchase* and will be assigned to some cost center corresponding to the department for which the consumable was purchased.

Thus a *cost element* represents a *particular type of cost* which the company wants to track. The management accounting process can charge occurrences of a cost element to an appropriate cost center. In management accounting speak, individual occurrences of cost elements can be *posted* to cost centers. (See the discussion of primary and secondary cost elements below for a more complete discussion.)

The above examples involved the posting of cost elements to cost centers. Cost elements can also be posted to other so called *cost objects* in SAP.

> **Review 16:** Through an example, bring out the difference between a *cost element* and an *occurrence* of a cost element.

Cost Element Accounting

Cost Element Accounting concerns the part of cost accounting involved in the recording and classification of the costs incurred during a given period.

Settlement Period

As we have already seen in many of the above examples, some costs are directly assigned to a cost center. Other costs, like the *utility* example above are incurred jointly and then *allocated* to various other cost centers.

The company might use the *Administration* cost center to accumulate all costs for, say, a month. Let us suppose this comes out to $100,000. Now this $100,000 has to be allocated to other areas of the organization because they used utilities and should bear their share of the cost.

In management accounting, we will take the costs in the *Administration* cost center and apportion the cost to various other cost centers on some basis. This apportionment process does not go on continuously. That is, as each cost element is used to add costs to the *Administration* cost center, it is not immediately apportioned to other cost centers. Instead, this might be done periodically. For example, companies might accumulate the electricity costs for a whole month, and at the end of the month, apportion the costs of this cost center to other cost centers.

In this example, each month is a *settlement period*. Thus all electricity costs incurred in the month of December 2014 will be allocated to other cost centers as allocations for the month of December 2014. Note that the settlement period need not always be a month. Some companies might do settlement weekly and others even daily (rare).

Sender and Receiver Cost Centers

In the above example, we saw that the costs accumulated in the *Administration* cost center for a particular *settlement period* are divided across many other cost centers that use utilities and hence must bear the costs. In this example, *Administration* is the *sender cost center* and the other cost centers that bear the total cost are the *receiver cost centers*.

> **Review 17:** A company has created a cost center called *CEO Office* to track the expenses of the CEO's office. At the end of each settlement period, it allocates these costs to ten different cost centers corresponding to the overhead expense for various divisions. When settlement occurs, what will be the sending and receiving cost centers?

Primary Cost Element

We have already seen that a cost element is a category of cost, whose occurrences can be charged to a cost center. Thus when the company pays rent of $3000 for the month of December 2014 to a particular party as a single payment, it represents an occurrence of the cost element rent payment. Financial accounting (FI) first records this as an expense. As of that time, the cost has not yet reached the management accounting (CO) module at all.

Management accounting clearly needs to get hold of the expense and assign it to some cost center.

The expense has to first flow from financial accounting to management accounting – as a cost.

The rent expense is first recorded in financial accounting as an expense. It only becomes a *cost* when it enters management accounting. How does the cost flow from financial accounting to management accounting (from FI to CO)?

We already know that there are various *expense accounts* in FI to record expenses. In SAP, expense accounts in financial accounting are directly connected to *primary cost elements*. Thus, as soon as an entry is made in an expense account, the system automatically uses an existing primary cost element to transfer it as a cost for management accounting (CO) to process.

This is the mechanism by which expenses in FI flow into CO. Whenever an expense is posted to an expense account, an instance of a primary cost element is created in management accounting – that is, there is a one-to-one correspondence between expense accounts and primary cost elements. The primary cost element instance resulting from an expense posting in financial Accounting gets posted to a specified cost center, as Figure 17 shows.

Secondary Cost Element

Continuing with the rent example, we see that a rent posting to an expense account in FI resulted in the use of the cost element *rent payment*. The cost was posted into (debited to) the cost center *Sales*.

As an aside, note that the posting using a primary cost element into a cost center is a *one sided* posting because it only resulted in a debit and no corresponding credit. This differs from postings in financial accounting which are always two-sided.

When an expense in FI enters CO as a cost, the cost is just entering CO, with no balancing posting. This is why it is a one-

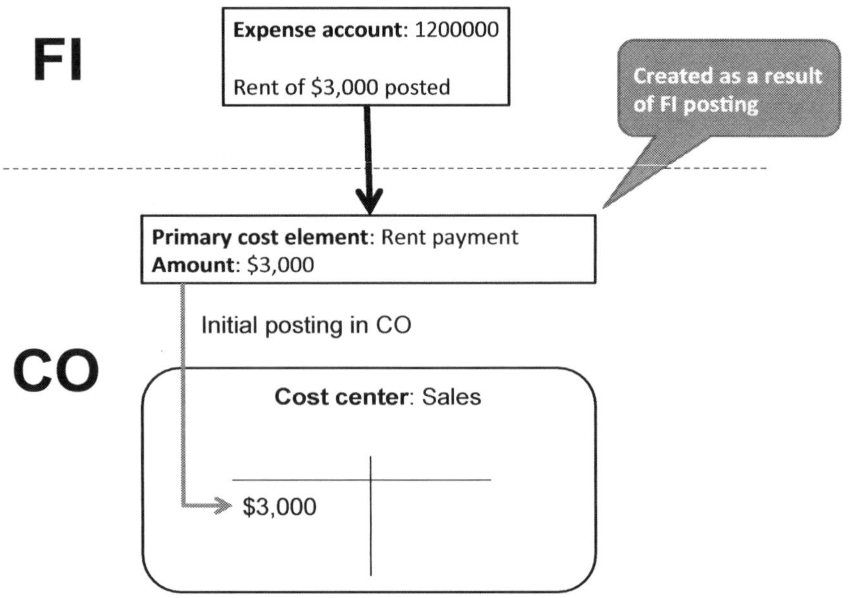

Figure 17: Flow of expense from financial accounting through a primary cost element

sided posting.

Suppose that the distribution and marketing departments occupy one building and each has a cost center to record its total expenses. Suppose the company pays rent of $6,000 for the month of December 2014 for that building in three different payments (Dec 7, Dec 14 and Dec 21).

Following the mechanisms outlined in Figure 17, these three rent payments will result in three postings to the cost center *Sales* as Figure 18 shows.

The Distribution and Marketing departments occupy the same building and have to share the rent of the building totaling $6,000 as above. Suppose the rent is allocated in proportion to the area occupied by these two departments and that Distribution occupies 4000 sqft and Marketing occupies 8000 sqft, then Distribution is responsible for $2,000 and Marketing for $4,000. Let us assume that Distribution and Marketing have appropriate cost centers for absorbing the rent allocated to them.

We already know that this allocation will occur at the end of the *settlement period*, say end of December 2014. Note that these postings create debit entries in the receiving cost centers and a credit posting in the sender cost center. The picture then is as shown in Figure 19 .

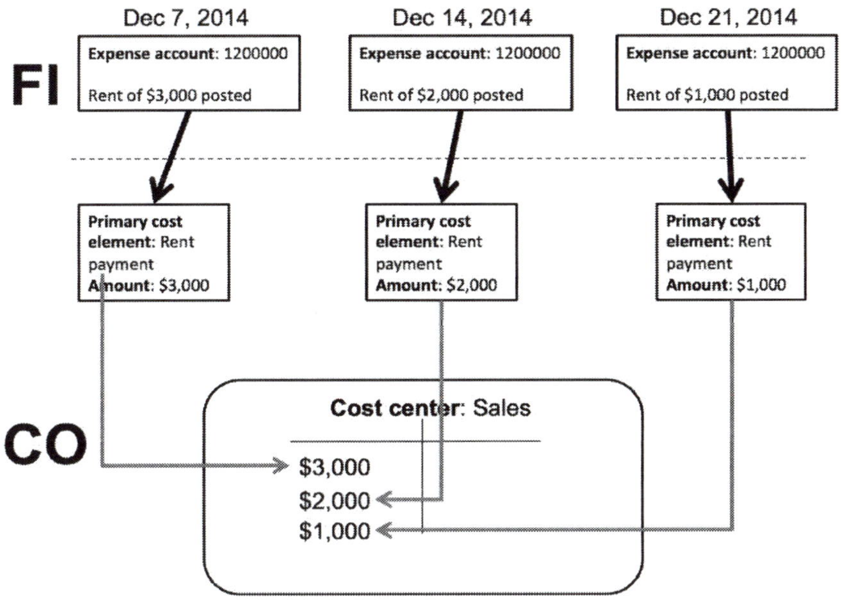

Figure 18: Flow of three rent postings from FI to CO. The primary cost element Rent payment has the same account number (120000) as the corresponding expense account.

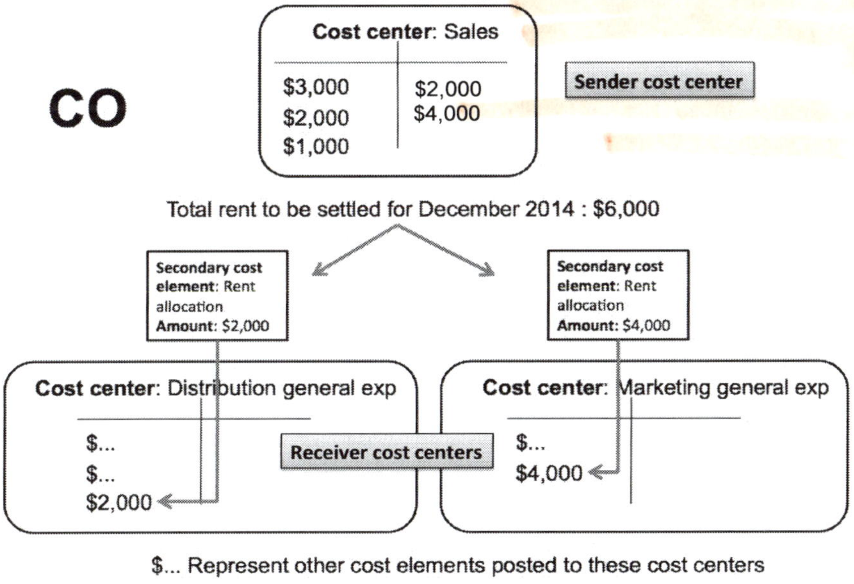

Figure 19: Settlement of total rent of $6,000 through postings within CO

From Figure 19 you can see that at the time of settlement, the accumulated costs from the sender cost center (for the settlement period) are split up into appropriate secondary cost elements, which are them posted into the receiver cost centers.

Controlling Area

In SAP, management accounting can result in cost allocations that cut across company codes within a client. This could occur because several company codes might share resources. For example, two company codes could share the same manufacturing facilities. Or there might be a purchasing organization that does purchasing for multiple company codes. In such cases, allocation of costs might cut across company codes.

This is why the top level organization unit for management accounting has to be above the level of a company code.

Controlling area is the top level organization unit for management accounting and can include multiple company codes within it.

However, note these two very important points:

- If multiple company codes are allocated to the same controlling area, the company codes must use the same operating Chart of Accounts and fiscal year variant.
- Cost movements in management accounting can only happen across company codes belonging to the same controlling area.

Order-related cost object controlling

We have seen earlier that *cost centers* can collect costs for possible redistribution. In SAP, cost centers are not the only objects that can accumulate costs. Consider a production order for making 100 units of some material. In order to compute the unit cost of that batch of material, we would need to accumulate all costs that go towards completing that production order. To facilitate this, the production order *collects* costs as it progresses. For example, when materials are issued, their cost is added to the production order. Later some labor time might be incurred on the production order and those costs are also added to the production order, and so on. Thus the production order acts as a *cost collector* and is an example of an *Order-Related Cost Object*.

In SAP, in addition to production orders, other orders like *maintenance orders*, *customer service orders* and *internal orders* (also called *CO orders*) can collect costs. These are also *Order-Related Cost Objects*. Though each of these orders is used for different processes, there are great similarities in the management accounting process that each goes through.

They all follow a standard sequence of steps from a management accounting viewpoint. Figure 20 shows the steps in the standard process that applies to all order-related costs objects. (Note: Each of these order types may have additional steps required that are unique to its own process.)

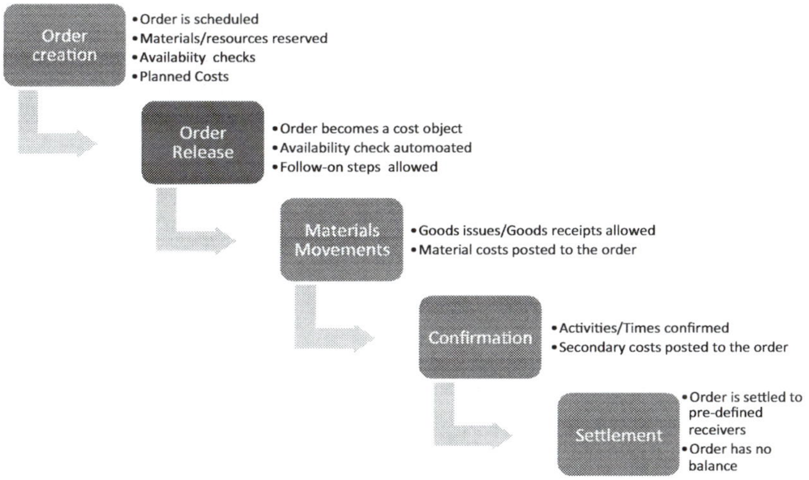

Figure 20: Generic process for *Order-Related Cost Objects*

During order creation, the order has not yet become a cost object. At this stage, this simply means costs cannot yet be posted to the order. However, the order is scheduled (as in the case of a production order) when resources necessary to perform work on the order become available. Thus, resources are then reserved for this order. The order may also require materials. Consider the example of a customer who brings in a defective item for repair. To repair that item, not only will resources be required, but materials are also likely to be necessary. Thus, materials are placed on reservation for the order. But what if there are no materials available? This isn't a problem for an

ERP system like SAP. The user could check inventory in the system to see if the materials exist. If not, the user can simply create a purchase order for what is missing. Ultimately when the order is created, all of the necessary materials and labor resources (as well as potential overhead costs) are calculated by the ERP system. In this way, the user is now made aware of the planned costs on this order.

The next step in order-related cost object controlling is the order release (highlighted in Figure 20). This is the most important step! If the order is not released, none of the follow-on steps can be completed. It is at this time that the order officially becomes a cost object. Actual costs can now be posted to this order and can be compared to the planned costs that were calculated in the previous step. If the user did not check material availability when the order was created, an ERP system like SAP automatically checks to see if materials are available. If they are not available (depending on the system settings) the system can block the order release until materials are available.

The step after the release of the order is generally a goods movement. The goods movement could be a goods issue from inventory to the order, or a goods receipt from a purchase order to the order. When these goods movements are posted, they are posted as expenses in financial accounting and a primary cost element posts the costs to the order in management accounting. These are actual costs which again can be compared to the planned costs in the order.

Material costs are not the only costs associated with order-related cost object controlling. There are additional costs, usually resulting from work completed on the order by one or more work centers. These costs are posted to the order when work centers confirm the work they performed. They could confirm this work in a number of ways, but the most common methods are to confirm the amount of time they spent working on the order as well as which activities they performed. These costs are considered secondary costs because they are not a result of direct expenses posted in financial accounting. Instead, they are costs that are allocated to the order from another cost object in management accounting. Recall that secondary cost elements are used to allocate such costs.

Finally, the order will go through the settlement step. Here, the costs collected in the order are normally settled to a predefined receiver. A receiver is an object that is ultimately responsible for the costs in the order. In management accounting, an order-related cost object can settle its costs to financial accounting general ledger accounts. Other receivers might be cost centers, projects, other orders, or profitability analysis. In the end, the order is settled so there are no remaining costs. In other words, the order has no balance on the debit or credit sides; its debit and credit entries balance out.

Chapter-end review questions

You can find suggested answers to these questions starting from page 229

To answer questions marked with ★, you will need to have read the official SAP TERP10 course material.

1. Which of the following questions might the Overhead Cost Controlling module of CO deal with? (two) ★

   A What is the unit cost of Product A?
   B How much did we spend on utilities in July 2011?
   C How should we allocate the costs of our IT department?
   D Did Profit Center X meet its target profit?

2. Which of the following questions might the Product Cost Accounting module of CO deal with? (two) ★

   A What is the unit cost of Product A?
   B How much did we spend on utilities in July 2011?
   C How much did production order Y cost as a whole?
   D Did Profit Center X meet its target profit?

3. Which of the following questions might the Profitability Analysis module of CO deal with? (one) ★

   A Did Profit Center X meet its target profit?
   B How profitable was company code 1000 in the Northern Region?
   C How much did we spend on utilities in July 2011?
   D How much did production order Y cost as a whole?
   E How much did project X cost?

4. Name one cost that might flow from each of the following modules to CO. Also indicate one sub-module within CO where it might be used.

   A FI (general)
   B FI-AA (Asset Accounting)
   C HCM (Human Capital Management)
   D MM (Materials Management)
   E PP (Production planning and execution)
   F SD (Sales and distribution)

5. Indicate one way in which CO might have an impact on FI.
6. Which organization element is concerned with Profitability analysis CO-PA? ★
7. Which organizational element is the top level for Overhead cost controlling? ★
8. Which organizational element is the top level for Product Cost Accounting CO-PCA? ★
9. Which organizational element is the top level for Profit Center Accounting EC-PCA? ★
10. A Business Area should be totally contained within one controlling area T/F?
11. One controlling area can have multiple company codes T/F?
12. One company code can belong to multiple controlling areas T/F?
13. A controlling area can have only one standard hierarchy (True/False).
14. A Client (in the SAP sense) has many controlling areas with each containing multiple cost centers. What restriction applies to the movement of costs across cost centers in this context?
15. Two company codes (1000 and 2000) in a given SAP client belong to the same controlling area. Account 100000 in company code 1000 is an expense account and account 200000 in company code 2000 is an asset account. What other facts can you infer from these two facts?

16. Explain the mechanism used to transfer information from FI to CO.

17. What type of cost elements can be posted to directly from FI and what type cannot?

18. Which Master Data Group is mandatory for a controlling area (not in SAP notes)? ★

19. What does the above contain? ★

20. What does the above group enable? ★

21. Unit price of an activity in Activity Based Costing is determined by ______________ and ______________. ★

22. A company has determined that rents will be allocated based on square footage used by various departments. The square footage is fixed across time periods. This is an example of a Type ______________ Statistical Key Figure. ★

23. You are preparing an assessment in SAP ERP Management Accounting. Which type of cost element is used to perform an assessment? (one) ★

    A Primary
    B Secondary
    C Revenue
    D Cost object

24. What must be created for every expense account in FI, which needs to be managed as a cost in CO. (one)

    A Primary cost element
    B Secondary cost element
    C Activity type
    D Activity price

25. A company accumulates the cost of its cafeteria and allocates this cost to other cost centers at the end of each month. What is this process broadly called?

26. What is the difference between CO postings to primary cost elements and to secondary cost elements in CO?

27. What are the four main elements of a controlling document apart from the document number? ★

28. What three conditions must be met for a journal entry posted to an expense account in FI to flow to a primary cost element in CO?

29. What is periodic allocation used for?

30. Which of the following cannot an example of periodic allocation? (select one) ★

    A Direct activity allocation
    B Assessment
    C Distribution
    D Periodic reposting
    E Template allocation

31. What is the purpose of using template allocation to allocate costs? ★

32. Which of the following might be a good use for an Internal Order? (three) ★

    A The company is going to produce finished goods and wants to have a mechanism to accumulate production costs.
    B The company is organizing a promotional seminar and needs to track all costs incurred for this purpose.
    C The company is buying a new machine and wants an object to which to charge the cost of the machine as well as future costs incurred on the machine.
    D The company is constructing a new parking lot and wants to accumulate the costs incurred.

33. A client in SAP has two different company codes 1000 and 2000 (among others). Company 1000 wants to track commitments but company 2000 does not want to do this. What should company 1000 do that company 2000 does not have to do?

34. What are the two different occasions at which an internal order can be settled? ★

35. Which of the following cannot be a receiver when the costs of an internal order are settled? (One) ★

    A Profit center
    B Cost center
    C Project

D Asset

E Profitability segment

36. What mechanism does SAP use to relate various controlling objects to profit centers? ★

37. What is the difference between a true cost object and a statistical object? ★

38. What is the purpose of a statistical object? ★

39. Which of the following are examples of characteristics used in profitability segments? (three) ★

A Sales region

B Cost of goods sold

C Sales revenue

D Product

E Customer

40. What is the effect on the material master of marking a material standard cost estimate? ★

41. What is the effect on the material master of releasing a material standard cost estimate? ★

42. What does the price control field on the material master determine? ★

43. What two things is the material price in the material master used for? ★

44. Which of the following is used in profitability analysis? (one) ★

A Standard price in the material master

B Standard cost estimate from product costing

Procurement

This chapter deals with purchasing various items for use by the company in carrying out its business. The main external entities with which this process interacts are vendors. This chapter provides a high-level overview of the topic so as to prepare you to be able to read the SAP course materials. The chapter does not get into too much detail as those can be found in the SAP course materials. In SAP, *procurement* is part of the Materials Management or MM module.

Process overview

Whether or not you have prior exposure to organizational purchasing processes, you might benefit at this point by listing the steps that you think should make up the process. As far as possible, try and list the steps chronologically.

Obviously business processes vary from industry to industry and even from company to company. In fact, even a single company could employ a few variations. In this module, we will discuss the basic purchasing process in SAP. As you might already have guessed, SAP allows lots of configuration options to enable a company to tailor the system to suit its specific needs.

Figure 7 on page 30 from the chapter The Big Picture discussed the process briefly. We reproduce it here for convenience in Figure 21, and amplify the earlier discussion.

1. **Purchase requisition**: Initially some department or process identifies that something needs to be purchased. This results in a *Purchase Requisition*.
2. **Source of supply**: The company then needs to find a source of

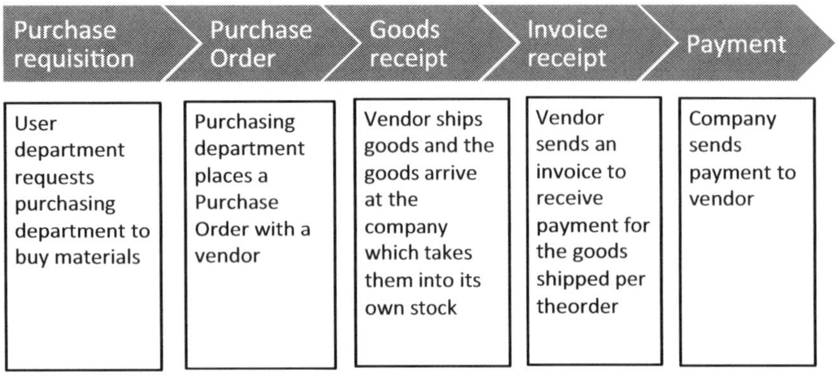

Figure 21: Outline of the Procure to Pay process

supply. This can happen in one of many ways:

- **Select existing vendor**: The company might have many existing vendors who can supply the item. In this case, the company can use performance history and select one from among its existing vendors.
- **Existing agreement or contract**: Often companies have standing agreements or contracts with a vendor for agreed quantities and prices. In this case, the company could simply order against an existing agreement or contract. SAP refers to such standing arrangements as *Outline Agreements* or *Contracts*.
- **Bidding process**: Sometimes a company might choose to invite bids and select a vendor based on the bidding process. In this case, the purchasing company could send out a *Request for Proposal (RFP)* or a *Request for Quotation (RFQ)* to each of several vendors and select a vendor based on their responses. SAP has support for issuing and managing *RFQ/RFP*.

3. **Purchase order**: At the end of the previous step, the company has identified a vendor with whom to place the order. At this point, the purchasing department creates a *Purchase Order* and sends it to the chosen vendor.
4. **Goods receipt**: Based on the *Purchase Order*, the vendor ships the goods. When the goods arrive, the company performs a *goods receipt*. The *goods receipt* process represents the steps to perform during the physical receipt of goods and the subsequent putting away of those goods into storage. Of course, in an integrated ERP system like SAP, just recording that the goods are in storage alone will not

suffice. Think for a minute about what else an integrated system might need to do while receiving goods.

- **Verification**: The first step in receiving goods would be to verify that the shipment is in fact related to something that we ordered. We therefore need to verify that the items supplied were in fact ordered and also note the quantity supplied. Thus, the goods receipt process will refer to the purchase order for verification.
- **Material document**: SAP and other ERP systems generally create a *document* to record the fact that a business transaction took place. When goods are received, SAP creates a *material document* with information about the items received and the storage location where the items were stored.
- **Put away in warehouse**: SAP clearly distinguishes between *Inventory Management* and *Warehouse Management*. Inventory Management deals with keeping track of how much of each item we have in storage in various storage locations. It deals with tracking quantities of items and also their value. *Warehouse Management* deals with the actual placement of items on storage and retrieval from storage shelves. It deals with knowing precisely where the items are and also with how to optimally put away and fetch multiple items from the shelves. You might have had the opportunity to see massive warehouses by the side of highways. Sometimes these warehouses span half a mile or more. Warehouses use forklift trucks and other mechanical equipment to handle material and have to manage their use of energy and manpower. Suppose the warehouse manager ordered a forklift operator to make a trip each time a piece of material was needed, the warehouse would be woefully inefficient. Typically, warehouse operations will bunch together many requests for materials and then use some optimizing algorithm to figure out the most efficient way to pick up all of the materials. For example, they might minimize the distance traveled to pick up all the items. When goods are received, the goods receipt process needs to let the warehouse know that there is some material to be put away in the shelves. This will enable the warehouse people to plan and operate efficiently. Thus the purchasing process needs to interface with warehousing.

Receiving the goods (which we most likely have not yet have paid for), causes our current assets to increase. Thus the process must also interface with Financial Accounting.

5. **Invoice receipt**: Having sent the goods, the vendor will send the purchasing company an invoice. The purchasing company then performs *invoice verification* to make sure that the invoice is in fact for

something that it ordered and something that the vendor actually shipped in the correct quantity. This step is sometimes called *three-point invoice verification* – purchase order, goods receipt and invoice. Sometimes, for simplicity, companies might not always perform a three-point verification.

6. **Vendor payment**: Once the invoice is verified, accounting can pay the vendor, and this completes the *Procure to Pay* process.

The first review question of this chapter appears below. You can find suggested answers to all the review questions in this chapter starting from page 235

> **Review 1:** Which of the above is the first step that has an accounting implication? Why?

> **Review 2:** What is the difference between a *Purchase Requisition* and a *Purchase Order*? Which of these do you think commits the company to something?

> **Review 3:** Based on the above discussion, which other SAP modules might integrate with Procurement? (Procurement is part of Materials Management or MM.)

Organizational Levels

The purchasing business process touches many organizational levels.

Figure 22 shows some – but not all – of the organization levels involved. These four organizational levels occur in all logistics modules in SAP – *Materials Management (MM), Sales and Distribution (SD), Production (PP) and Enterprise Asset Management (EAM).*

We already know about two organizational levels related to MM – ***client*** and ***company code***.

A company code can have many ***plants***. Note that *plants* in SAP are not always production plants. Plants could also be locations from which services are provided. In a consulting

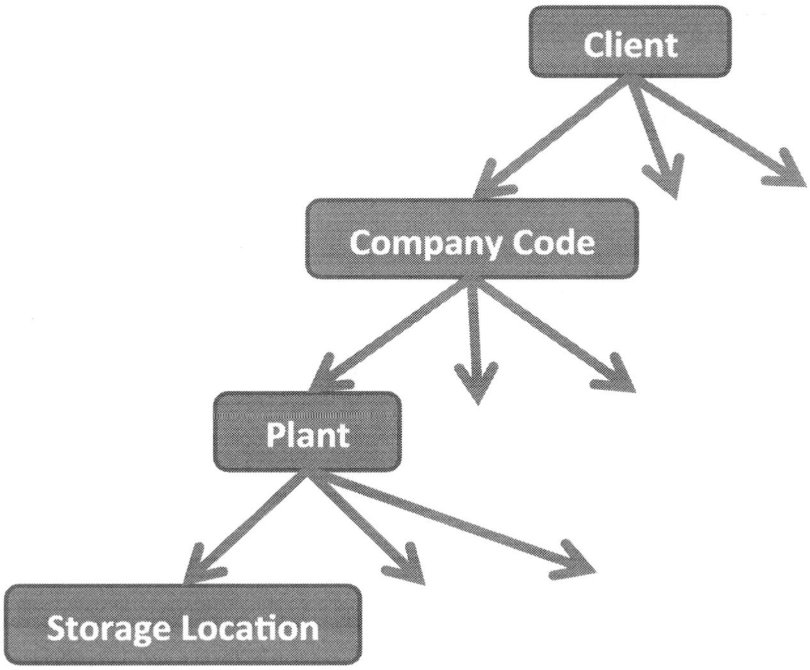

Figure 22: Some of the organizational levels involved in the purchasing process

organization, an office could be treated as a plant from which a customer is serviced.

In SAP, materials are managed at the ***plant*** level. A plant can have many ***storage locations***. A *storage location* is a location where stocks are maintained. Thus we might have 10,000 units of a particular material in a company code, but these might be kept in several different storage locations across different plants, all of which belong to the same company code.

Purchasing organizations in SAP allow a company to strategically manage the purchase process. A *purchasing organization* can negotiate with vendors across many company codes. (Terminological note: In SAP, actual purchasing work is done by *Purchasing Groups* – groups of people. *Purchasing organizations* are the organization levels responsible for managing the negotiated terms with vendors.) A *purchasing organization* can thus serve several company codes.

Alternately we could have a purchasing organization that negotiates with vendors for just one company code or for even just one plant within a company code.

Figure 23 shows the three possibilities.

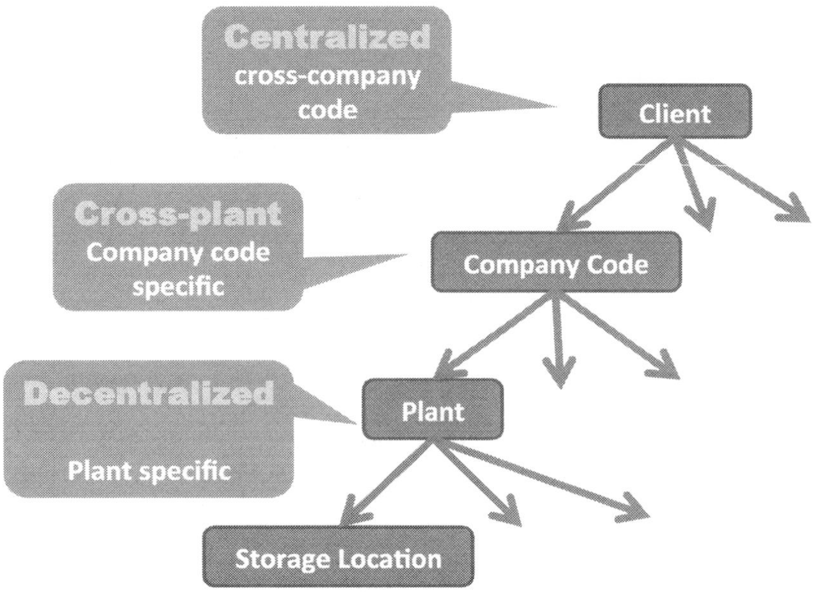

Figure 23: Possible levels at which a purchasing organization can operate

The SAP course materials provide more details.

Purchasing group refers to a set of people who actually carry out purchasing related activities.

Inventory Management Vs. Warehouse Management

Inventory management is the process of keeping track of how many units of each material we have in each storage location. It is concerned with just quantities and values of materials and with storage locations.

Do not confuse inventory management with warehouse management. Whereas inventory management is concerned simply with how much of each material we have on hand and where, warehouse management is concerned with physically managing the storage and movement of materials in storage. Which bin in which shelf in which aisle contains what material? What is the most effective way for us to store a set of items or to pick up a set of items from the warehouse? These are the concerns of warehouse management. The steps associated with the physical management of materials are collectively referred to as *Logistics Execution*.

Procuring for Stock

A company can buy materials whose usage can be looked at in two different ways. One is when a company buys material which it places in stock and then uses as needed.

For example, a company might buy 10,000 units of a particular raw material (say material X) and place it in stock. At this time, these materials have not yet been used for anything and hence the cost of these cannot yet be allocated to any cost center or other *cost object*. That is, when materials have been purchased and placed in stock for later use, they exist in the form of current assets that have not yet been expensed. Since no department or business process has yet consumed the material, the company has actually not yet incurred any *expense* on account of these materials – from a financial accounting viewpoint.

At some later point in time, the company might need to use the material X in stock to make some finished products. For example, let us assume that the company is about to initiate the production process. The company will create a *Planned Order*. Just as a *Purchase Requisition* could be the basis for a *Purchase Order*, a *Planned Order* could form the basis for a *Production Order*.

To execute the *Production Order*, someone might issue 500 units of material X from stock. These 500 units are issued against *Production Order* – therefore the production order is now responsible for the cost of these materials. That is, the cost of the material will be included in the cost of finished goods produced for this *Production Order*.

The key point is that when the material was originally purchased, we knew that the material would be used, but had no idea exactly which object is going to bear the cost. That becomes known only when some object comes along and *consumes* the material – like our production order did.

The above illustrates *purchasing for stock*. In summary, when materials are purchased for stock, their cost is not allocated to anyone or anything at the time of purchase. These materials just form part of the current assets and only impact the balance sheet of the company when the purchase process is executed.

They have not yet become expenses for the company – that is, they have still not had an impact on the income statement of the company. That will happen when they are consumed.

Procuring for Consumption

A company might also procure many materials *for consumption*. This happens when materials are purchased for a specific use and the cost of the material is immediately allocated to some *cost object* – for example, a *cost center*. When the material for such a purchase arrives, it is not placed in inventory for later use, but is instead treated as *consumed* directly.

Even at the time of purchase, it has already been determined which object will be responsible for the cost of the items. In such cases, the cost of the material is directly treated as expenditure and hence does not appear as part of current assets.

Most importantly, when we procure materials for consumption, the cost of such materials is assigned to some *account assignment object* when the purchase order is created. A good example of an account assignment object is a cost center.

Let us take a concrete example. Suppose the accounting department wants to buy a case of printing paper for its internal use and the procurement department buys it for them. Now this case of printing paper is not going to be kept in stock like a raw material and then issued to the accounting department when it asks. This case of printing paper is being purchased specifically for the accounting department and the expense will be absorbed by its cost center right away. Looked at another way, this is an expenditure, and it hits the income statement immediately. The value of the case of printing paper is not part of the company's assets.

Taking the example further it is quite likely that the company would want to keep track of the case of printing paper that was purchased for the accounting department. The company might have purchased such items for other departments and, on earlier occasions, even for the accounting department itself, and might want to keep track of the quantities of such items, but not their monetary value as an asset on the balance sheet.

Inventory management in SAP deals with keeping track of materials. In *value-based inventory management*, we track the quantities and the monetary value of materials – typically those that form part of the assets of a company. In *quantity-based inventory management*, we track only the quantities of the concerned materials and do not keep track of their monetary value. The case of printing paper purchased for the accounting department in our earlier example would likely be subject only to quantity based inventory management – if any inventory management is done for those materials at all. In SAP, individual materials might be subject to *value based inventory management*, *quantity based inventory management* or not subject to inventory management at all.

The key difference between procuring for stock and for consumption is that the latter requires that we specify an *account assignment object* at the time we create a purchase order.

Another example of an account assignment object is an *asset* – like a piece of machinery. Suppose we are buying spare parts for a specific piece of equipment – say a truck. In this example, the cost of the spare part does not hit the income statement immediately, but will do so when depreciation is charged for the asset (truck) at some future point in time. Other examples of account assignment objects are *project* and *internal order*.

The distinction between procuring for stock and for consumption has another implication. When an invoice for an item that is purchased for consumption arrives, any small price difference regarding the amount is charged to the appropriate account assignment object (like cost center). Therefore the process interfaces with management accounting (CO).

Goods Movements

When we procure material, we receive material and place them in stock in some storage location. *Goods receipt* is an important step because it brings into a storage location material that was not there earlier. Receipt of goods into a storage location is a *goods movement*.

SAP recognizes several types of goods movements. Each movement is assigned a number to indicate what type of movement it is. The *movement type* determines how the accounting postings are made.

Goods can be received into *unrestricted use* stock. This means that these materials are ready for use and can be issued to users.

On the other hand, some material might be such that we have to inspect them before using. In this case, we will receive the material into *stock in quality inspection*.

Sometimes goods might be received into *blocked stock*. In all cases, the goods are *valuated*. That is, the value of these goods is part of the current assets of the company. All of these are movement type 101.

We can distinguish between goods movements that are actually physical movements and some which are considered movements, but involve no physical movement of the goods. Suppose we receive 200 units of some raw material into unrestricted use stock and place them in some storage location. However, later we come across information to the effect that goods supplied by the concerned vendor have been faulty. We now decide that we should inspect those materials before using them.

Thus we now have to re-categorize those materials as being in *quality inspection* and not in *unrestricted use* stock. This re-categorization involves no actual physical movement. The materials are going to sit in the same place, but we now record that they are in quality inspection. This re-categorization is also a form of *goods movement* although it involves no physical movement.

Generally, goods movements involving physical movements are called *stock transfers* and those that do not involve physical movement are called *transfer postings*. The unit on Inventory and Warehouse Management explores this in greater depth.

Chapter-end review questions

You can find suggested answers to all these questions starting from page 236

To answer questions marked with ★, you will need to have

read the official SAP TERP10 course material.

1. Which of the following represent organization levels at which stock can be tracked? (three) ★

   A Storage location
   B Client
   C Business area
   D Company code
   E Controlling area

2. Which of the following represent valid options for purchasing organizations? (three)

   A Cross client
   B Cross company code
   C Cross plant
   D Dedicated to a single plant
   E For a single storage location

3. How many plants can a storage location be attached to?

4. How many storage locations can a plant have?

5. How many plants can a company code have?

6. How many company codes can a plant belong to?

7. What information is needed to uniquely identify a plant within an SAP client? ★

8. What information is needed to uniquely identify a storage location within an SAP client? ★

9. What is the difference in customizing when creating a centralized purchasing organization and when creating a decentralized purchasing organization? ★

10. Which of the following represent levels at which material master data is defined? (three) ★

    A Plant
    B Client
    C Company code
    D Purchasing organization
    E Storage location

11. Which of the following represent levels at which vendor master data is defined? (three) ★

   A Plant
   B Client
   C Company code
   D Purchasing organization
   E Storage location

12. Which master data contains information about the combination of a material and a vendor? ★

13. Describe the condition under which the price of a material on a purchase order might come from the Purchasing Info Record. ★

14. Which of the following processes is not part of SAP procurement? (one)

   A Supply source determination
   B Goods issue
   C Purchase order monitoring
   D Invoice verification
   E Goods receipt

15. Which of the following is not a feasible option in SAP procurement? One cannot create a purchase order for: (pick one) ★

   A Procuring a stock item with a material master record
   B Procuring an item without a material master record for consumption
   C Procuring an item with a material master record for consumption
   D Procuring a stock item without a material master record

16. Which of the following represent ways by which a purchase requisition might be created? (four) ★

   A By SAP SRM
   B By SAP CRM
   C By SAP SCM
   D Manually
   E By MRP
   F From a purchase order

17. A purchase requisition can be created in one of many ways. What in the purchase requisition enables us to find out how a purchase requisition was created? ★

18. What could be one reason for maintaining a material master record for a material for which we intend to perform no inventory management whatsoever? ★

19. What could be one reason for maintaining a material master record for which we intend to perform inventory management only for quantity, but not value?

20. When purchasing material for which there is no material master, how does the material description get populated on the purchase requisition? ★

21. Which of the following purchasing situations require us to provide an account assignment object? An account assignment object is mandatory for procuring: (pick two)

    A Any material that is subject to value based inventory management

    B Any material that is not subject to value based inventory management

    C Any material without a material master record

    D Any material for stock which will later be consumed for production of finished goods

22. Which of the following represent valid account assignment categories? (four) ★

    A Cost center

    B Profit center

    C Vendor

    D Project

    E Asset

    F Order

23. What is the difference between an account assignment category and an account assignment object? ★

24. In terms of immediate financial accounting impact, how do purchasing to stock and for consumption differ?

25. What name is given to an internal purchase order that is used to move stock? ★

26. While checking the status of a purchase order, SAP supports status checking for the order as a whole and for individual items T/F? ★

27. Which of the following is not part of a purchase order? (one) ★

    A Header
    B Items
    C Schedule lines

28. Which item category represents vendor-owned material kept in a company's storage, and will be billed based on actual usage only? (one) ★

    A Standard
    B Subcontracting
    C Consignment
    D Third party
    E Stock transfer

29. Which item category represents material that a company provides to a vendor to incorporate in a product that we are buying from the vendor? (one) ★

    A Standard
    B Subcontracting
    C Consignment
    D Third party
    E Stock transfer

30. Which item category represents material that a company asks the vendor to ship directly to an entity different from the company placing the order? (one) ★

    A Standard
    B Subcontracting
    C Consignment
    D Third party
    E Stock transfer

31. Which of the following does not represent a consequence of a goods receipt from a vendor against a purchase order? (one) ★

A Creation of a material document
B Posting to a vendor account
C Creation of an accounting document
D Update of the purchase order

32. A company wants to ensure that all goods receipts of a specific material from all vendors are first inspected before use. Where can this be set? ★

33. A company wants to ensure that all goods receipts of a specific material produced in-house are first inspected before use. Where can this be set? ★

34. In general, what are the four different places within SAP where one can specify that particular material should first be inspected before use? ★

35. When material is received into stock in quality inspection, will the value of stock increase before it clears inspection? ★

36. Stock overview is said to be a static view. What does this mean? ★

37. A material was in a storage location and awaiting quality inspection. It was inspected in place and cleared for unrestricted use. What type of goods movement occurred – stock transfer or transfer posting?

38. A company has activated inspection processing in its quality management system. What implications does this have for inventory management? ★

39. Will a stock transfer of a material from one storage location to another in the same plant have any financial impact? ★

40. All goods movements result in material documents T/F?

41. If warehouse management is active, how might a goods receipt impact warehouse management?

42. What impact might a goods receipt have on the material master? ★

43. What is the impact of a goods receipt if QM is active? ★

44. What step completes the logistics steps in the procurement process?

45. What is the difference between purchase order based invoice verification and delivery based invoice verification? ★

46. Under what conditions would an invoice posting need to update the moving average price in the materials master? ★

47. Which of the following could represent characteristics used in reporting structures for procurement? (two) ★

    A Purchasing organization
    B Order quantity
    C PO value
    D Vendor
    E Delivery quantity

48. Which of the following could represent Key Figures used in reporting structures for procurement? (three) ★

    A Purchasing organization
    B Order quantity
    C PO value
    D Vendor
    E Delivery quantity

Material planning

This chapter introduces the material planning business process as relevant for the TERP 10 certification examination. It introduces key terms and provides background knowledge that will prepare readers for SAP's course material.

The *Material Planning* business process deals with the integrated planning of the procurement of raw materials used in manufacturing finished products. Think for a moment about the various things that the process of planning raw material procurement must consider (see Figure 24):

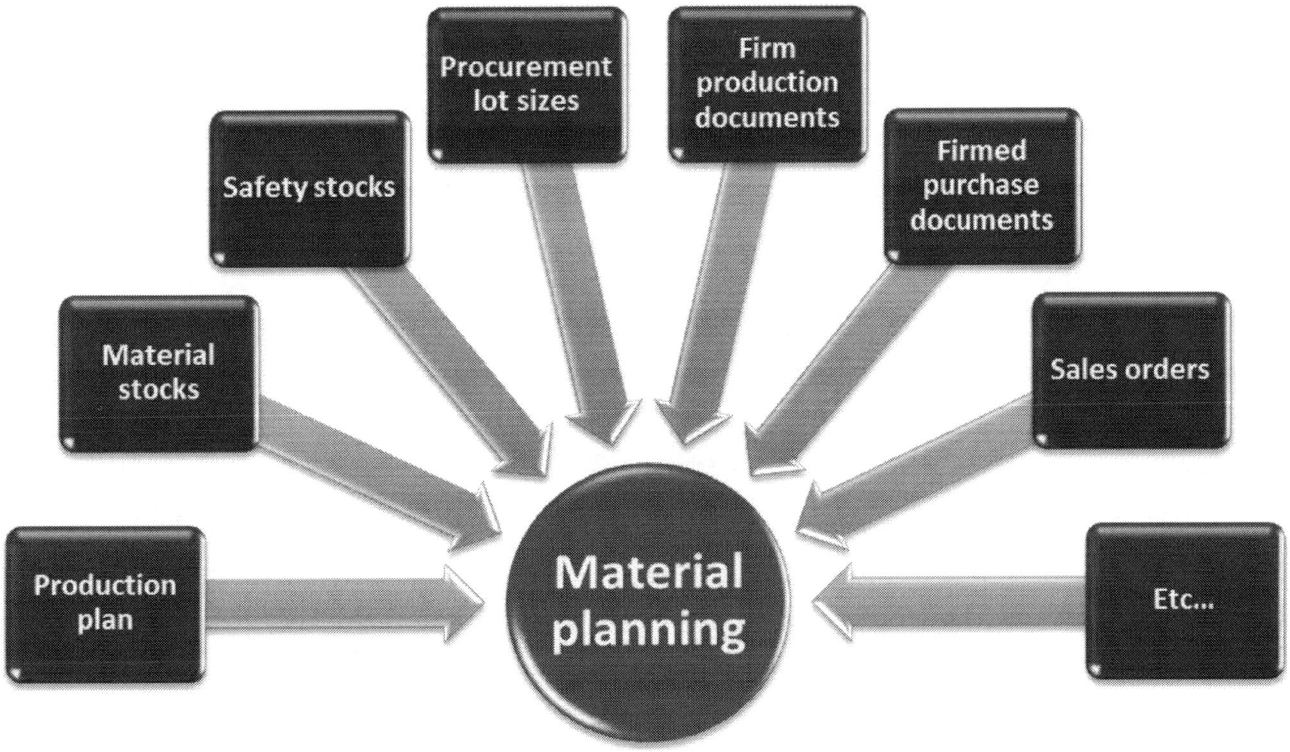

Figure 24: Inputs for the material planning process

- Production plans for the relevant planning horizon.
- Material stocks at various locations.
- Safety stocks of various materials.
- Procurement lot sizes for various materials.
- Finalized or firmed up production orders that will consume materials currently in stock.
- Purchase orders and other means of procurement that are already in the pipeline and against which the company will receive materials.
- Confirmed sales orders for made-to-order items (that is items that the company does not produce for stock and instead only manufactures against firm orders).

We can see that unless the process takes all of the above into account, the end result might not be as good as it could be. Even moderate sized companies deal with many finished goods, each of which uses many raw materials. On top of that numerous purchase orders could be in various stages of fulfillment and several production orders could be in a firmed state.

The process includes additional complicating factors that the above list does not show. Given all of these, planning for materials could be a very complicated process consuming lots of time and effort. The *Material Planning* process serves to integrate and automate this complicated activity.

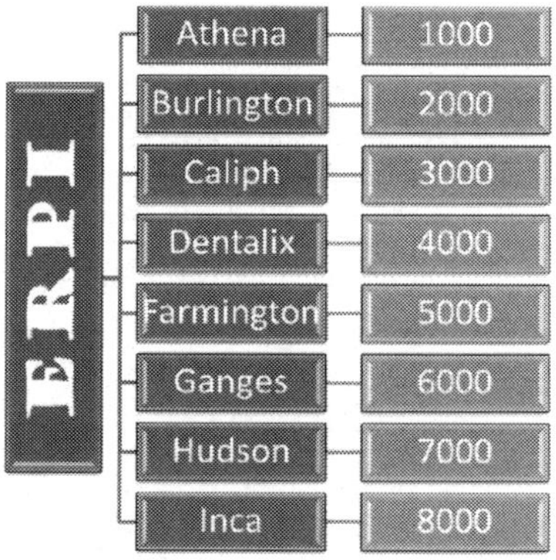

Figure 25: Client and company codes

Organization Levels

Material Planning involves the following organization levels:

- **Client:** Client is used in almost all modules and business processes. (see Figure 25)
- **Company Code:** Also used in most of the modules and business processes.
- **Plant:** In SAP, materials are managed at the plant level and thus plants play an important role in material planning.
- **Storage Location:** Materials are physically stored in various storage locations and stocks are also tracked primarily by storage location. Thus storage locations play an important role in material planning. (see Figure 26)

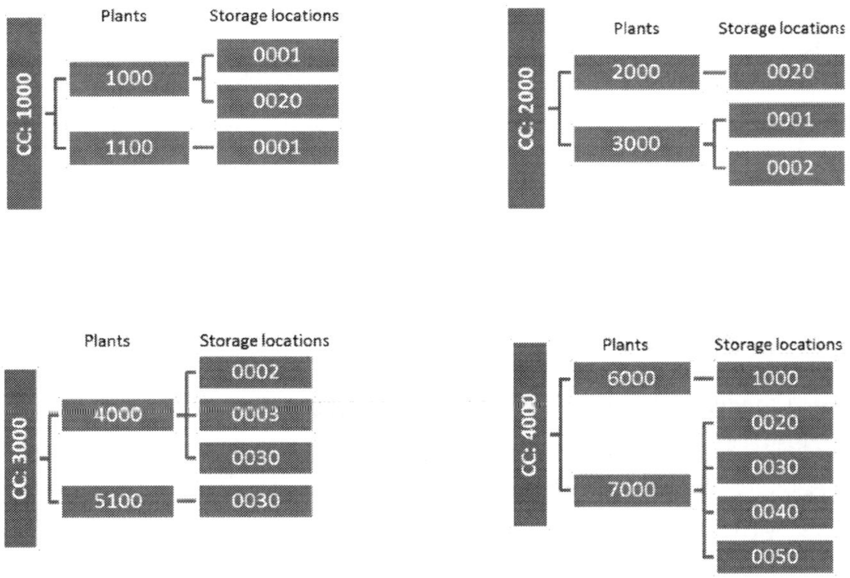

Figure 26: Company codes, plants and storage locations

Master Data

Business processes in SAP make use of various items of master data. The material planning business process uses the following:

- **Material Master:** Contains information about each material – including material number, name, units of measurement, and such.
- **Bill of Materials or BOM:** For every finished product, its BOM specifies what raw materials and how much of each goes into the product.

  A BOM does not just specify what raw materials go into each finished product. It actually specifies the complete hierarchy of sub assemblies and raw materials that make up each finished product. From the BOM, one can figure out exactly how much of each material is needed to make a certain number of units (or quantity) of a product.
- **Routing:** Routings specify the steps in the production process for a finished product. For each step, the routing specifies the work center where the step will be performed, the time it takes to set up the machine, the time it takes to process a single piece and so on. Why is the routing important for material planning?

  It looks like routings are more concerned with the actual process of production rather than for material planning. After all, so far as material planning is concerned, what does it matter where an operation is performed or how long it takes? Actually it does matter, because in material planning, we are concerned not just with how much of a material is needed, but also with *when* it is needed. Not all materials might be needed when the process starts. If a particular material is needed only in the fourth step of an operation which might start a week after the first step starts, then procurement can be planned accordingly.

Material Planning (MRP)

In this book we will look at a simple outline of the process to emphasize the key aspects. The SAP course materials go into greater detail. Once you understand the simple sketch of the process, you should be in a good position to take on the additional details in the official course material.

At the very outset, let us establish some important terminology.

- In a **make-to-stock** scenario, a company makes finished products and stores them as finished goods stock. Then the company sells finished products as customers place *sales orders*.
- In a **make-to-order** scenario, a company first receives sales orders from customers and only then manufactures finished goods to fulfill the *sales orders* already received.

What are the pros and cons of each strategy? In **make-to-stock**, a company takes on greater risk because it is producing in advance. What if some of the manufactured products do not sell? There is scope for finished goods to go to waste. In **make-to-order** a company takes on no risk of a finished product going unsold, but the downside is that its delivery lead time will be higher since it will produce only after receiving the order. A competitor who can ship quicker could have an advantage.

In this book we assume that a company could be using a mix of the two approaches. Perhaps for some of the products the company could use *make-to-stock* and for others, use *make-to-order*.

Companies also use a third hybrid option that serves to get the best of both worlds and this is called **subassembly planning**. In **subassembly planning** companies might produce sub assemblies (components using which the final products are assembled) to stock, and perform only the final assembly or other final step based on actual sales orders.

At its core, the material planning business process aims to make materials available in time for production processes to be completed on schedule to fill planned sales. The material planning process has to be repeated at regular time intervals.

Suppose a company does material planning once every month for all its materials (a simplification of reality, no doubt, because companies could have different planning cycles for different materials and for different plants). At the start of each month, the company might make a three-month material plan. Although, at the start of January, the company would have planned its materials through the end of March, we have to remember that the company would have made its plans based on various forecasts and estimates. At the start of February, things would hardly have gone exactly according to plan and thus the material plan done at the start of January would need to be modified for February and March. When the company plans its materials again at the start of February, it can correct for the deviations from the plans.

The material planning process (MRP) plans for materials for manufacturing and must therefore be driven by planned production activities. Production plans, in turn, must be driven by estimates of sales – for products and sub-assemblies that the company makes for stock, and by actual sales orders for products that the company makes to order.

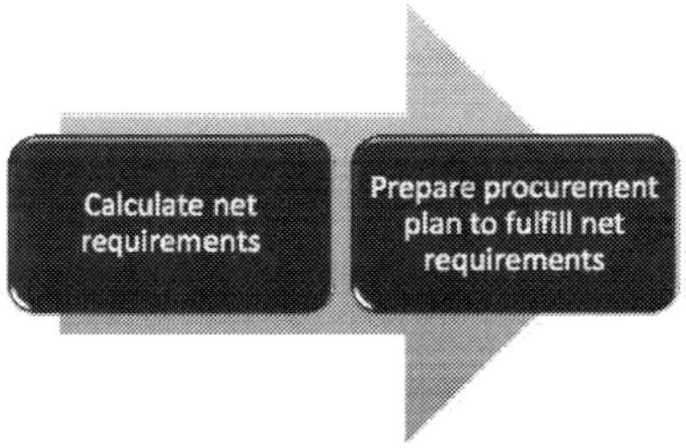

Figure 27: High level view of material planning

Very coarsely speaking, the material planning process has two high level steps that we outline below and describe in slightly greater detail later (see Figure 27).

- **Calculating *net requirements*:** In this step, MRP determines the material shortfall for each day of the planning horizon, taking into consideration all *requirements* (see Figure 28).

- **Preparing *procurement proposals*:** In this step, MRP prepares a plan for how to fill the shortfall. Since the material planning process does integrated planning, it starts out with the shortfall in finished goods and works backward using the BOM to calculate the requirements and shortfall of all sub-assemblies and raw materials. Filling the shortfall could therefore involve purchasing raw materials as well as producing sub assemblies and finished goods. (see Figure 29)

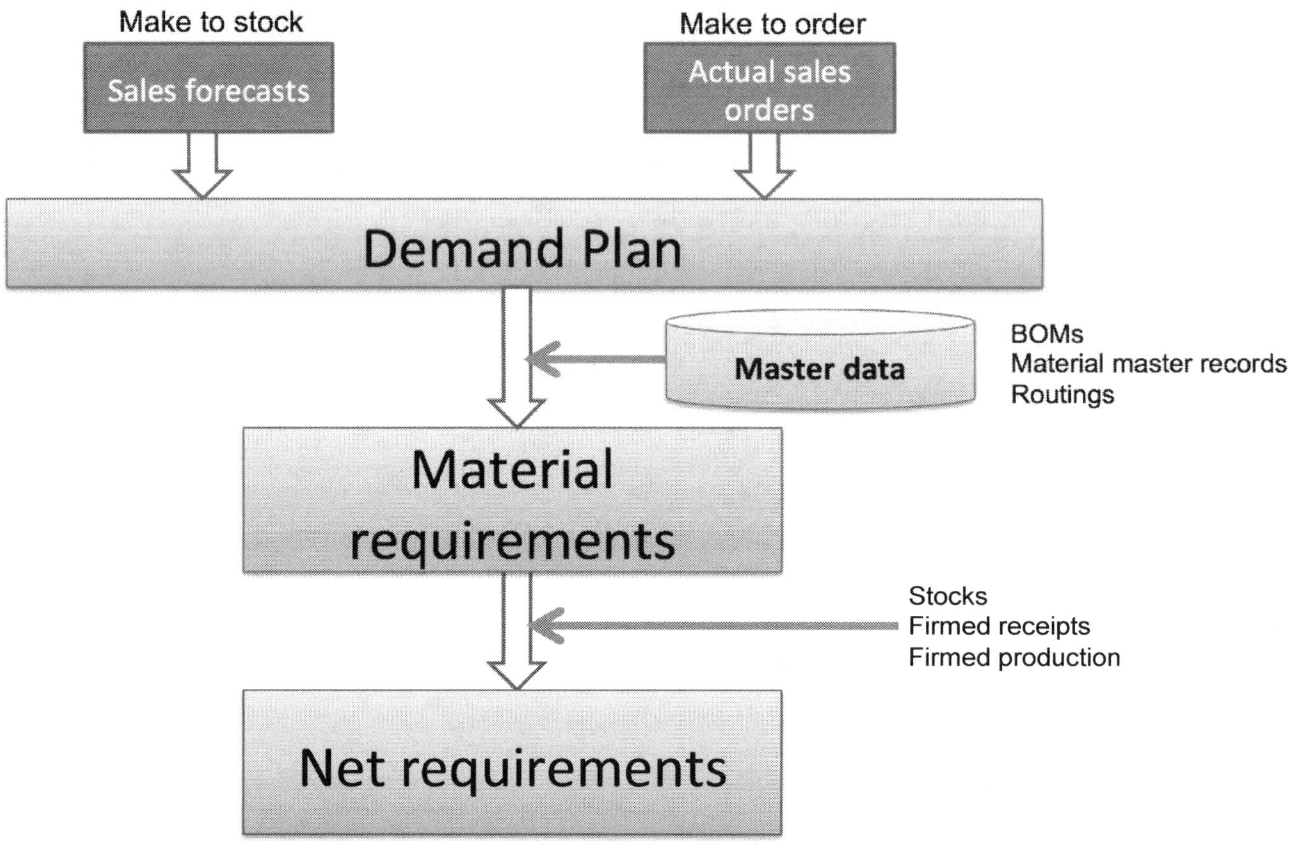

Figure 28: Simplified view of net requirements calculation

Once MRP has determined the net requirements, it will identify how to fill those requirements. Here we have to consider the different types of materials that a company would deal with. *finished goods*, *raw materials* and *semi-finished goods*. Furthermore, it is possible that a company would buy some of the materials only from vendors and might only make some of the materials (especially finished goods and semi-finished goods in-house). Often though, companies make some goods in-house and also buy the same materials from vendors when needed.

For materials that are only bought from vendors and never made in-house, MRP often generates *purchase requisitions*. These purchase requisitions would be created in such a way that they take into account when a material is needed as well as purchasing lot sizes and other considerations. The purchasing process

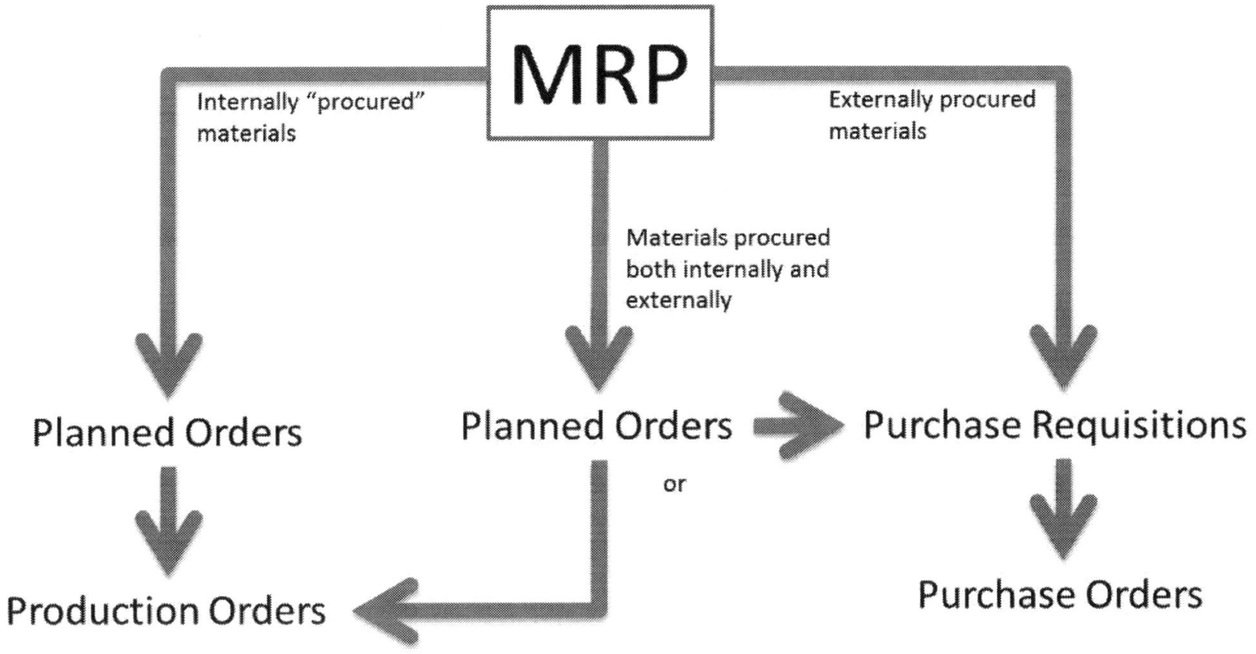

Figure 29: MRP procurement proposals and subsequent processing

could then be used to convert these purchase requisitions into purchase orders.

Similarly, for materials that the company only makes in-house, MRP creates *planned orders*. The manufacturing process could then be used convert these planned orders into production orders.

For materials that a company both makes in-house and also purchases from vendors, the process generates planned orders. Later on when the time comes, the company could decide to convert the planned orders into either purchase requisitions or into production orders.

MRP Type

Thus far we have generally assumed that MRP does material planning for all items based on BOMs. This need not always be the case. Companies might plan for some materials based on BOM – that is first consider how many finished products or sub assemblies need to be made and then explode the BOM to calculate the quantities of raw materials needed. However, planning for all materials need not be done this way. For some materials that are inexpensive, such an elaborate process might not be worthwhile – for example, small nails, generic screws, small generic fasteners and glue. Other materials might actually not go into the finished product at all even though they might be used in the manufacturing process – for example, cleaning supplies and rag cloth. For such items, rather than planning based strictly on BOM, companies use **consumption based planning**. How the planning for a material is to be done is stored in the material master in a field called its **MRP Type**. Broadly, the MRP Type can be either **MRP** or **consumption based planning**.

For materials with MRP type *MRP*, the process utilizes BOM explosion to determine quantities needed of such materials. For materials with one of the *consumption based planning* MRP types, the process determines the quantity needed based on their consumption pattern rather than on BOM explosion. Typically this enables companies to automate the process and reduce processing costs. This also enables companies to focus on costly and critical materials while preventing less important materials from taking up valuable time. There are many types of methods for consumption based planning. Some examples appear below:

- **Reorder point planning – VB:** In Reorder point planning, companies determine the following for the material: *safety stock, reorder point* and *reorder quantity* or *lot size*. Companies keep using these materials until the stock reaches the reorder point. At this stage the company reorders the material and the quantity ordered is the reorder quantity or lot size. Because of the time pattern of how the material stock looks, this is also called the saw-tooth model of inventory management. See Figure 30.

- **Forecast based planning – VV:** In this, companies independently forecast the consumption of the material and act accordingly.

- **Time based planning – R1** In this, companies simply procure a certain quantity at regular intervals.

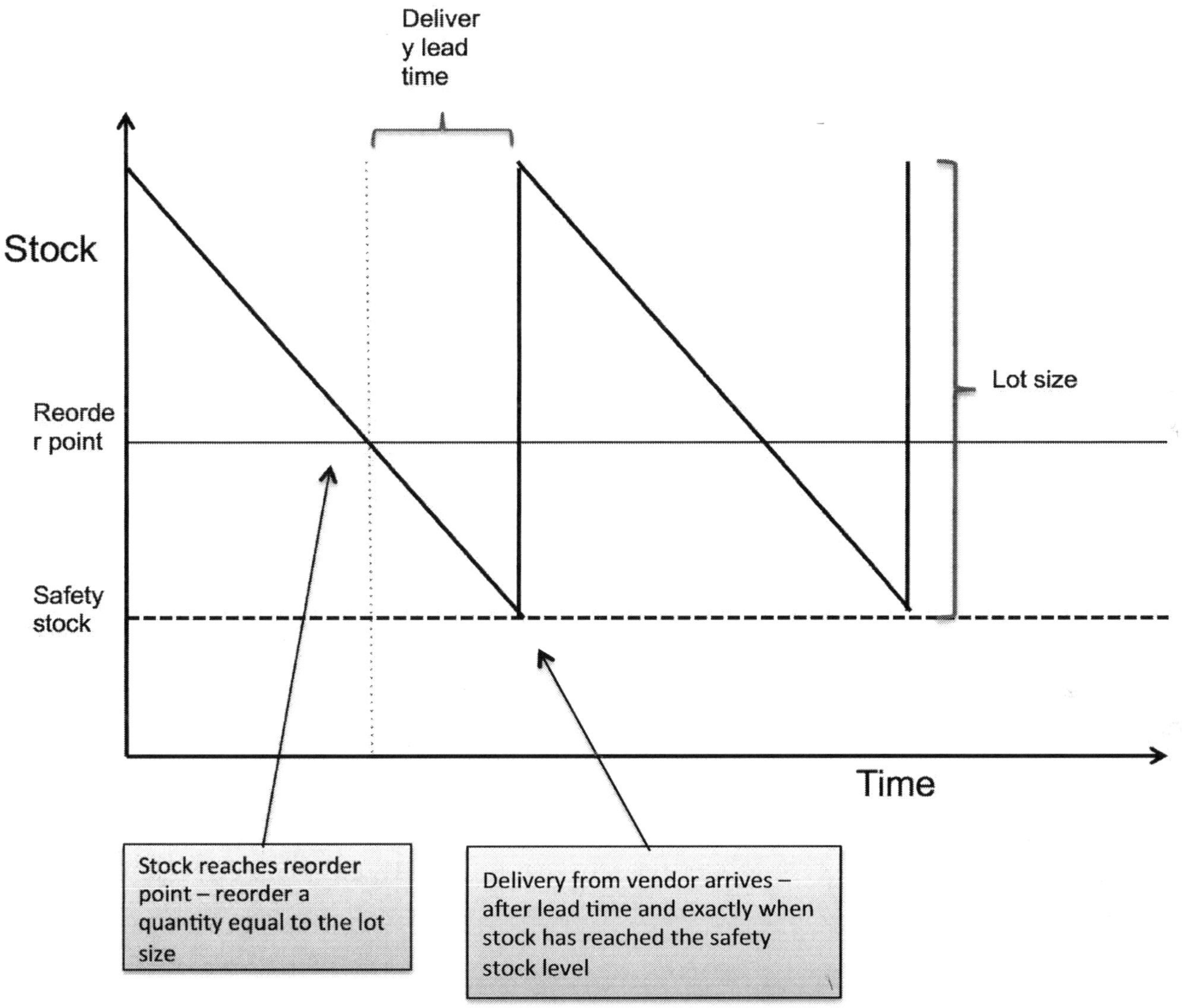

Figure 30: Example of consumption based planning: Reorder point planning

Chapter-end review questions

You can find suggested answers to all these questions starting from page 243

To answer questions marked with ★, you will need to have read the official SAP TERP10 course material.

1. At which organizational level is material planning generally performed? (one)

   A Client
   B Company code
   C Plant
   D Storage location

2. Which of the following represent master data required in Materials Planning? (three)

   A Materials
   B Work centers
   C Routings
   D Bill of materials

3. Which of the following represent plant-specific views in the material master record? (three) ★

   A MRP
   B Work scheduling
   C Accounting
   D Forecasting
   E Quality management

4. Explain how each of the following fields in the material master is used: ★

   a MRP Type
   b Procurement type
   c Strategy group

5. Which of the following represent valid material types for the material master? (three) ★

   A In house production
   B Raw material
   C Finished good

D Externally procured

E Operating supplies

6. When creating a material master record, you have to assign it a material type. What does the material type determine? (two) ★

    A What screens are displayed for maintaining the material

    B How the material number is assigned

    C The strategy group assigned to the material

    D The MRP Type for the material

7. BOMs in SAP can be multi-level T/F?

8. What is the difference between the quantity in the header and those in the item level of a BOM?

9. In SAP it is possible for a material to have multiple BOMs. Explain why this might be necessary. ★

10. What does the BOM usage field in the BOM header determine? ★

11. Which of the following represent valid item categories in BOM? (three) ★

    A In house production

    B External procurement

    C Stock item

    D Non-stock item

    E Variable-size item

12. Can a consumable material be included as a component in a BOM? ★

13. SAP provides a planning table for Sales and Operations Planning. There is a planning table for each ________________. ★

14. When we create a product group, SAP creates a material with type ________________ ★

15. The lowest level of a product group hierarchy contains ________________. ★

16. The proportion factors in a product group definition can be created ________________ or be ________________. ★

17. Which of the following values are calculated by the system when using a planning table? (one) ★

A Sales
B Production
C Stock level
D Target stock
E Days supply
F Target days supply

18. Sales data in the planning table can be created: (three) ★

A Manually
B By calculating backwards from prior yearsâĂŹ consumption of raw materials
C By transferring from CO-PA
D By calculating from production and stock level
E by running forecast models in the system

19. Disaggregation of product group level plans is not automatic T/F? ★

20. While disaggregating data for a product group which of the following options are valid? (two) ★

A We can disaggregate the stock of the higher level group
B We can disaggregate the sales plan of the higher level group
C We can disaggregate the production plan of the higher level group
D We can disaggregate the production or sales plans of the lowest level elements in the hierarchy

21. With respect to requirements in MRP, which of the following statements are true? (two) ★

A Planned independent requirements represent customer orders
B Customer independent requirements are based on forecasts and plans
C Planned independent requirements can be based on forecasts and plans
D Customer independent requirements are sales orders
E Dependent requirements can be based directly on forecasts and plans

22. Demand management results in the creation of independent requirements. What does MRP create for these independent requirements? (one) ★

A Planned orders
B Purchase requisitions
C Production orders
D Schedule lines

23. Which of the following is considered demand when MRP runs the net requirements calculation? (one) ★

A Purchase orders
B Safety stock
C Firmed planned orders
D Firmed purchase requisitions

24. What is the goal of Master Production Scheduling? ★

25. MRP type ______________ is based on independent requirements and type ______________ is based on past consumption. ★

26. For what kinds of materials is reorder point planning suitable?

27. Which of the following can represent procurement proposals generated by MRP? (three)

A Sales orders
B Planned orders
C Purchase requisitions
D Schedule lines
E Purchase orders

28. Which of the following is not part of net requirements calculations in MRP take into account: (one)

A Planned sales
B Firmed purchase requisitions
C Current stock
D Safety stock
E Lot size

29. Which of the following does not represent MRP relevant changes to a material? (one) ★

A Change in BOM
B Goods receipts against existing purchase orders
C Unplanned goods issues

D New sales orders

30. What is the main difference between the stock/requirements list and the MRP list? ★

Demand planning

Independent and dependent requirements

Manufacturing

This chapter introduces the manufacturing execution business process as relevant for the TERP 10 certification examination. It introduces key terms and provides background knowledge that will enable users to read and understand SAP's course material. The chapter does not aim to duplicate content from the official SAP course materials. Instead it describes the broad framework in an easily understandable form and lays the foundation for students to delve deeper into the detailed course materials.

The *Manufacturing Execution* business process covers all the steps and interactions involved in producing finished products from raw materials and sub-assemblies. The official certification course material uses many technical terms. Without clearly understanding the context and relating the terms to reality, the official course material might appear much more complicated than necessary.

After all, the manufacturing process uses some raw materials to produce finished goods. To do this, it uses certain facilities, labor and other resources. All this is, of course, happening in the context of a demand plan that has determined the quantities of finished products to be produced at various times. While the details of this can get complex on the shop floor, we only need to grasp the big picture – which is not at all complex. So, as you read this chapter and SAP's official certification course material, focus your energies on clearly understanding the big picture and relate the various terms that the course material uses to the real-world.

In the real world, many different types of production processes have evolved.

- **Manufacturing based on *Production Orders*** The easiest would be a process where we want to make some finished products using some raw materials and we *ask* the manufacturing department to produce x pieces of a product. In small organizations this *asking* could be just that – verbally asking. However, larger organizations need to do things more formally to avoid waste and inefficiency. They follow formal processes and track and control the processes through various documents. They initiate the production process by creating a formal document. In SAP, we initiate most processes by creating some kind of *Order*, and a *Production Order* formally initiates production.

- **Repetitive Manufacturing** deals with the situation where materials continuously flow through an assembly line.

- **Process Manufacturing** is concerned with process industries where the end products are not discrete products. Here typically fluids (or gases) flow through the process.

Each type of manufacturing presents different issues and challenges. **This chapter covers only manufacturing based on *Production Orders*.**

Master Data

A few important pieces of master data used in manufacturing are:

- **Material Master** – Used to get appropriate information about the materials used as relevant to manufacturing.

- **Bill of Materials** – Specifies what materials are needed and in what quantities to make other materials.

- **Work Center** – Provides the capacity needed to perform work. A work center could be a machine, a group of machines, a person or a group of people.

- **Routing** – Steps or *operations* to make a product, and the specification of each operation, including the time required and the work center needed for the operation.

- **PRT** – *Production Resources Tools*. Some operations will require the use of special equipment (other than the work center itself). These could be special jigs and fixtures or specialized measuring instruments and so on.

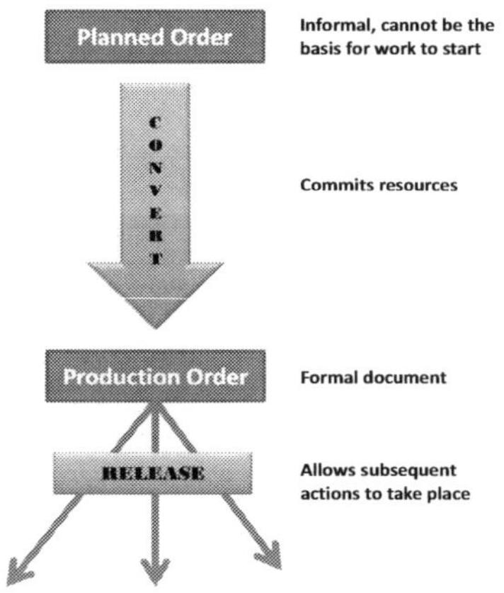

Figure 31: Planned Order and Production Order

Process Overview

As mentioned earlier, a *Production Order* formally starts the process. However, in SAP, a formal order is almost never the first step in a process. SAP always provides the capability of an informal step before the formal one. For production, a *Planned Order* usually (but not always) precedes a production order. A *Planned Order* does not formally authorize production. None of the formal steps for manufacturing can be accomplished simply based on a *Planned Order*. It represents just a preliminary planning step.

The *Planned Order* remains an informal document with no actual impact until someone or some automated step *converts* it into a *Production Order* (see Figure 31). This allows the organization to *commit* resources to it – resources like machine time, labor, and materials. However, actual work on the Production Order cannot begin until it is *released*. *Releasing* a Production order authorizes subsequent activities to take place; for example, only after release can materials be issued against the production order. Recall from order-related cost object controlling that only after release does the production order becomes a cost object.

Common sense tells us that certain things must be in place before converting *Planned Orders* into *Production Orders* and before releasing *Production Orders*. Think a little bit about what must be in place before it would make sound sense to perform these steps.

When a *Planned Order* is converted into a *Production Order*, various other business processes will assume that this order will now be executed. For example, materials management will assume that some amount of material will be consumed. Capacity planners will assume that this order will take up some machine time and labor and so on. Thus, converting a planned order has real consequences and can result in inefficiency if not done carefully.

Before converting a *Planned Order* into a *Production Order* and before *releasing* a *Production Order*, we must ensure that the materials and resources needed for the order (machine capacities, labor, PRT, etc,) are available. This process is called

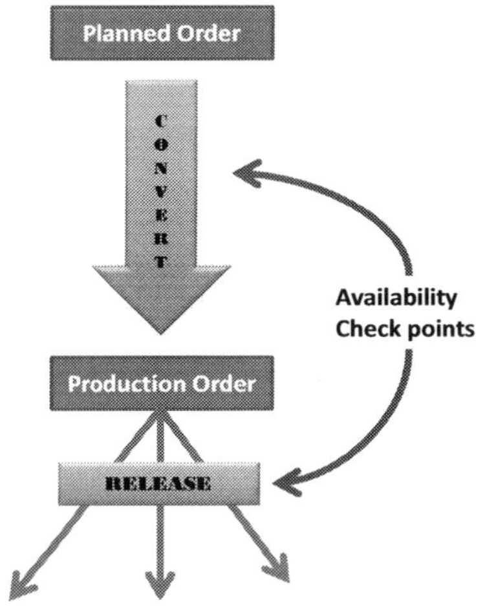

Figure 32: Availability Check

Availability Check. Of course the steps can be completed even if the *Availability Check* fails – there is room for judgment – but the system alerts us of any non-availability. (See Figure 32.)

Having seen how the Production Order comes into being, let us go further. A *released* production order has kinetic energy and can cause actions to take place. Materials necessary for completing the production are now issued from inventory; Work Center *Capacities* are allocated; any special tools (called *Production Resources Tools or PRTs*) are also issued. When a production order is released, the system can also print any documents needed for the work to be done on the shop – for example, any drawings, instructions and other shop documents can be printed. In cases where numerically controlled machines or robotic machines are being used, we might need to upload appropriate programs as well to these machines. (See Figure 33)

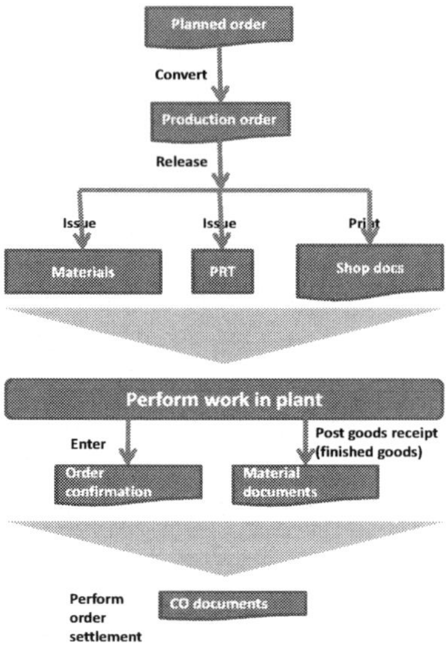

Figure 33: Manufacturing process flow

Once all the materials needed to complete the order are issued, work can begin – we assume that the required capacities like machine time and labor hours are available.

At this point in the process, the work centers assigned to the operations begin their work on the production order. As and when work gets completed, the SAP system comes to know about this through the entry of *confirmations*. To make it concrete, suppose we issued a production order to make 50 chairs. The concerned people issued the materials needed and went off to work on the chairs. When they finish making these chairs, they will enter an *Order Confirmation* in the system indicating how many they were actually able to make, how much time the process took, how many pieces did not pass quality checks, and so on. The information from these confirmations also provide management with knowledge concerning efficiencies and costs.

Once the production process completes, the finished materials manufactured have to be placed in *finished goods stock*. Thus a *goods receipt* operation occurs in inventory management. After that is completed, the newly produced finished goods show up in the books as assets in finished goods stock. Before this they were only work in progress inventory.

After the goods receipt, everything seems complete as far as the manufacturing process is concerned – after all we have finished producing the goods and handed them over to inventory. However, the business process has one more step remaining. The production order has been happily consuming resources – using up materials, machines, labor and so on. Prudent management accounting would require that the cost of using all of these direct and indirect resources be properly allocated. Technically, these costs have been allocated to the production order during the manufacturing execution process. After all, a production order follows the order-related cost object controlling steps. When the goods receipt step described above is completed, the value of the product that was placed into inventory is offset by taking that same value out of the production order. What remains is considered a variance. As you perhaps remember from the Management Accounting chapter, some costs collected on cost objects (including variances in production orders) are likely to be settled during the settlement period. Depending on company practices, the settlement period could be a fortnight or a month or whatever. Thus this production order's variance will be settled when the settlement period arrives. Figure 33 shows this step as *Order Settlement*.

Interfaces with other SAP Modules

The SAP TERP10 course emphasizes *integration*, that is, the interconnections across modules. After all, *enterprise* is the operative word in ERP. ERP systems aim to increase efficiency and effectiveness by integrating various business processes.

Let us look at the various ways in which Manufacturing Execution (PP) integrates with other modules:

- **Materials management (MM)**: Clearly, when PP consumes materials and PRTs, and when MM receives finished products, PP interfaces with MM. From the materials planning unit, we also saw that MRP might create *Planned Orders* or *Purchase Requisitions* which are used in the MM Procurement process.
- **Management Accounting (CO)**: A released *Production Order* is a cost object in CO. Thus costs on the order can be managed in CO. *Settlement* also provides another integration piece between PP and CO. The official certification course material shows other touch points.

Other Salient Points

- **Origin of production orders**: Most often, production orders result from planned orders being converted. However, we can also directly create production orders. order release can also be automated.
- **Sources of planned orders**: So far we have seen that planned orders come from MRP. However, planned orders can also be manually created. Additionally, SAP has a *Supply Chain Management (SCM) module* and planned orders could be the output of this process. Whether a specific company uses the MRP or SCM application depends on the complexity of their processes and on what they choose. A common scenario in the ERP landscape is for companies to use *best of breed* components for various business processes. For example, a company could be using SAP for MM and PP, but use another vendor's product for MRP. In this case some work is needed to integrate these systems.
- **Automating Inventory Postings** For efficiency, sometimes companies automate good issue and/or receipt postings. Thus, when a Production Order is *released*, the corresponding goods issues could be posted without requiring an additional manual step. Similarly, along with *order confirmation*, the posting of goods receipt for finished goods can be automatically completed.
- **Backflush goods issue postings**: In the interest of efficiency, some companies do not post the issue of certain materials separately. A good example is a repetitive manufacturing process like the manufacturing of automobiles. Suppose a company produces 40 units of a specific model of car during a certain time period. When order confirmations are entered for these, they clearly know that 160 tires of a certain kind must have been used. Thus they can post goods issue for that quantity automatically. This saves time and effort.
- **Material usage**: In the *Procurement* chapter, we had noted that when materials are purchased for stock, the cost of such materials is not immediately reflected as expenses. These materials simply go into the raw materials stock and affect only balance sheet accounts. During manufacturing execution, when raw materials are issued against a released production order, these materials are finally accounted for as expenses. The production order is responsible for the cost of the materials it uses. This is necessary for accurate product costing.
- **Order confirmation options** We had earlier mentioned that confirmation of a production order occurs when the order completes. Actually SAP provides many more options for finer tracking if needed. For a production order, we can enable tracking at the level of each operation. Which means that confirmations can be entered

as soon as an operation is complete. In fact, confirmation is even possible at specific points *within an operation*.

Chapter-end review questions

You can find suggested answers to these questions starting from page 249

To answer questions marked with ★, you will need to have read the official SAP TERP10 course material.

1. At which organizational level are costs managed in a production order? (one) ★

   A Client
   B Controlling area
   C Company Code
   D Plant

2. During the manufacturing execution process, which steps include a material availability check?

3. When a production order is created, costs are planned and the order is scheduled. Which master data is responsible for the scheduling of the order? (two) ★

   A Material
   B BOM
   C Routing
   D Work center

4. When a production order is created, materials are reserved. Which master data is responsible for these reservations? (one) ★

   A Material
   B BOM
   C Routing
   D Work center

5. A production order can be confirmed before the release of the order. (T/F)

6. What is the procurement type in the material master for finished goods that we only make?

7. What are task lists and what are the different types of task lists in SAP? ★

8. What are PRTs?

9. What field in a work center master record controls the types of activities in which it could be used? ★

10. Data stored in the work center master can be used for which of the following: (three) ★

    A Actual cost determination
    B Scheduling
    C Costing
    D Capacity planning

11. What mechanism enables connecting a work center to CO? ★

12. What name is given to a task list in: ★

    a Discrete manufacturing
    b Assembly line manufacturing
    c Process manufacturing

13. What is the analog of Production order in process manufacturing? ★

14. Give an example of a fixed time element in a routing operation. ★

15. Give an example of a variable time element in a routing operation. ★

16. BOM components not assigned to an operation in a routing are assumed by the system to be required when? ★

17. In addition to BOM components, name one other thing that can be assigned to an operation. ★

18. Which of the following things do Formula Keys in work centers help with? (three) ★

    A Calculation of costs
    B Calculation of capacities
    C Activity based costing
    D Scheduling
    E Determining the task lists in which a work center can be used

19. When a work center is assigned to an operation in a routing, what part (view) of the information from the work center master might be used to determine the operation time? ★

20. Production Resources Tools might be needed to produce a finished product. In which master data pertaining to the product are they included?

21. Which of the following steps in the manufacturing process can be automated? (two)

    A Order creation
    B Order release
    C Material staging
    D Material withdrawal posting
    E Order archiving

22. Is it possible to create a production order directly without a planned order? If so, mention a few variations.

23. Which of the following can be assigned to operations on a production order? (three)

    A Materials
    B Cost center
    C PRT
    D Trigger points
    E Profit center

24. Under what controlling scenario would we assign a settlement rule and calculate planned costs and track actual costs for a production order? ★

25. At what level are costs for an order determined and at what level are they managed? ★

26. What has to take place before one can issue goods for a Production Order?

27. At what two time points can availability checks be performed for a production order?

28. Availability checks for production orders can check for availability of: (select three)

    A Spare parts
    B Material

C PRT
D Machines
E Warehouse resources

29. What impact can goods issue for production have on material reservations?

30. Which of the following accounts are affected when goods issue occurs against a production order? (two)

A Stock
B Product
C Overhead
D Consumption

31. The production order is updated when goods are issued against a released production order T/F?

32. Can goods issue against a production order generate a controlling document? Why or why not?

33. What two main possibilities exist for order confirmation?

34. Which of the following represent possible detailed options for production order confirmation? (two) ★

A Time at which setup was initiated for an operation
B Work center related
C Reaching a milestone
D Material related

35. Explain how automated goods receipt postings against a production order might work – at what point will this occur?

36. Explain how automated goods issue postings against a production order might work – at what point will this occur and what is this mechanism called?

37. What linkage to the warehouse management system might exist with goods receipts from a production order?

38. Which accounts are updated when goods are received against a production order? ★

39. When a production order is settled, it is credited/debited?

40. Which of the following scenarios might be well suited to use order-related cost object controlling? (two) ★

A Production of large quantities

B Flexible production environment

C Manufacture of co-products

D When quality is very important

E When the cost variance across orders is low

Sales Order Processing

This chapter introduces the *Sales Order Processing* (also referred to as the *Order to Cash*) business process as relevant for the SAP TERP10 certification examination. This business process encompasses all the steps starting from pre-sales activities all the way to the generation of a billing document which results in the customer being invoiced. Processing the customer's payment occurs in the financial accounting (FI) module. Although pretty easy to understand because of our general familiarity with the process, it would still be a good idea for you to read this chapter before proceeding to the SAP certification course materials.

The Order to Cash business process covers all the steps and interactions involved in pre-sales activities up to and including invoicing the customer. The process comprises the following main steps:

- Pre-sales
- Sales Order
- Outbound Delivery
- Post Goods Issue
- Billing the Customer
- Payment processing

Pre-sales activities

Although a *Sales Order* represents the formal document that triggers the shipping of goods to customers, the selling process usually does not begin with a *Sales Order* – although it can. In its simplest form, pre-sales could involve a prospective or existing customer making an inquiry. For example, a customer might inquire about specific products, possible delivery dates and prices. In response, the company might respond to the customer with details. A *Sales Inquiry* results. A customer could then take the process further by converting the *Sales Inquiry* into a formal *Sales Order*. SAP supports other pre-sales activities as well, like a company bidding on a customer's Request for Proposal (RFP) or having standard agreements with customers for providing materials under agreed upon terms and conditions. We will look at these later.

Sales Order

A *Sales Order* represents a formal, legally binding document through which a customer orders products from our company. SAP provides means by which pre-sales documents – like *Sales Inquiries* can be directly converted into *Sales Orders* – thus avoiding the need to re-enter much of the same information again.

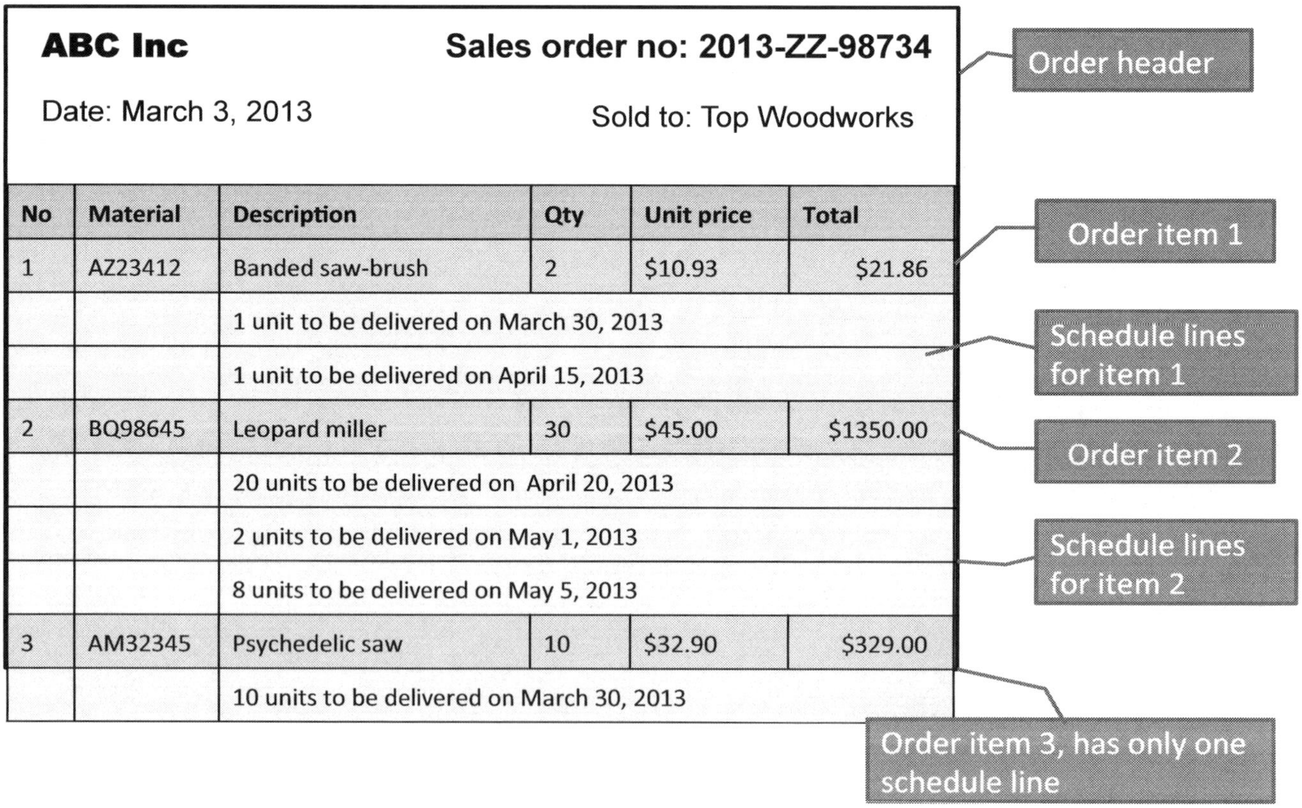

Figure 34: Structure of a sales order

While creating a *Sales Inquiry* or *Sales Order*, SAP makes available complete pricing or *conditions* support. Seemingly simple, determining the price applicable for a product on a sales order can be very complex. For instance, we could have specific prices for a customer for a particular material – like customer X gets product Y at $5 per unit, whereas customer Y pays $5.25 per unit. Rather than stating a specific dollar amount, the above two conditions could specify discounts (percentages or dollar values). Alternately, we could be offering a promotion on a particular product during specific dates. The promotion could again be a specific dollar price or a dollar or percentage discount. Numerous other possibilities exist. A price could be based on the geographic region where a sale occurs or could be based on total dollar value of sales order and so on. Price often represents a very important tool used by companies and hence calls for utmost flexibility. Broadly speaking, the price applicable on a sales order for a particular product is determined by various *conditions* as illustrated above. This is why SAP uses the term *condition* when talking about prices.

While creating a sales order or sales inquiry, SAP also makes available features to determine the delivery dates for items on a sales order. Delivery dates can be determined not just based on available stocks, but also based on production orders – for finished goods, on purchase orders – for trading goods, or based on customer needs. (Recall that *finished goods* are products that a company makes and sells whereas *trading goods* are goods that a company simply buys and sells.)

Structure of a sales order – A sales order has an *order header*, a set of *sales order items* and, for each sales order item, *possibly one or more schedule lines*. (See fig 34.) From the figure, you can observe the following:

- **Sales Order Header** – A sales order contains one order header with information that is common to the entire order (information like order number, customer number, and order date).
- **Sales Order Items** A sales order can have several sales order items – but must have at least one.
- **Schedule Lines** Each order item can have one or more schedule lines to indicate the delivery dates for various quantities of the material ordered on the order item. It is possible for all the units

ordered on an item to be required on the same date, or for the total quantity to be broken up across several delivery dates.

While creating a sales order, SAP also makes the credit management module available. Since we are discussing sales against credit, the system has to ensure that we do not allow customers to exceed their credit limits. SAP will track this and automatically block a sales order if the order will cause the customer's credit limit to be exceeded. SAP provides this functionality in *Credit Management*, which is part of its Financial Supply Chain Management (FSCM) component. SAP can track credit utilization and limits for a customer by sales area, by company code and overall, at the level of the client. Thus we can set an overall enterprise-wide credit limit for a particular customer cutting across company codes. This will help to prevent over-exposure of the whole enterprise at the *client* level.

Outbound Delivery

SAP uses the term *Outbound Delivery* in a way that might not be immediately clear, but you will do well to understand precisely what the term stands for. The term *Outbound Delivery* sound like it refers to an activity. However in SAP, the term actually represents a *document* that signals the start of the process of making a delivery. In the *Order to Cash* process, this document signals the start of the process of shipping goods for each schedule line of a sales order.

So a sales order like the example in Figure 34 would require multiple outbound deliveries.

Thus *Outbound Delivery* is represented by a *document*. By creating this document, someone is authorizing a shipment. We highlight this point because SAP course materials generally assume that readers understand this. Much confusion arises from a misunderstanding that the term refers to a process.

Post Goods Issue

Once the *Outbound Delivery* document has initiated the shipment process, this enables warehouse operations to be carried out. The required materials can be physically removed from the warehouse and readied for shipment. Removing items from the warehouse represents a purely physical operation. Though the materials might have moved physically, they are still in the company's possession and comprise part of the current assets of the company.

The *Post Goods Issue* step formally removes the materials from stock. At the end of this step, the quantity on hand of the material goes down. Current assets decrease, and the goods are technically in transit from that point on. This is the first step in the order to cash process that impacts financial accounting.

As a matter of fact, have you noticed that in the *Procure to Pay* and in the *Manufacturing Execution* processes, the first financial accounting impact occurred with the first goods movement? In the *Order to Cash* and *Manufacturing execution* processes, the first goods movement is a goods issue, resulting in a reduction of stock. In the case of the *Procure to Pay* process, we performed a goods receipt, resulting in an increase in stock.

While we might think that the customer owes us money at this point, that is incorrect – the customer will owe us money only after we have invoiced the customer.

Billing the customer

Once we have posted the goods issue, we can create a *Billing Document* which is a company-internal document signifying the fact that the goods have been shipped and have become the customer's property. At this point the customer owes us a payment. The billing document then authorizes the creation of the customer invoice, which is an external document to be sent to the customer, and on the basis of which the customer will make a payment. The terms *Billing Document* and *Invoice* are sometimes used interchangeably, but the former is an internal document and the latter is sent to the customer.

Post Customer Payment

This step is carried out in accounting. Once the customer receives our invoice, the customer will most likely send us a payment. Accounting receives the payment and applies it to the customer's account.

Organization Levels

Figure 35 shows some of the organization levels that Sales and Distribution (SD) shares with several other logistics modules.

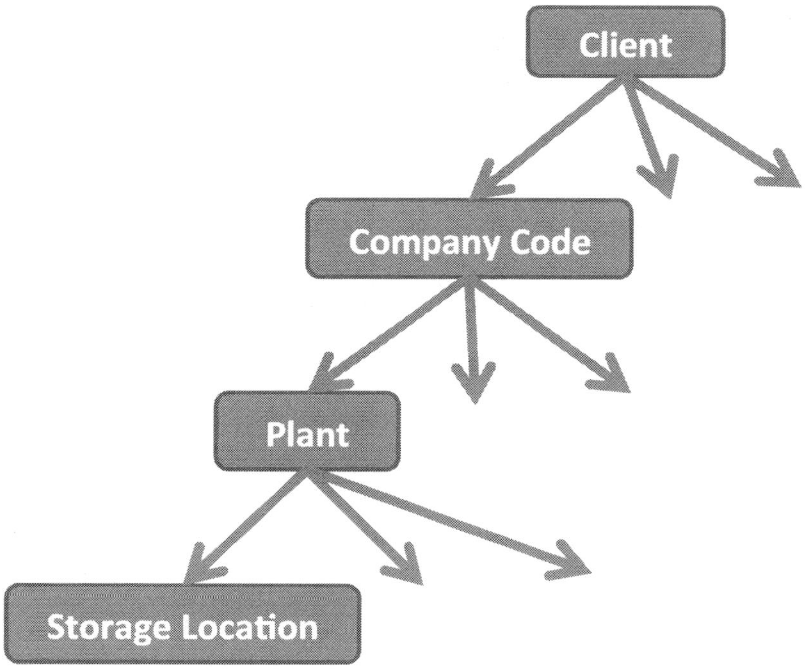

Figure 35: Some of the organizational levels that SD shares with other logistics modules

SD has its own dedicated organization levels as well.

- **Sales Organization:** A company code could have many *Sales Organizations*. Each *Sales Organization* can belong to exactly one company code. A *Sales Organization* is responsible for the distribution of goods and services, negotiating the terms and conditions of sale and for issues arising out of the sale of a product – like product liability. All SD documents are created in a *Sales Organization* and it is also the highest summarization level for sales reports.
- **Distribution channel:** This represents the means to reach customers. Examples would be *retail, wholesale* and *Internet*.

- **Division:** A division usually represents a product line.

It is possible to combine *Sales Organization, Distribution Channel* and *Division* in many ways; each such unique combination is called a *Sales Area.*

Other Salient Points

- **Availability Check** – While creating a sales order, delivery dates have to be specified as well. To promise delivery dates, SAP has to ensure that materials are available. The screen for sales orders has features to perform a material availability check before assigning delivery dates. While performing the availability check, the system can consider not only stocks on hand, but also anticipated stocks based on production and procurement schedules. In this sense, this is a *dynamic availability check.*

- **Forward and Backward calculations** – If the customer has specified required delivery dates for an item, SAP first calculates *backward* from the customer's dates and applies the various lead times (manufacturing lead time, shipping lead time, etc.,) to determine if the customer's delivery requirement can be met. If so it assigns the date. If the date cannot be met, the system calculates *forward* from the current date and determines the earliest possible shipping date.

- **Relationships between sales order items, schedule lines, outbound deliveries, billing documents and payments** – From the foregoing, it is clear that a single sales order could have several sales order items. In addition, a single sales order item can contain more than one schedule line. Thus each sales order item can have more than one outbound delivery. For example, if a sales order item is for 10 units, we can break it into multiple shipments, thus requiring multiple outbound deliveries. Under certain conditions, it is also possible to combine more than one sales order into a single outbound delivery. Can you guess what might be required that would allow for this?

  We might choose to create a single billing document for an outbound delivery or create multiple billing documents. One customer payment might cover a single billing document or cover several of these. Similarly, a single billing document might be cleared by multiple customer payments as well. All of these represent practical situations and SAP supports these common scenarios.

Chapter-end review questions

You can find suggested answers to all of these questions starting on page 255

To answer questions marked with ★, you will need to have read the official SAP TERP10 course material.

1. Which of the following are used to define a sales area? (three)

   A Division
   B Sales organization
   C Sales Group
   D Distribution channel
   E Plant

2. Which of the following organization levels are dedicated to SD? (two)

   A Shipping point
   B Sales Order
   C Sales organization
   D Sales location
   E Product Group

3. How many sales organizations can a company code have?

4. How many company codes can a sales organization belong to?

5. Which of the following can represent a distribution channel? (two)

   A Internet sales
   B Wholesale sales
   C Distribution center
   D Shipping point
   E Loading dock

6. What does a division represent?

7. Which of the following statements are true about sales areas? (two)

   A One division can be part of only one sales area

B A single sales organization could exist in several different sales areas
C A division can be used in defining several different sales areas
D The same combination of sales organization, distribution channel and division can occur in multiple sales areas

8. How many sales areas can a plant be associated with?

9. How many plants can a sales area serve?

10. What is the role of the plant in SD?

11. Give an example of a plant for a service organization.

12. Regarding the relationship of shipping points and plants, is the assignment of shipping points to plants one-to-one, one-to-many, or many-to-many?

13. Which component in SAP determines a customer's credit-worthiness when a sales order is created? (one)

A Quality Management
B Management Accounting
C Financial Accounting
D Financial Supply Chain Management

14. In which step of the standard sales order process will the first financial posting occur? (one)

A Creation of the sales order
B Creation of the outbound delivery
C Goods Issue
D Billing

15. Which of the following represent master data used in a sales order? (three) ★

A Plant master
B Customer master
C Output master
D Condition master
E Price master

16. Which of the following represent mandatory partner functions in the customer master? (two) ★

A Sold to party

B Contact persons

C Ship to party

D Billing party

E Forwarding agent

17. At least two different partner functions appear in a sales order. T/F? ★

18. Which of the following pieces of information might appear on the customer-material info record? (two) ★

A Moving average price

B Customer material number

C Delivery tolerances

D Average monthly sales

19. What master data determines how documents are communicated or sent to various parties? ★

20. The _______________ master is used to define material prices for various complex combinations of criteria.

21. Which of the following represents the standard sequence of steps in the sales order process? (one)

A Sales order> Inquiry> Billing> Payment

B Inquiry> Sales order>Delivery> Billing> Payment

C Inquiry> Sales order> Billing> Delivery>Payment

D Sales order> Delivery> Payment> Inquiry

22. Which of the following documents can a sales order reference? (two) ★

A Sales Inquiry

B Purchase order

C Quotation

D RFQ

E RFI

23. Which of the following represent benefits of using pre-sales features? (two) ★

A Ability to track lost sales

B Enables better tracking of billing

C Advantage when doing business with customers who want to document the whole sales process

D Speedier delivery times

24. Which of the following must be specified in order to create a sales order? (three) ★

A Sales group
B Sales area
C Customer
D Required delivery date
E Customer material number

25. Which of the following represent possible ways in which a sales order can be created? (two) ★

A A purchase order can be the reference document for a sales order
B Can be created independently of any other sales document
C Multiple pre-sales documents can be combined into one sales order
D Can be based on prior scheduling agreements

26. Which of the following represent item types on a sales order? (two) ★

A Material item
B In house production
C Free of charge item
D Externally procured

27. Which of the following scenarios would require separate schedule lines for a single line item in a single sales order? (one)

A Customer orders 500 units of a material and wants them to be delivered in two different sets of 250 units on two different dates
B Customer orders two materials in one order and specifies a different delivery date for each material
C Customer places two separate sales orders with separate delivery dates, and one item on each order. Customer wants all the pieces of the materials on each order to be delivered on the date specified in the respective orders.

28. While placing a sales order, the system determined that the requested date for a material could not be met. What kind of scheduling did the system use to determine this?

29. In the above scenario, what kind of scheduling might the system use to propose a delivery date?

30. The ______________ can be used to find out required fields that have not been supplied in creating a sales order. ★

31. Sales orders can become ______________ requirements in MRP. ★

32. Under which of the following conditions can an availability check be triggered for a sales order? (two) ★

    A It has been set in *customizing* for the specific customer
    B It has been set in *customizing* for the specific material
    C It has been set in *customizing* for the specific user
    D It has been set in *customizing* for the transaction
    E It is specified in the material master for the item

33. Which of the following documents can have schedule lines? (one)

    A Billing documents
    B Invoices
    C Sales orders
    D Outbound deliveries
    E Inbound deliveries

34. Picking lists can be created from which of the following documents? (one) ★

    A Transfer orders
    B Transfer requirements
    C Sales orders
    D Outbound deliveries
    E Billing documents

35. Under what conditions a transfer requirement would be created for an outbound delivery? ★

36. You are in the process shipping an item against a sales order. You have created an outbound delivery and look at the stock/requirements list. In a different session, you go ahead and post goods issue for the outbound delivery. You then go back and refresh the stock/requirements list. What changes would you see on it? ★

37. Which accounts are affected when a goods issue occurs against a sales order?

38. Which accounts are affected when a billing document is generated against a delivery?

39. Which feature of SAP supports seeing all related SD documents on one screen and allows the user to navigate to any one of these documents? ★

40. Which of the following modules has an integration with SD? (three)

    A Materials management
    B Warehouse management
    C Manufacturing execution
    D Material planning

41. How can ad-hoc reporting requirements be met? ★

42. When a valid sales order is saved, it affects which of the following worklists? (one) ★

    A Picking worklist
    B Billing worklist
    C Shipping worklist
    D Goods issue posting worklist

Inventory and warehouse management

This chapter introduces *Inventory and Warehouse Management* concepts as relevant for the SAP TERP10 certification examination. **Inventory Management** deals with keeping track of stocks quantities and stock valuation of materials. **Warehouse Management** is responsible for physically putting away materials into storage and retrieving them from storage. As with the other chapters, you might benefit from reading this document before proceeding to SAP's certification course materials.

Any ERP system must enable a company to keep track of its materials. How much do we have on hand of each material? More specifically, we need this information for each storage location and not just the aggregate figure. Knowing quantities alone does not suffice – we also need to know their values as well. ERP systems also need to enable a company to keep track of movements of stock.

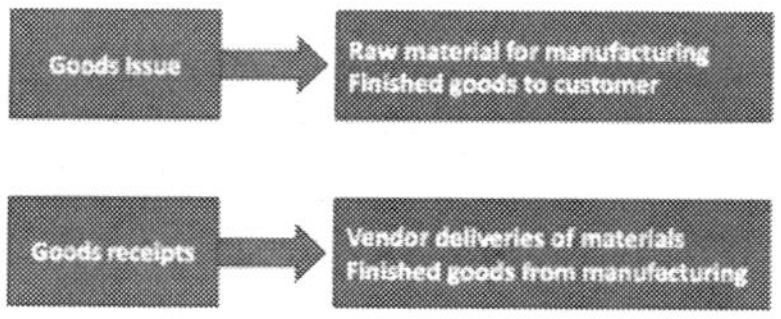

Figure 36: Examples of goods issues and receipts

In addition to keeping track of quantities and values of materials, organizations also need to efficiently handle the physical logistics of actually moving materials into and out of storage as well as keep them in physical locations in such a way as to promote efficiency. In this module we look at the following topics:

- **Types of goods movements** – SAP defines several types of goods movements, not all of them involving physical movement of goods. The obvious types of movements involve *good receipts*, putting materials into stock and *goods issues*, taking materials out of stock for some use. (see Figure 36) *Good receipts* mostly (but not always) occur when the company receives shipments from vendors and when the manufacturing process produced finished goods that have to be taken into stock. *Goods issues* mostly occur when raw materials and semi-finished goods are issued for manufacturing against released production orders and also when finished goods are to be shipped out to a customer to fulfill a *Sales Order*. Remember that the words *receipt* and *issue* are written from the perspective of *inventory*. So when we say *goods receipt* we are talking about *inventory* receiving goods and when we talk about *goods issues* we are referring to goods being issued from *inventory*. Apart from the above two obvious types of goods movements, we have *transfer postings*, which are technically considered *goods movements*, but do not involve any physical movement of material. We will look at goods movements in greater detail soon.

- **Options for goods movements** – Any ERP system has to carefully track goods movements. Goods are often moved from one storage location to another. When this happens, a good issue occurs at the sending storage location and a goods receipt occurs at the receiving storage location. Under some conditions, for efficiency, SAP allows, (but does not force), these two postings to be performed in a single step. Goods movements can occur between two storage locations of a single plant, or between storage locations belonging to different plants or even across company codes.
- **Stock Transport Order** – When moving goods across different plants, SAP provides two options. The first is to use goods issues and receipts. the second approach is to use a *Stock Transport Order*, which is like an *internal purchase order*. Recall that a normal purchase order is something that a company sends to its suppliers and those suppliers deliver goods based on the purchase order. In the case of a *Stock Transport Order*, the supplier is not a vendor, but another plant within the enterprise. Thus it is like a purchase order, except that it is a completely internal document and does not go to a vendor. Instead it goes from one plant to another. We will soon see the conditions under which a *stock transport order* makes sense.
- **Warehouse management** – We can easily get confused between the two terms *Inventory Management* and *Warehouse Management*. The former deals simply with keeping track of stocks and their values. Thus *Inventory Management* keeps track of how much of each material is in a storage location and also the value of the material. Inventory management also periodically reconciles book inventory and actual physical stocks. Inventory management has nothing to do with the physical processes of putting away material into storage areas and removing them from storage areas. *Warehouse Management* deals with the physical logistics involved in efficiently retrieving materials from, and putting away into warehouses. The physical logistics mentioned here are often referred to as *Logistics Execution* in SAP. *Warehouse Management* also keeps track of precisely where a material is within the warehouse – which shelf, in which aisle and in which area (see Figure 37).
- **Physical inventory procedure** – Periodically companies have to match their book inventory with actual physical inventory because

differences could arise due to material shrinkage (evaporation, for example) or from pilferage and theft. Physical inventory is important to ensure accurate financial information as well as accurate inventory quantities for MRP calculations.

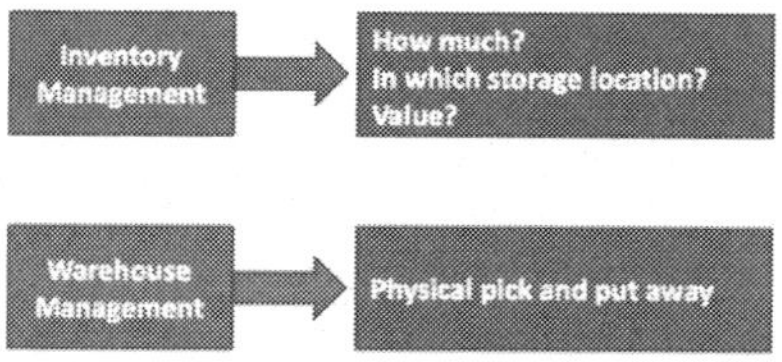

Figure 37: Inventory Management and Warehouse Management

Types of goods movements

As we have already mentioned, goods issues and goods receipts comprise the two obvious types of goods movements involving getting material into stock and issuing material from stock. We already know that SAP creates a *document* to record the occurrence of any business event. This also applies to goods movements. SAP generates *material documents* to document goods movements. For example, if 500 units of a material are issued for manufacturing, SAP creates a *material document* recording the details of this goods issue.

SAP also allows for some types of movements which do not represent actual physical movement of goods. The goods remain exactly where they were, but acquire a different designation. The best example of this occurs when some material, originally designated as *unrestricted use stock* is now designated as *goods in quality inspection*. The goods have not moved physically, but SAP considers this as a *goods movement*. The above represents a *transfer posting*. Physical goods movements are *stock transfers*. The TERP10 course materials will reference other examples of *transfer postings*. Be sure to check out the following types of transfer postings: *stock to stock*, *material to material* and *consignment to warehouse*. (see Figure 38)

Options for goods movements

As we saw earlier, SAP creates a *material document* to document any goods movement that occurs. Every physical goods movement need not result in a *material document*. For efficiency, under some conditions, SAP allows a single material document to document multiple movements. For example, an issue and the subsequent receipt could both be documented in a single document when these two goods movements occur using a single transaction. The goods issue and goods receipt were handled

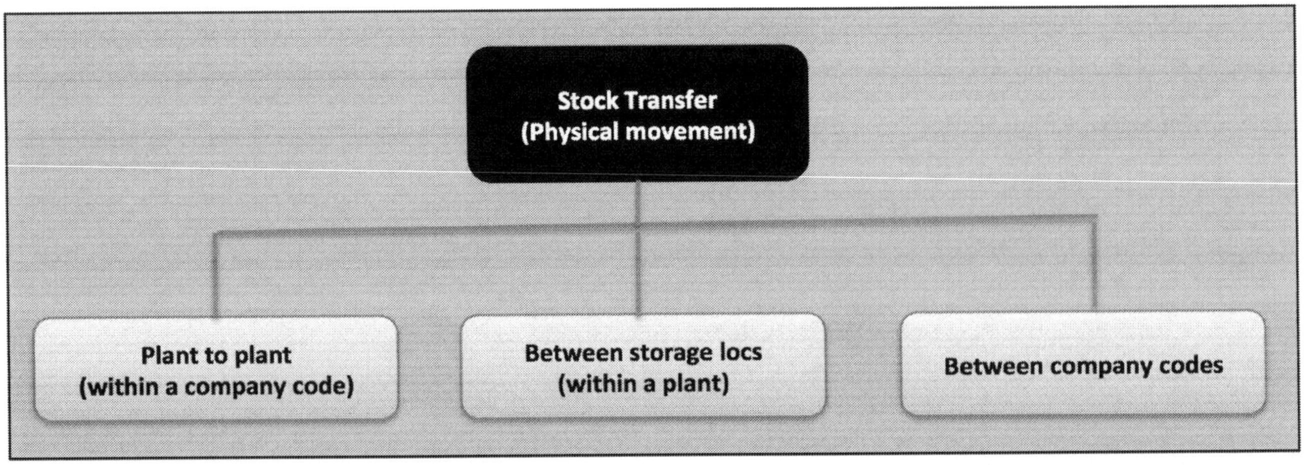

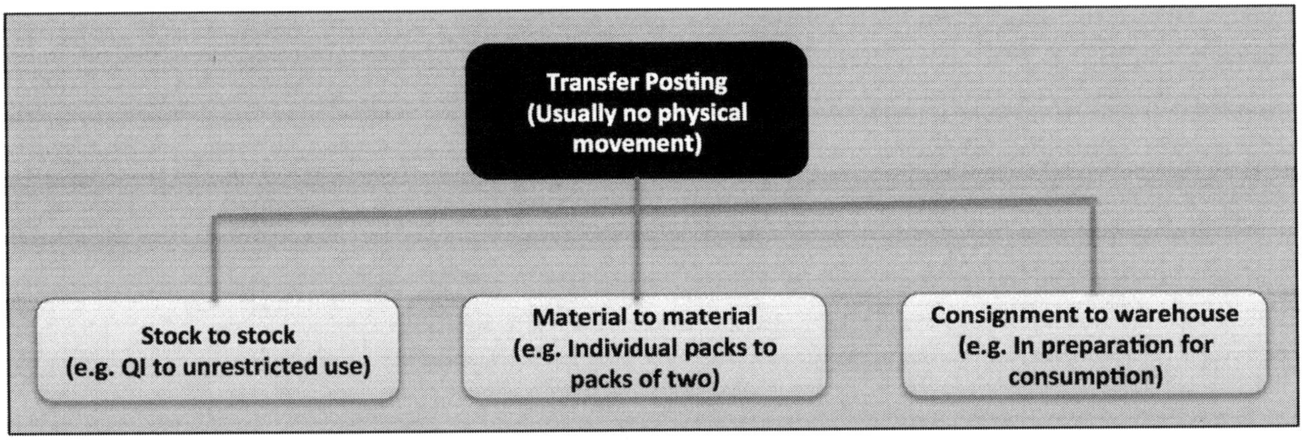

Figure 38: Stock transfers and transfer postings

in the single transaction. However, physically, the materials would be taken out of inventory and placed into inventory as two separate tasks.This is defined as a one-step stock transfer.

Goods movements *usually* generate an accounting document (there are occasions when this is not the case).

For example, receipts of goods from a vendor will generate both a material document to document the goods receipt, but will also generate an accounting document, because our current assets increase as a result of receiving the materials. Similarly, goods issue for a customer also generate both a material and an accounting document, because quantity of material and its value are both affected.

SAP uses *movement types* to specify the type of movement that takes place. *Movement types* are represented with three-digit numbers. Each movement type indicates precisely what kind of movement took place. For example, the movement type 311 indicates movement of stock in unrestricted use at one storage location to unrestricted use at another storage location. Movement type 101 is used for a goods receipt related to a purchase order to receive goods into unrestricted use stock. 103 is used for non-valuated goods receipt, which is one of those exceptional cases when a material document is created, but not an accounting document.

You need not memorize these numbers. SAP internally uses these numbers to ensure that the correct postings occur.

We know now that when goods move from one location to another, SAP certainly has to generate material documents to document these flows so that the location and quantity of the material can be tracked. SAP generally creates an accounting document to track the change in valuation resulting from the goods movement. However, an accounting document would not be needed if the goods movement involves the movement of materials between two storage locations within the same plant.

Since materials are valuated at the plant level in SAP, this movement would not affect the current assets position and thus no accounting document would be necessary. Under certain circumstances, companies value goods differently within the same plant (called *split valuation*). If stocks move from one storage location to another within the same plant and the company employs different valuation for the material in the two storage locations – *split valuation* – then SAP will generate an accounting document.

When goods move between company codes, SAP will generate a material document and will always generate two accounting documents to reflect the change in valuation of assets in both company codes. As an example, when a goods issue occurs in the originating company code and a goods receipt occurs in the receiving company code, the current assets of both company codes are affected. Therefore, accounting documents are generated in both.

The certification course discusses *one and two-step goods movements*. As mentioned earlier, in some situations, SAP allows us to make two postings – goods issue and goods receipt – with just a single material transaction, for efficiency. Be sure to understand those concepts as well from the TERP10 course materials.

Stock Transport Order

A company can move goods between plants (either within the same company code or across company codes), through the usual process of a goods issue at the sending end and a goods receipt at the receiving end. However, sometimes when we need to track the transfer more closely, SAP allows the use of a special process called a *Stock Transport Order* which is like an internal purchase order. From the procurement module you will recall that SAP allows us to track purchase orders. At any stage, we can see how much material has been delivered against a PO, how much has been invoiced and how much has been paid. SAP updates all of these statuses in the PO as the company records goods receipts and invoice receipts, and makes payments. *Stock Transport Orders* behave almost exactly like regular purchase orders, except that *Stock Transport Orders* are internal documents going from one plant to another.

As the receiving plant receives goods against a *Stock Transport Order*, SAP updates the status of a *Stock Transport Order* just as it would the status of a purchase order, thus enabling tracking. When the status of a goods movement needs to be tracked closely, *Stock Transport Orders* turn out to be a good choice. Another major advantage is that MRP can take Stock Transport Orders into account when computing net requirements. Other advantages also exist and are discussed in the TERP10 certification course.

Warehouse Management

Warehouse management deals with the physical logistics of removing materials from stock (*picking*) and placing them into stock (*putaway*). You must pay careful attention to the difference between *inventory management* and *warehouse management*. The former is concerned only with tracking the quantity and value of material stock at various storage locations and with periodic reconciliation of physical inventory with book inventory.

Of course the two are closely linked and SAP achieves the linkage by allowing us to *enable* warehouse management for storage locations. Not all storage locations need to be warehouse management-enabled. Some might be and others might not be – based on how a company wants to handle this. Some storage locations might be small and not require any warehouse management at all. For example, a storage location could be just a room for storing a few hundred items and hence not need any warehouse management at all. Other storage locations might be huge facilities with several square kilometers of space, and could need extensive warehouse management to function efficiently. We could also have special storage needs like refrigerated/freezer storage.

So, in SAP, we talk about a storage location being used with or without warehouse management. Storage locations under warehouse management have a *Warehouse Number* associated with them, and that warehouse number is not solely linked to the storage location, but is actually associated with the Plant/Storage Location combination. Figure 39 highlights certain important points:

- Storage location numbers can be duplicated across plants, but the combination of plant number and storage number has to be unique. In other words, one plant cannot have storage locations with duplicated numbers under it.
- Warehouse number 0001 is linked to two storage locations from the same plant. Warehouse number 0002 illustrates the point that a single warehouse number can be linked to storage locations from multiple plants.
- Storage locations that are not linked to any warehouse number are not under warehouse management. In figure 39, storage location 40 in plant 2000 and storage location 30 in plant 3000 are not under inventory management as they are not linked to any warehouse numbers.
- Goods movements related to storage locations that are under warehouse management (that is, storage locations linked to a warehouse number) generate *transfer requests*, which trigger warehouse operations. Goods movements related to storage locations that are not under warehouse management do not trigger transfer requests.

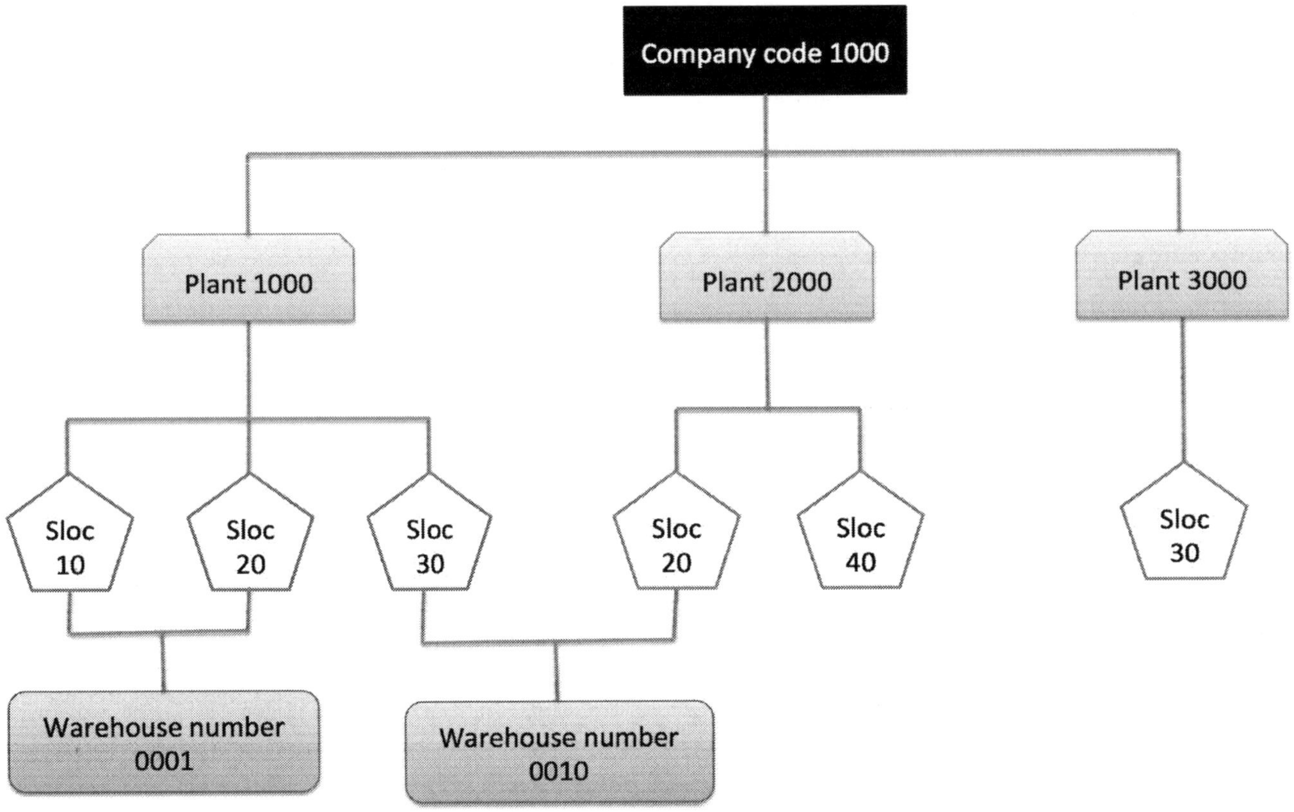

Figure 39: Linkage between Inventory Management and Warehouse Management

Recall that in SAP, some kind of *order* controls almost every operation – we have already seen *purchase order*, *sales order*, *production order* and *stock transport order*.

A *Transfer Order* initiates warehouse operations.

When a goods issue or goods receipt occurs in a storage location that is under warehouse management, then SAP requires a *Transfer Order* to signal to warehouse management that it has some work to do.

With huge warehouses, retrieving materials from and putting materials into the warehouse should not be done haphazardly because that will end up being very inefficient and costly. Instead, warehouse management software tries to perform these operations as efficiently as possible using mathematical techniques. However, in order to plan warehouse operations, warehouses need advance information about the expected material movements.

Outbound delivery documents and *Inbound delivery documents*

may occur before planned goods movements and assist in the warehouse management planning process. We have already seen *Outbound delivery documents* in the Order to Cash business process. After a Sales Order is saved, we initiate the shipment process by first creating an *Outbound delivery document* for some or all of the items in the sales order. This document can enable warehouse management to plan the picking of the item from the shelves.

Similarly *Inbound delivery documents* occur when a planned goods receipt is set to occur. Although the certification course does not specifically cover *Inbound delivery documents*, they can be used to initiate planned goods receipts. For example, suppose we are moving goods from one plant to another, then we could create an outbound delivery to initiate the process and could also create an inbound delivery document to signal an impending goods receipt and enable warehouse management to plan ahead.

Often POs are handled without a delivery document. Thus warehouse management operations might be required for material movements that occur against delivery documents or movements without any associated delivery documents.

When a goods issue or receipt occurs, we need to perform inventory management operations – updating the quantity and value of materials – as well as warehouse management operations – picking or put away. In what order should these operations be performed?

Figure 40 illustrates the sequencing. When a goods movement is performed *against a delivery document* (inbound or outbound) then warehouse operations are performed first; otherwise inventory management operations are performed first. In the figure, ovals represent warehouse operations and rectangles represent inventory management operations.

In cases where the Goods Receipt or Goods Issue occurs first, SAP automatically creates a *Transfer Requirement*. The *Transfer Order* for the warehouse workers is then created from this *Transfer Requirement*.

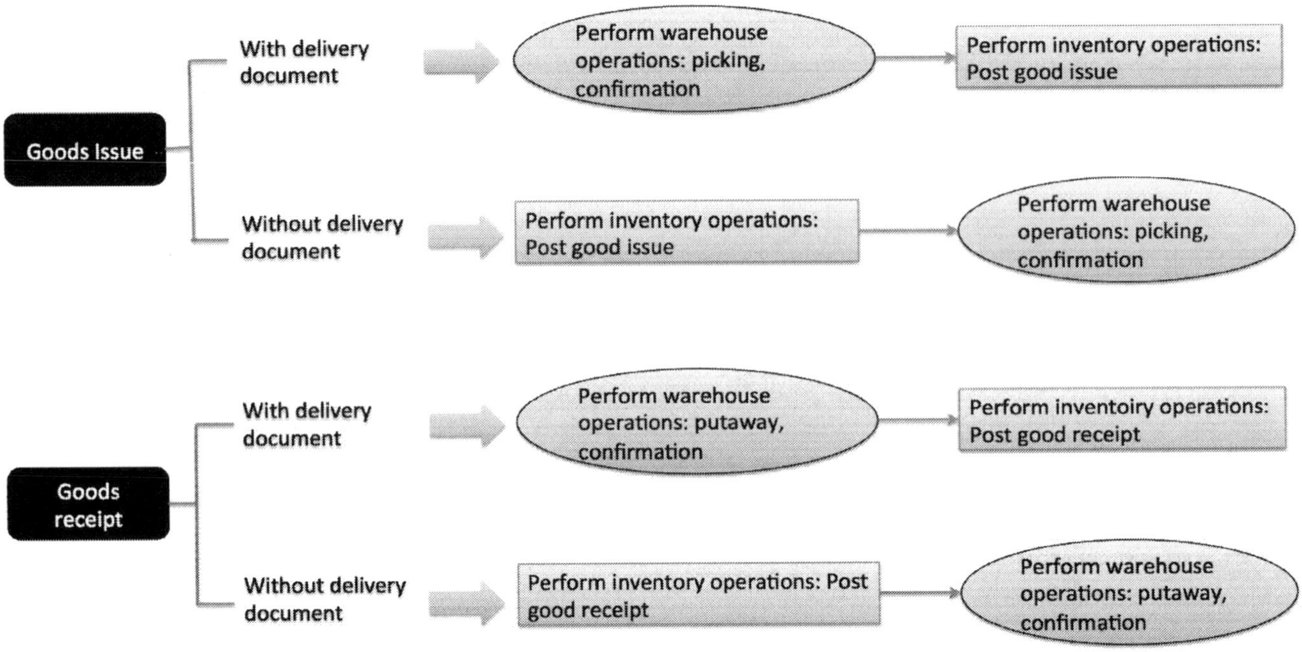

Figure 40: Sequencing of Inventory Management and Warehouse Management operations: When an operation occurs against a delivery document, then warehouse operations are performed first; otherwise inventory management operations are performed first.

Chapter-end review questions

You can find suggested answers to all these questions starting from page 261

To answer questions marked with ★, you will need to have read the official SAP TERP10 course material.

1. Which of the following can result in a goods receipt posting in our company? (three)

   A Receipt of shipments against purchase orders raised by us
   B Receipt of raw material by an employee against a production order
   C Receipt of goods returned by customers to us
   D Receipt of our shipment by a customer of ours
   E An outbound delivery document

2. Which of the following can result in goods issue postings in our company? (two)

   A Issue of raw material by an employee against a production order
   B Deposit into stock of finished products from production
   C Issue of goods by a vendor to fulfill our purchase order

D An outbound delivery for a sales order

E Receipt at our plant of a Stock Transport Order from another plant

3. Which of the following could represent a transfer posting? (two)

A The warehouse confirms a transfer order for an inbound delivery

B We take some materials from consignment stock into our possession

C We move stock from one plant to another within the same company code

D Some material to be inspected in a storage location clears quality inspection

4. Which of the following are true about one and two step stock transfers? (two) ★

A One step stock transfer creates two material documents

B One step transfer creates one material document with two items

C Two step stock transfer creates two material documents with two items on each

D Two step stock transfer creates two material documents each with one item

5. What is an advantage of the two-step stock transfer process over the one-step process?

6. In two-step stock transfer where is the stock shown on the stock overview between the time it leaves the first location and is checked into the second? ★

7. If there is valuation involved in a two-step transfer process, at which step does valuation take place? ★

8. Under what conditions is an accounting document created for a stock transfer?

9. What impact does the two step process have on physical inventory? ★

10. Under what conditions can an accounting document be created for goods movements across two plants of a single company code?

11. Under what conditions can an accounting document be created for goods movements between two storage locations within a single plant?

12. If a stock movement happens across two storage locations in one plant and simultaneously changes stock type from goods in quality inspection to unrestricted use, this involves stock transfer and a transfer posting. T/F?

13. Which of the following is required in two step stock transfers across storage locations in a single plant? (one) ★

    A Unrestricted stock from the origin can be moved to stock in QI at the destination

    B Unrestricted stock from the origin can be moved to blocked stock the destination

    C Unrestricted stock from the origin can be moved to unrestricted stock at the destination

    D Stock in QI at the origin can be moved into stock in QI at the destination

14. Suppose stock is transferred from one company code to another. Which two G/L accounts will be affected in the sending company code? ★

15. Suppose you are planning to move stock from one plant to another and would like to include additional costs such as freight charges associated with this move. What mechanism would be best? What other benefits does this approach provide over the alternative approach available?

16. If MRP creates a Purchase Requisition it can be converted into a purchasing document. Which two options exist for this conversion to a purchasing document?

17. How is inventory management connected with warehouse management?

18. Is posting a goods issue a part of inventory management or warehouse management?

19. Is the execution of a transfer order part of inventory management or warehouse management?

20. For what reason might a stock transfer not involve warehouse operations?

21. Your company has received a sales order and has created an outbound delivery for it. In what order will the inventory and warehouse operations be performed?

22. Your vendor has given you advance notification of a shipment and you have created an inbound delivery in anticipation. In what order will the inventory and warehouse operations be performed?

23. With respect to warehouse management, which of the following statements is valid? (one)

    A Multiple storage locations from multiple plants can all be assigned to a single warehouse number

    B All the storage locations assigned to a warehouse number must belong to the same plant

    C Different storage locations of a given plant cannot be allocated to different warehouse numbers

    D If one storage location of a plant is allocated to a warehouse number, then all have to be allocated to warehouse numbers, but not necessarily the same one

24. Transportation planning points are allocated at which organization level? ★

25. Under what conditions would a goods receipt generate a transfer requirement?

26. What three things determine a specific location in a warehouse?

27. When a goods receipt results in the creation of a transfer requirement, where will the material appear in the warehouse? ★

28. Explain the hierarchical sub structure of a warehouse. ★

Enterprise Asset Management

This chapter introduces *Enterprise Asset Management* concepts as relevant for the SAP TERP10 certification examination. **Enterprise Asset Management** – formerly referred to as *Plant Maintenance* – deals with servicing the physical assets of a company and remains completely internal to a company. These assets include plant and machinery used for manufacturing, as well as other assets that could need maintenance.

The topic deals with both *preventive maintenance* and *breakdown maintenance*. *Preventive maintenance* refers to the routine maintenance of an asset (to prevent failure) – similar to when we change motor oil in our cars regularly, even in the absence of a tangible malfunction. A machine does not need to fail or break down for preventive maintenance to occur. Companies perform **Breakdown Maintenance** – as the name clearly suggests – when a machine actually fails. This unit covers the SAP business processes involved in breakdown maintenance. As with the other chapters in this book, you might benefit from reading this chapter before proceeding with the TERP10 course materials.

Proper care and maintenance of physical assets, commonly referred to as *Enterprise Asset Management (EAM)*, plays an important role in the success of manufacturing organizations, despite not being directly involved in revenues or profits. A complete ERP system must therefore support the related business processes. SAP provides extensive support to manage the business processes related to this function in the *EAM* module.

Organization levels

As with most other units, EAM has its own organization levels and the process also interacts with other organization levels.

- **Maintenance Plant**: The term refers to any plant in which physical assets are installed. Although the term might seem to refer to a plant that performs maintenance work, it does not. You might recall from prior chapters that SAP uses the term *Plant* rather flexibly to refer to any unit that produces products or services customers. Thus the regional office of a consulting company would be defined as a *plant*, even though it might not have any production equipment. A typical manufacturing plant would also be a plant in SAP. To differentiate between these kinds of plants, SAP uses the term *Maintenance Plant* to refer to plants that actually house equipment that might need to be maintained.
- **Maintenance Planning Plant**: This term refers to the plant responsible for planning for the *Enterprise Asset Management* function.

SAP allows for various ways of organizing the planning for maintenance tasks.

- **Decentralized**: Each maintenance plant plans its own activities.
- **Centralized**: We have a single maintenance planning plant that plans for every other maintenance plant.
- **Hybrid**: Many maintenance planning plants with each one responsible for planning for a set of maintenance plants.

SAP also allows us to organize the actual execution of maintenance activities similarly.

Master Data

In addition to the organizational levels, we again need to address the master data relevant to *Enterprise Asset Management*. One example of master data needed for *Enterprise Asset Management* is *Work Center*. Just like production, work centers provide the capacity to perform work. In *Enterprise Asset Management*, work centers are used to perform maintenance activities. The other master data for *Enterprise Asset Management* are, broadly termed, *Technical Objects*.

We discuss three types of *technical objects*.

- **Functional Location**: This term refers to a physical place within the plant. It could be as simple as an office or as complex as a physical location where many pieces of equipment are installed.
- **Equipment**: A piece of *equipment* is something that might require maintenance and is also something that needs to be tracked autonomously. It is a unique item that can be installed in a *functional location* or exist in inventory. As an example, we may have a lathe machine (equipment) that is installed in a specific place (functional location) within the plant. From time to time, the lathe may require maintenance. The lathe would be managed as a unique item. To put things in perspective, keep in mind that plants can be huge and could include thousands of pieces of installed equipment. Proper tracking of where the equipment is installed requires that we create functional locations to identify their precise location. This leads to efficiencies in the maintenance process. *Functional locations*, by themselves, could also require maintenance, such as the painting of walls or replacement of broken lights.
- **Assembly**: To simplify the planning of materials needed to repair equipment or perform maintenance on functional locations, planners utilize *Assemblies*. *Assemblies* are the same as bill of materials, except that the purpose of assemblies is not to facilitate manufacturing, but rather to plan parts needed for maintenance. Assemblies are available for functional locations and equipment. In some cases, to simplify master data creation, material BOMs (bill of materials) can be used as assemblies for equipment.

Process

As we have already seen, business processes in SAP reflect a broad similarity in that we usually have a preliminary step that identifies the need for an action (*Sales Inquiry* in the sales process, *Purchase Requisition* in the purchasing process, *Planned Order* in the manufacturing process and *Transfer Request* in warehouse management). When the action is to be formally started we have an ***Order*** of some kind (*Sales Order* in the sales process, *Purchase Order* in the purchasing process, *Production Order*in the manufacturing process and *Transfer Order* in warehouse management).

In EAM, a *Maintenance Notification* starts the process. It indicates that somewhere, something needs to be maintained. A notification could identify a specific equipment at a specific functional location, a functional location itself, or be generic –

because it might not always be possible to zero in on the location of a problem or to trace it to a specific piece of equipment.

A *Maintenance Notification* also contains a brief textual description of the problem. The notification could then be converted into a *Maintenance Order* that would be used as a basis for planning its execution and for estimating costs and as a general document for authorizing further steps in the process. For example, the maintenance operation could require the use of some materials – these can be issued against the maintenance order. The task could involve the procurement of some specific material (as a consumable).

Recall from our discussion in management accounting that a maintenance order, *once released*, becomes a cost object and can collect costs.

A Maintenance Notification differs from other preliminary documents in that the maintenance notification serves as a place where people add textual updates as the work on the corresponding order progresses. The notification initially contained a description of the problem and as work progresses, people update the notification to include progress on the maintenance item.

Chapter end review questions

You can find answers to these questions starting from page 266

To answer questions marked with ★, you will need to have read the official SAP TERP10 course material.

1. When creating a maintenance order, which of the following represent two examples of master data that might require maintenance? (two)

   A Structure

   B Functional location

   C Planner group

   D Equipment

2. Prior to creating a maintenance order, which of the following documents might be created to support the maintenance process? (one)

A Purchase requisition
B Transfer order
C Maintenance notification
D Maintenance requisition

3. Which of the following is considered master data in *Enterprise Asset Management*? (two)

A Maintenance plant
B Work center
C Technical object
D Maintenance planning plant

4. Which of the following are examples of technical objects? (three)

A a. Work centers
B BOMs
C Functional locations
D Equipment

5. What is the role of a functional location?

6. What is the role of equipment?

7. What is the role of assemblies?

8. What is the role of a planner group?

9. What is the role of a maintenance planning plant?

10. What is the role of a notification?

11. What is the role of a maintenance order?

12. What is the significance of releasing a maintenance order?

13. What is the difference between *Enterprise Asset Management* and *Asset Accounting*?

14. Which of the following are examples of equipment? (three)

A Cafeteria
B Oven
C Steamer
D Cooler

15. When the maintenance order is created, the maintenance notification is deleted. (T/F)

16. Which of the following are different types of maintenance described in this chapter? (two)

    A Preventive maintenance

    B Overall maintenance

    C Breakdown maintenance

    D Material maintenance

17. Explain the main differences between centralized and decentralized maintenance planning.

18. A maintenance plant is an example of master data. (T/F)

19. Which of the following is considered master data that is responsible for performing maintenance activities? (one)

    A Maintenance plant

    B Work center

    C Technical object

    D Maintenance planning plant

20. Which of the following is considered master data that is used by planner groups to plan materials on a maintenance order? (one)

    A Functional location

    B Work center

    C Equipment

    D Assembly

21. A maintenance order is managed using order-related cost object controlling. (T/F) ★

Human Capital Management

This chapter introduces *Human Capital Management (HCM)* concepts as relevant for the SAP TERP10 certification examination. HCM is broader than the commonly used business term, *Human Resources Management*. HCM, among other things, involves having the right number of employees, with the right skill sets, in the right places, at the right time, and at the right price. When it is put in those terms, it can seem a bit simplistic, but do not be fooled. It can involve rather detailed steps and processes to make all of that happen effectively, especially when we incorporate HCM into our ERP environment. As with the other chapters, you might benefit from reading this before proceeding with the TERP10 certification course.

Human Capital Management Cycle

There are a number of different processes that make up what we will call the HCM Cycle. Unfortunately, there is no easily identifiable beginning and end to this cycle. (See Figure 41)

As we can see, there is a lot involved in the HCM cycle. One might think the cycle begins with recruiting, but it could easily be argued that an enterprise could not recruit employees without having an organizational structure (departments) in which to hire employees. Furthermore, whether or not an organizational structure exists, needs to be eliminated, or needs to be created depends heavily on planning processes. We could go on and on arguing where the HCM cycle begins and ends, but that is not the purpose of this chapter. The purpose of HCM is to effectively manage these processes in a way that allows an enterprise to have the right number of employees, with the right skill sets, in the right places, at the right time, and at the

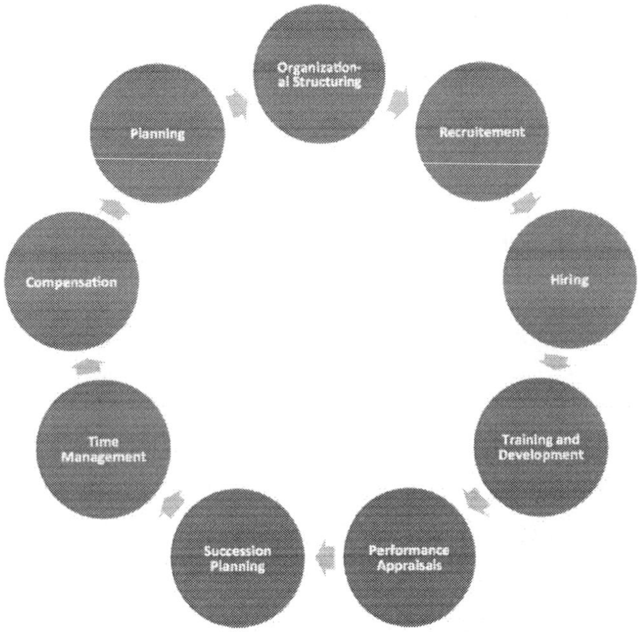

Figure 41: Human capital management cycle

right price.

Organizational Structuring in HCM

For years, there have been different philosophies on how enterprises should be structured organizationally. AN organization's structure is depicted as an organizational chart. The most common approach to an organizational chart is the hierarchical structure of the enterprise. An example appears in Figure 42.

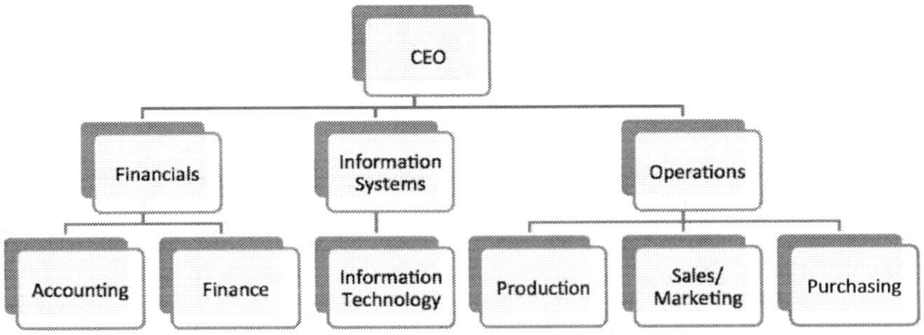

Figure 42: A typical organization structure

Having an organizational chart like the one in Figure 42 is a good start at understanding organizational structuring. However, in an ERP system like SAP, it can get complicated rather quickly. Because ERP systems are integrated, there is much more that goes into organizational structuring. For purposes of demonstrating this, let us use the production department from the example organizational chart in Figure 42 . In SAP, a production department must be created in the SAP system. Additionally, it must be created to exist within the hierarchy; therefore it must be linked to the *Operations* department. There are several questions which then need to be answered. Those questions may include: How will we track costs for this department? How many different types of jobs will be performed in this department? Are any special skills required for these job types? For all of the different types of jobs, how many positions will be needed? Will these positions be full-time or part-time positions? How will we pay our employees? What type of an employee will we need? A great deal of planning is required to do this effectively. Now you understand why planning is also a step in the HCM cycle.

For purposes of understanding how this works, let us simplify things a bit by addressing some of the questions listed above.

- **How will we track costs for this department?** To track costs in SAP, we could use a *cost center* for the Production department. We discussed *cost centers* in the *Management Accounting* chapter of this text. A *Cost center* is a part of an organization which incurs costs, and to which costs can be allocated.
- **How many different types of jobs will be performed in this department?** In SAP, Jobs are generic descriptions of what people do. A Job should be created and described to be as general as possible, and as specific as necessary. A department could require many different Jobs. As an example, the Production department could require managers, planners, shop stewards, and shop workers. Each of these would need to have a *Job* created in the SAP system to describe it.
- **For all of the different types of jobs, how many positions will be needed?** Once we know the descriptions of work that will be performed – *Jobs* – we can then begin planning how many Positions we will need for each of these *Jobs*. In SAP *Positions* are described by *Jobs*. One *Job* can have several *Positions* associated with it in a department. For example, as we discussed above, the *Production* department could require a Job called *Manager*. The *Production*

department may need three managers, thus it will create three *Positions* described by the *Job Manager*. Some or all of these positions could be full-time positions. Others maybe part-time positions.

- **How will we pay our employees?** Not all employees will be paid in the same manner. As an example, some employees may be paid a salary and receive their paycheck only once a month. Others may be paid a wage and receive their paychecks on a weekly basis.
- **What type of employee will we need?** Just as we may pay employees differently, employees also are categorized differently. For instance, we are likely to have full-time employees and part-time employees. We may also have employees who are contracted on a temporary basis. Another example could be interns. Some interns may receive compensation, while other do not.

These are just answers to some of the questions regarding organizational structuring. There are many other considerations. But for now, the following statement holds true: "An enterprise will hire a *Person*, into a *Position*, which is described by a *Job*, and belongs to a *Department*."

Recruitment in HCM

Recruitment in HCM can involve different activities. First, there is the matter of advertising openings for positions. Generally speaking, the advertisements should include a description of the position as well as some requirements associated with these positions. So where do these descriptions and requirements come from? Recall from above that *Positions* are described by *Jobs* and that many *Positions* can be described with a single *Job* in SAP. To simplify the creation of descriptions for every position in the enterprise, one could use the *Job* descriptions and then modify those descriptions to satisfy advertisement needs. For example, suppose an Accounting department in the College of Business at a university has an opening for a "Management Accounting Lecturer". In theory, this open Position would be described using a Job labeled, "Lecturer". That job may be used to describe all lecturer positions at the university. The advertised description for this position could then be modified as needed to customize it to meet the needs of the Accounting Department. *Jobs* may also list specific requirements that can also be associated with an advertised position.

There are likely to be some requirements for a position that candidates must meet in order to be eligible to be considered for employment. These requirements would also be included in the advertisement. Using the example of the "Management Accounting Lecturer" position, a candidate could be required to hold a Masters Degree or higher in the field of Accounting.

Part of the recruitment process also involves evaluating candidates. It's only natural that there will be applicants whose qualifications don't meet the requirements of the position. To assist managers, applicants can easily be screened using a tool. In SAP this tool is called the *Profile Matchup*. Other software vendors have similar tools with different names, but the concept is basically the same. Recall, the enterprise advertises open positions and includes the description as well as the requirements of that position. It's expected that all candidates who apply meet these requirements, but as we noted, that is not true in all cases. A simplified example of a profile matchup can be seen in Figure 43. Here we will once again use the example of the lecturer position in the Accounting department. Suppose we receive information from an applicant. Figure 43 shows the position requirements on the left, and the applicant's qualifications on the right. You can see that this applicant fails to meet all of the requirements of the advertised position. This simple example makes it easy to see how management can use the *Profile Matchup* in evaluating applicants. Those who fail to meet the requirements should no longer be given any consideration for hire into that position.

In today's business environment, it has almost become a mandate that companies provide some form of electronic access to advertise these position openings. Once upon a time, a company would do this advertising in newspapers and in rare cases, on radio or in other print media like magazines. Today we go to the Internet to find open positions. There are many online companies like CareerBuilder and Monster to assist enterprises by providing a space where they can post their positions and make them available to the public. Other companies like Gulfstream create their own space (http://www.gulfstream.com/careers/) on the Internet where potential candidates can create a profile and search available

Position requirements	Applicant's Qualifications
Master's degree or higher in accounting	☑
Minimum of three years' teaching experience	☑
Fluent in English and French languages	☐
Hold a certification in accounting (CPA or similar)	☑

Figure 43: Applicant profile matchup

openings. However, posting available positions is not exclusively intended for the public. Enterprises realize the value in promoting employees from within. It is a very common practice these days to have a presence on an internal site where current employees can also look for opportunities where they work.

Having an online presence can simplify the transition from the recruitment process to the hiring process. Data collected from applicants can be used for automatic transfer during the hiring process to minimize the data entry at hiring. In addition, applicants often have the capability of monitoring and updating their applicant status and information.

All of this discussion about advertising positions does not imply that this is all there is to recruitment in HCM. Recruitment could also involve recruiters from the HR department attending career fairs or universities to recruit students. At such events, recruiters could accept resumes from applicants and even screen them using the Profile Matchup and/or interview them for current or future position openings. This is a proactive approach often used by enterprises to help reduce the time and expense required to fill vacancies when they occur.

Hiring in HCM

The hiring process is the next logical step in the HCM Cycle. After applicants are evaluated, the enterprise has to make a decision and hire an applicant into a position. The hiring process joins the complexities discussed in Organizational Structuring with the Recruitment phase in the HCM Cycle. The applicant is hired into a position, described by a job, belonging to a department. Earlier in this chapter, we again referenced Cost Centers, which is a part of SAP Management Accounting (CO), describing where costs occur in an organization. A simple approach for an enterprise is to associate the department where this employee works with a cost center (as described in the Organizational Structuring in this chapter). In doing so, when running payroll for this employee, any labor costs associated with the person being hired will immediately be linked to that cost center. Because management accounting isn't the only thing impacted by payroll, we also need to ensure the financial accounting integration with ERP is properly recorded.

Enterprises are also going to want to maintain a *Personnel File* for employees they hire. A *Personnel File* is a record of their personal information as well as other information relating that employee to the enterprise. The personnel file contains information that the Humans Resource department needs to maintain for an employee. Some examples include, but are not necessarily limited to: address information; employee banking information; pay rate information; and organizational structuring information (see Figure 44). Keep in mind, some of the information applicants entered in the recruitment phase can be copied over into the hiring phase. What does all of this mean? It means an enterprise has to ensure that this new employee is properly hired into the organizational structure and that necessary information about the employee is maintained.

To manage some of these complexities, SAP uses a form of master data called an *InfoType*. They exist to help maintain all of the information the enterprise needs to record for an employee. An *InfoType* is a collection of related data. The categories (Personal Information, Banking Information, Pay Rate Information, and Organizational Structuring) presented in Fig-

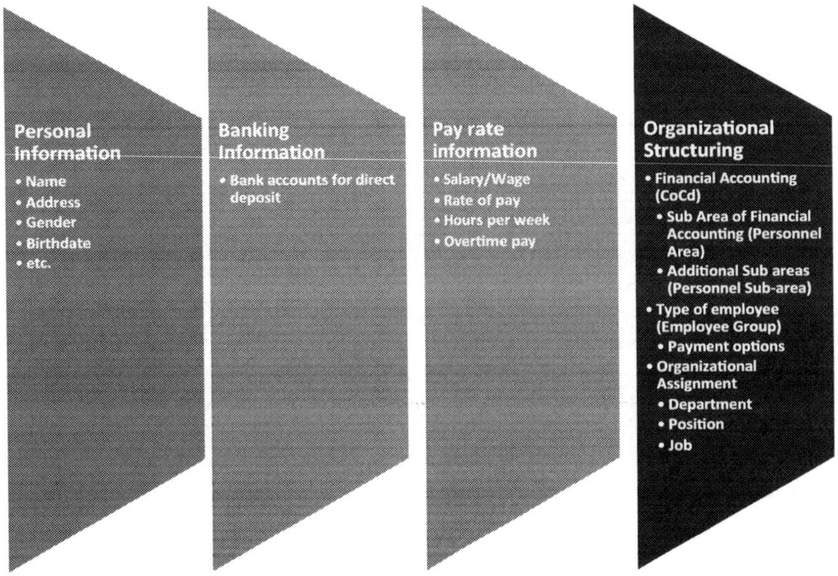

Figure 44: Personnel information

ure 44 further demonstrate this. Each of the categories is an example of what could be considered a unique *InfoType* in SAP. The collection of all *InfoTypes* for an employee makes up their *Personnel File*.

Maintaining *InfoTypes* in SAP can be performed with something called an *Action*. Hiring is an example of an *Action* and would result in the maintenance of *InfoTypes*. Often during hiring, the enterprise would like to maintain many *InfoTypes* at one time. If you can imagine, maintenance of *InfoTypes* could become a challenge. An enterprise needs to maintain *InfoTypes* for many reasons (i.e., Actions) other than hiring. Another type of an Action would be termination, which would require further maintenance of *InfoTypes*. Other reasons could also exist that would require updating an *InfoType*. Suppose an employee receives a wage increase. Only one *InfoType* for one employee would need to be maintained. On the other hand, we could have several employees who have received a wage increase. It would make sense then to be able to maintain that single *InfoType* for several employees at one time. To satisfy each of these scenarios, SAP provides three options for *InfoType* maintenance (see Figure 45). To maintain several InfoTypes for one employee at one time, SAP provides the option of using what they call, Personnel Actions. For the purpose of maintaining only one

InfoType at a time for one employee, SAP offers Single Screen maintenance. Finally, to maintain a single *InfoType* for many employees at one time, SAP offers Fast Entry maintenance.

Infotype maintenance need	Option
One employee – many InfoTypes	Personnel actions
One employee, one InfoType	Single screen
Many employees, one InfoType	Fast entry

Figure 45: InfoType maintenance options

Some InfoTypes can be maintained by employees themselves. For example, if an employee's address changes, it would be inefficient to have management make this change. SAP offers a tool called *Employee Self-Service (ESS)* to enable these types of authorized changes. ESS could also be used for employees to view paychecks and download tax documentation when needed.

To summarize the Hiring phase, it is fair to say hiring is supported by the Recruitment phase and integrates directly with the Organizational Structuring phase in the HCM Cycle.

Training and Development, Performance Appraisals, and Succession Planning in HCM

Training and Development, Performance Appraisals and Succession Planning (Figure 46) are so closely related in the HCM Cycle that it makes sense for us to talk about all three of them at the same time. To begin our discussion, we should note that training and development are not necessarily the same thing. Training could be used for current employees or new hires to improve their skills. To be hired into a position, the employee held the necessary qualifications to meet the position requirements. This does not however mean that new employee is job

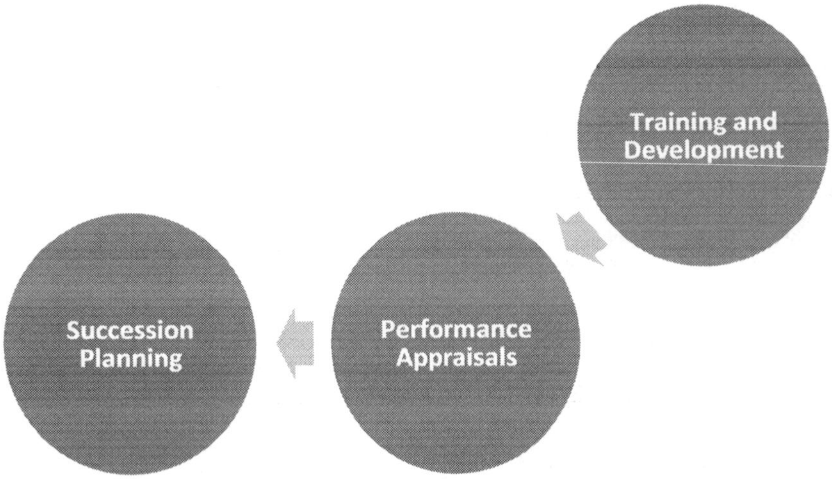

Figure 46: Training development, Performance appraisals and succession planning in SAP

ready. The new employee might need some training to improve on their qualifications to suit the needs of the enterprise. Development is different. Development is often used to prepare current employees for future opportunities within the enterprise and to increase their potential value to themselves and to the enterprise.

Training and Development assumes there is a need for either or both. This assumption is what creates the close relationship between them and with Performance Appraisals and Succession Planning. Let's begin by discussing training. Training for the sake of training is generally fruitless. To provide effective training, the enterprise should perform a type of needs assessment. For new hires, this needs assessment generally takes place during the recruitment process. Management, while evaluating and selecting the new employee for the position, makes a determination of this person's capabilities. If they responsibly made this hiring decision, they would have a very good understanding of the new employee's training needs. Current employees also have training needs. The needs assessment for current employees can stem from the use of Performance Appraisals. These appraisals serve many purposes, but one of them is to assist with defining training needs for current employees. Appraisals are primarily based on the requirements of the position held by the employee. The appraisal helps keep the employee informed as to how well he/she is performing in their position. Appraisals also serve other needs, such as compensation decisions; documenting employee successes; documenting employee shortcomings; and building development plans for employees. We will discuss development next.

As noted, development is designed to prepare current employees for future opportunities within the enterprise and to increase their potential value to themselves and to the enterprise. Part of the employee appraisal could include developing a current employee for promotion. The appraisal would help identify the desire for development, but doesn't do a very good job of identifying the development needs. Since appraisals are designed to evaluate an employee's performance in their current position, it is not optimized for development. An effective way to build development plans for employees is to once again take advantage of the *Profile Matchup*. During the appraisal process, the appraiser (supervisor) or the employee might express an interest in the promotion potential for that employee. A position could be identified and the *Profile Matchup* is used to determine which qualifications an employee currently lacks to be eligible for that position. Let's use the earlier example of the *Profile Matchup* (see Figure 47), but this time we will put it into a different context.

Position requirements	Employee's Qualifications
Master's degree or higher in accounting	☑
Minimum of three years' teaching experience	☑
Fluent in English and French languages	☐
Hold a certification in accounting (CPA or similar)	☑

Figure 47: Employee profile matchup

Notice in Figure 47, the qualifications column is now labeled, "Employee's Qualifications". This is so because we are not evaluating an external applicant, but rather an existing employee. Suppose the Accounting department in the College of Business has an existing part-time employee who teaches accounting classes as an adjunct lecturer. This adjunct would like to be considered for promotion to a current or future opening of a full-time lecturer's position in the Accounting department. A development plan should be built which addresses qualifications that are missing. In this case, the adjunct lecturer would need to develop his/her language skills to become fluent in both English and French language. If the adjunct currently speaks English, he/she should consider attending available French classes as part of their development plan to meet the development needs.

It becomes apparent that the primary objective of the above example certainly addresses the needs of the employee. However, there are also situations in which the primary objective is not to develop employees for their personal benefit, but to develop employees because it benefits the enterprise. Using the same *Profile Matchup* in Figure 47, let's again change the context. This time, suppose a current full-time lecture in the Accounting department has announced that he/she will retire at the end of the academic year. The enterprise now has a need to fill a vacancy that will happen in the near future. Planning to fill this vacancy is an example of *Succession Planning*. In this scenario, the head of the Accounting Department might approach the adjunct lecturer and ask that person to consider applying for the future vacancy. However, the adjunct lecturer does not have the qualifications at this point in time. Addressing this need early on in the process helps to get the right person in the right place at the right time. The adjunct lecturer would once again have a development plan which includes attending French classes to satisfy that part of the position requirement. In this example, the primary objective is for the enterprise to have someone readily available and prepared to enter that position as soon as it becomes vacant. This makes a lot of sense, but can be difficult to manage. If you think deeply enough, you might soon realize that if a current employee is being prepared to fill a future vacancy, that means their position is also about to become vacant. And so, there will be a spiraling effect associated with *Succession Planning* that will have to be effectively managed by the enterprise.

Time Management and Compensation in HCM

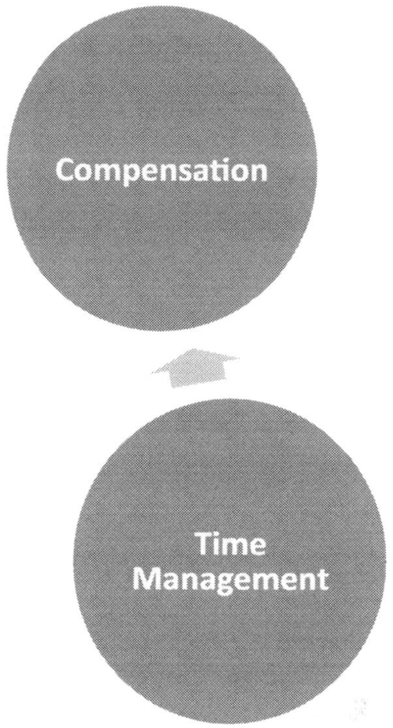

Figure 48: Time management and compensation

Time Management and Compensation are also closely related, so again it makes sense to include both of them in a single discussion. In the HCM Cycle, *times* play an important role on several levels. One of those involves using working times to help process payroll. Compensation also involves more than simply using recorded times to pay employees for hours they work. Compensation has a number of functions in the HCM Cycle as well.

If you were asked a question about how *times* are used in the HCM Cycle, it would only be natural for you to state that times are used for payroll. You would be correct, but that statement is too broad. In the HCM Cycle, we need to look more deeply into what these times are that an enterprise uses for payroll. Of course we need to record times that people work. These work times are extremely important for calculating pay for an employee. However each employee is different. If you recall in the hiring phase, we discussed that SAP uses *InfoTypes* when hiring employees. Among these *InfoTypes*, the enterprise maintains information about what type of employee the person is, how they get paid (wage, salary, etc.,), and their pay rate. The collection of working times may be used differently depending on the information maintained in their *InfoType* records. As an example, a wage worker may receive a rate of pay for all recorded hours up to forty hours. After that, the wage worker may receive a different rate of pay (overtime rate). On the other hand, a salaried employee would receive the same pay regardless of how many hours they work. But that doesn't necessarily mean the enterprise doesn't need to record working times for the salaried employee. Salaried employees could be required to record working times for other reasons. Perhaps the enterprise would like to know how many hours salaried employees work to make sure they are properly being compensated for the amount of work they perform. Or it could be that the salaried employees working times are recorded so they can be used to bill their times to customers. As you can see, working times can be used for more than just payroll.

There are additional forms of time other than working times that an enterprise would also collect in the HCM Cycle. These times include, but are not necessarily limited to: sick time, vacation time, overtime, leave time, maternity time, paternity time, time on sabbatical and travel time. If times are that important in the HCM Cycle, then it's equally important to have an effective tool for recording times. In SAP, there is a tool called, *CATS, Cross-application Time Sheet*. *CATS* allows employees, employers, and others to record various times for various business applications, hence its name – *Cross-application Time Sheet*.

By now, it should be quite evident that *Time Management* is closely integrated with *Compensation*. Up until this point, we've discussed compensation being a result of recording working times. So how does an enterprise determine how much to pay its employees? How is pay rate determined for wage workers and how are salaries determined for salaried employees? A common approach to this is *Job Pricing*. To learn how job pricing works, we need to reflect on some of the things we've learned so far. The term *Job* in SAP is used to describe various positions that can be linked to it. Thus *Jobs* describe the work that people in those positions will perform. In addition to this, we looked at *InfoTypes* for an employee and we learned that an employee is assigned in the organizational structuring. Part of this assignment is for Financial Accounting purposes. You can see in Figure 49, there are sub areas within the Financial Accounting part of *Organizational Structuring* (*Personnel Area* and *Personnel Sub-area*).

Let's use an example to understand how *Job Pricing* works. In Table 17, you see two employees, Employee A and Employee B.

Employee	Job	Country	City	Pay Rate
Employee A	Painter	USA	New York City, NY	$35/hr
Employee B	Painter	USA	Des Moines, Iowa	$25/hr

Table 17: Information for job pricing

Both employees work for the same enterprise and have some things in common. They both perform the same job and both work in the United States. However, you can see they do not

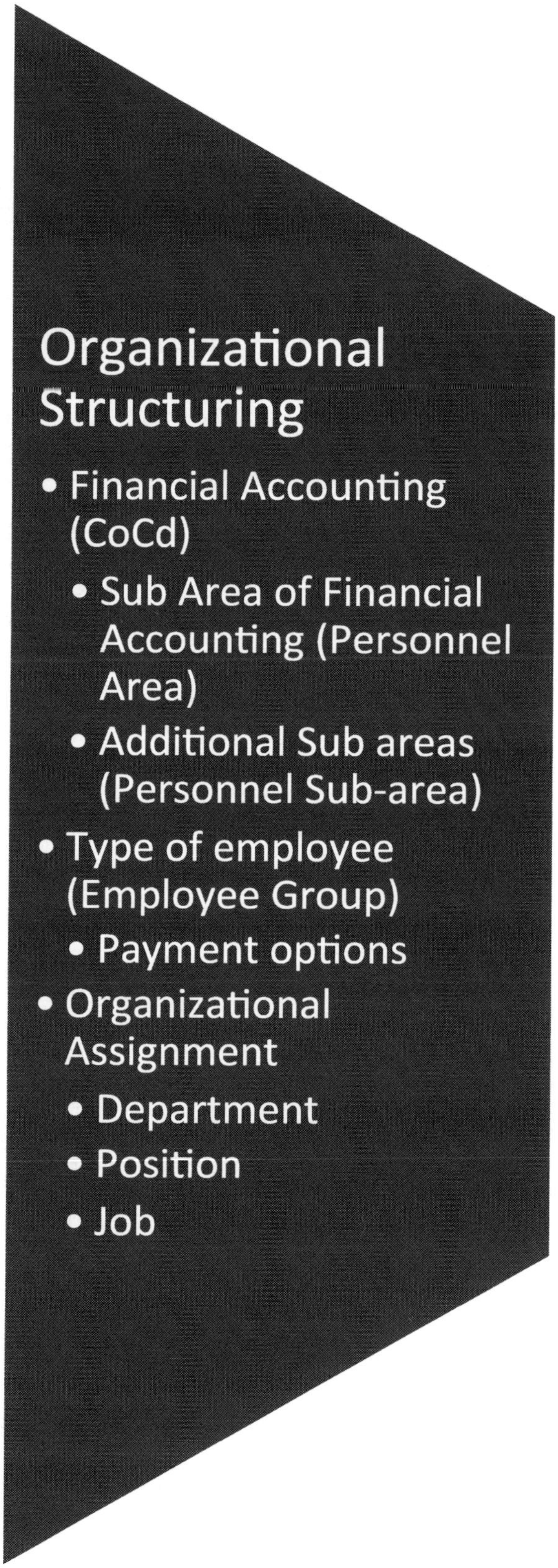

Figure 49: HCM and Financial accounting

receive the same pay rate.

Though both perform the same job, they work in different cities, demonstrating that where you work can impact your rate of pay because cost of living is different in these two cities. From a Financial Accounting point of view, both employees work in the United States, so their payroll expense will report to the same company code. However, the city represents the Personnel Sub Area within the United States (CoCd). It makes sense to have a different pay rate for the same job. *Job Pricing* allows the enterprise to analyze a job and to find a pay rate for that job that is competitive within the local market. Recall that HCM involves having the right number of employees, with the right skill sets, in the right places, at the right time, and at the right price.

Pay isn't the only form of compensation. Benefits provide additional forms of compensation. There are many types of benefits for employees. Benefits include health insurance, life insurance, retirement, vacation schedules, leave benefits and others. In some respects, benefits can be used to attract candidates. Should an applicant have more than one job offer, the applicant looks at more than just the rate of pay. The applicant will also consider various forms of benefits that are included in the job offer. The benefits could make the difference between whether or not the applicant accepts the job offer or takes a different offer elsewhere. Benefits also influence retention rates in an enterprise. As an example, an enterprise might provide a fully vested schedule for a retirement benefit after an employee completes ten years of service. If that employee has worked six years and has another job offer from another company, the retirement benefit mentioned may be enough to influence the employee to remain with their current employer so they could meet the requirements to become fully vested. Benefits can then be considered incentive packages that are a form of compensation. They can be used as a retention tool in the HCM Cycle.

One final form of compensation that bears some discussion is reimbursement. As part of an employee's position requirements, they may need to travel from time to time. The enterprise has to consider this and have a mechanism in place by which an employee would be reimbursed for any business expenses they personally paid out-of-pocket for during travel. Reimbursement is handled as part of compensation and can be included in the employee's paycheck when payroll is run. An employee would complete a travel expense form within the HCM system and those expenses would need to be evaluated and approved before reimbursement occurs. It's important to note that the reimbursement of these expenses has both a Financial and Management Accounting impact in the system.

Regarding time management and compensation, you should now be aware that these two phases mean more than simply paying employees for the time they work. There is a lot of strategy, integration, and planning that go into these concepts. As for planning, that is next.

Planning in HCM

Though this is the last phase of the HCM Cycle that we will be discussing, it does not mean that it is the last step in this cycle. Recall from our opening conversation that the HCM Cycle has no clear beginning or end.

There are a couple of aspects of planning that need to be addressed here. To begin, let's focus on organizational structure planning. Of course, planning any changes to the Organizational Structuring phase of the HCM Cycle involves a great deal of integration with the other ERP modules. Changing structures means creating new structures, modifying others, and in extreme cases, the elimination of some. The decisions around these changes are generally driven by profitability. Increased costs could result in restructuring as could increases in revenue. Most cost and revenue planning takes pace in Management Accounting, so there will be a close relationship between HCM and Management Accounting when it comes to planning.

Planning in HCM also involves planning personnel costs. Personnel costs are dependent on Organizational Structuring. If an enterprise eliminates a department, that will obviously impact personnel costs. Some employees in that department might be absorbed into other departments, but it is very possible that many of their positions will be terminated. Likewise, the creation of a new department may result in an increase in positions. Another input into personnel cost planning is performance appraisal. Performance appraisal could result in offering pay raises for employees. It would therefore make sense to include performance appraisal in personnel cost planning as well.

Sometimes external events will also impact the planning. Suppose a competing company just opened an office in the same city or in a nearby location. There is likely a threat that some employees may take jobs with the competing company. To offset that threat, the enterprise may re-evaluate their job pricing strategy to become more competitive in hopes of retaining their employees. Furthermore, they might also consider changes to benefits for the same reason. These changes are going to impact future costs and should also be given careful consideration in personnel cost planning.

Planning in the HCM Cycle requires intense management decision making. So managers must have tools to be able to access the information they need. In SAP, the *Manager's Desktop* is a useful tool that provides managers with the insight and reporting tools to enable these decisions. Management also needs tools to be able to support other aspects of HCM, and in general these tools are referred to as *Manager Self-Service (MSS)* tools.

Chapter-end review questions

You can find suggested answers to these questions starting from page 270

To answer questions marked with ★, you will need to have read the official SAP TERP10 course material.

1. Which of the following is not part of the HCM cycle? (one)

   A Recruitment
   B Performance appraisals
   C Time management
   D Work center planning

2. Define the beginning and end to the HCM cycle.

3. When a person is promoted into a new position, a vacancy occurs. Planning to have that vacancy filled efficiently and effectively is part of. (one)

   A Recruitment
   B Hiring
   C Succession planning
   D Performance appraisals

4. Keeping track of how much vacation an employee currently has is part of which process in the HCM cycle? (one)

   A Time management
   B Compensation
   C Organizational structuring
   D Planning

5. The Profile Matchup compares which two things?

   A Candidate's requirements
   B Candidate's qualifications
   C Position requirements
   D Position qualifications

6. Which processes in the HCM cycle use the Profile Matchup? (two)

   A Personnel development
   B Compensation
   C Recruitment
   D Planning

7. Explain how SAP supports the keeping track of costs for various organizational units in SAP HCM.
8. Explain the use of Jobs in SAP HCM.
9. Explain the use of Positions in SAP HCM.
10. The Hiring component in the HCM cycle supports the internal postings of positions for internal candidates. (T/F)
11. Explain how the SAP ERP system supports the integration of data between the Recruitment and Hiring components in the HCM cycle.
12. When someone is hired into a position, explain how this new employee is associated with a cost center.

13. Which transaction in HCM will result in the posting of a cost to a cost center? (one)

    A Hiring
    B Payroll
    C Recruitment
    D Planning

14. Which of the following best describes an Info Type? (two)

    A A collection of related data about an employee
    B A collection of related data about a cost center
    C Organizational data
    D Master data

15. Explain a personnel file.

16. Which of the following are possible examples of Info Types? (three)

    A Personal information
    B Banking information
    C Work center information
    D Pay rate information

17. Which of the following are methods for maintaining Info Types? (three)

    A Multiple screen
    B Single screen
    C Fast entry
    D Personnel actions

18. Explain personnel actions info type maintenance.

19. Explain single screen info type maintenance.

20. Explain fast entry info type maintenance.

21. It is not possible for an employee to maintain any of their own info type information. (T/F)

22. Training and development in HCM also takes advantage of the Profile Matchup. (T/F)

23. A company is preparing an employee to fill a future vacancy. As a result, they also need to prepare for the vacancy left behind by this employee. This is an example of ________________. (one)

A Succession planning
B Development
C Training
D Appraisals

24. A current employee is interested in being promoted to a higher position. The employee works closely with his/her manager to create a plan for achieving this. This is an example of _______________. (one)

A Succession planning
B Development
C Training
D Appraisals

25. A manager meets with an employee on an annual basis to discuss their performance. This is an example of _______________. (one)

A Succession planning
B Development
C Training
D Appraisals

26. Wages, salaries, benefits, and insurance are all examples of _______________ (one)

A Pay scale
B Job pricing
C Compensation
D Promotion

27. Explain CATS.

28. List various types of times that are used in HCM.

29. Explain the concept of Job Pricing in HCM.

30. Planning is the last phase of the HCM cycle and therefore ends the HCM process. (T/F)

31. Which of the following is available to assist managers in making planning decisions in HCM? (one)

A Employee desktop
B Manager's desktop
C Planning table
D Sales and operations plan

Project Management

This chapter introduces Project Management (PS) concepts as relevant for the SAP TERP10 certification examination. While reading through the information in this chapter, it is important to note that the objective of this chapter is to inform you of tools available for project management and how SAP uses those tools for managing projects. Learning how to manage projects and how to become a project manager is NOT an objective here. As with the other chapters, you might benefit from reading this before proceeding with the TERP10 certification course.

Project Characteristics

Projects can serve many purposes and there are many things that can influence a project. From an SAP perspective, it is important to note that the *Project Systems (PS)* module does not have any organizational levels directly associated with it. Projects get their organizational levels from the other SAP modules with which Project Systems integrates. From an enterprise perspective, projects have some defining characteristics. Projects are generally capital intensive and time intensive. They are usually complex in nature and involve many different functional areas. In addition to these characteristics, projects have a definitive beginning and a definitive end. Identifying the beginning and end of a project can be a lot more challenging than you think. For purposes of demonstration, let us discuss planning and managing a wedding as a project. If you have gotten married, planned a wedding, or know someone who has, you will understand the complexities involved in planning a wedding. If you ask ten different individuals to define the beginning of the wedding and end of the wedding you are likely to get ten different answers. Whereas this chapter will not help you figure out how to define the beginning and end of a project, it provides you with information on which tools are available that can help manage the project. The beginning, middle, and end of a project can be measured with time, but are better represented using other forms of measurement. These other forms of measurement are *Work Breakdown Structure (WBS) Elements* and *Activities*.

Work Breakdown Structure (WBS) Elements and Activities

Projects have various components which help project managers and teams measure and manage various aspects such as dates, costs, budgets, activities, payments, among other things. If we continue with our example of managing a wedding as a project, we can identify some basic elements which make up the wedding. Figure 50 shows these.

Wedding
- Wedding Ceremony?
- Wedding Reception?
- Wedding License?
- Who will be in the Wedding Party?

Figure 50: Some important elements in a wedding

The wedding itself is defined as the top level element, which defines the project. The items below it represent other elements that must be given consideration to manage the wedding (Note: this is just a rudimentary example for demonstration purposes only, and doesn't necessarily reflect all aspects of a wedding). These elements are called *Work Breakdown Structure (WBS) Elements*. From a project perspective, we can structure these elements in a hierarchical form to give us a visual representation as Figure 51 (rough-cut) shows.

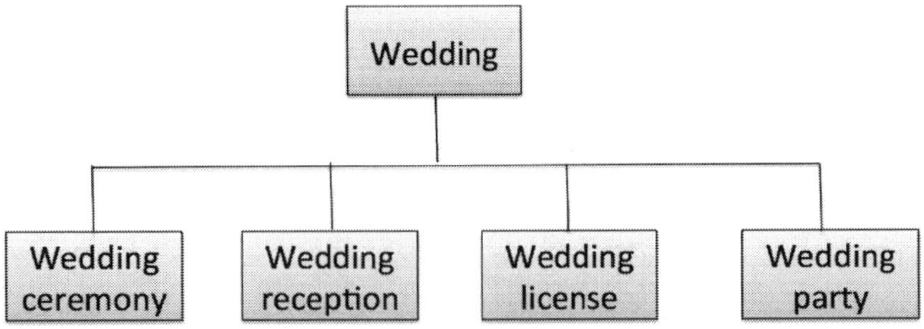

Figure 51: Rough cut work breakdown structure for a wedding

Figure 51 represents a *Work Breakdown Structure (WBS)*. Thus a WBS is a hierarchical representation of the project. Realistically, this WBS is a high-level WBS, meaning there are likely to be several additional levels. For example, the *wedding ceremony* WBS Element could involve other aspects such as the location, wedding official, flowers, music, etc. Likewise, the wedding reception WBS element may also have additional aspects associated with it, while the wedding license and wedding party WBS Elements may not. Figure 52 shows the WBS hierarchy in greater detail.

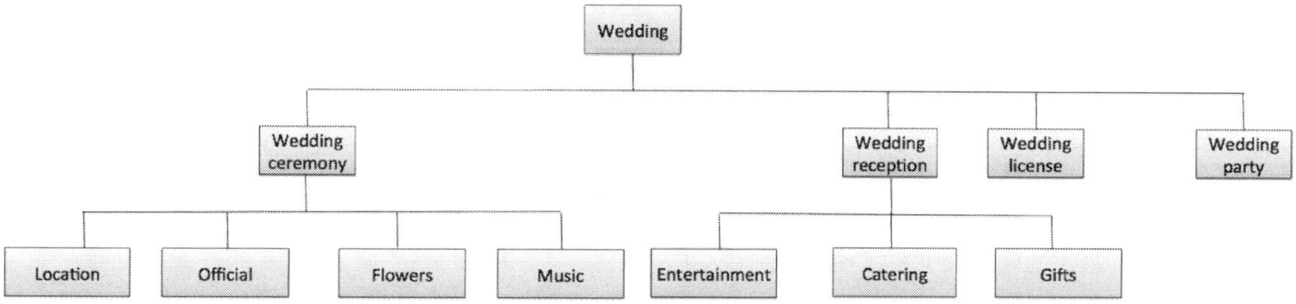

Figure 52: More detailed work breakdown structure for a wedding

The difference between the three previous figures is dependent upon the project phase. At first, the bride and groom to-be might begin working on their wedding by planning it at a very high level. This is considered the *concept* phase. During the concept phase, there is just some discussion about the wedding, with no detail. That would simply be represented with the top level *Wedding* as seen in Figure 50. When the planning of the wedding reaches the next phase, it is considered a rough-cut phase. The rough-cut phase would be represented as shown in Figure 51. Ultimately, the wedding progresses to the detailed planning phase. It is the detailed phase that we see in Figure 52 above.

Interestingly, we have used the term *planning* to describe these three phases. What does that mean? It means that the WBS can be used to plan the project. The more detailed our WBS, the more detailed the plan. We will discuss other phases of the project a little later in this chapter. For now, these three phases help provide a framework for how *WBS Elements* shape a project.

Activities represent the work or steps that need to be accomplished to complete the project. The activities of a project can be linked to one another in a precedence diagram. The precedence diagram describes the relationships (dependencies)

between the activities, and the order in which they must be completed. The precedence diagram is called a *Network* (Figure 53).

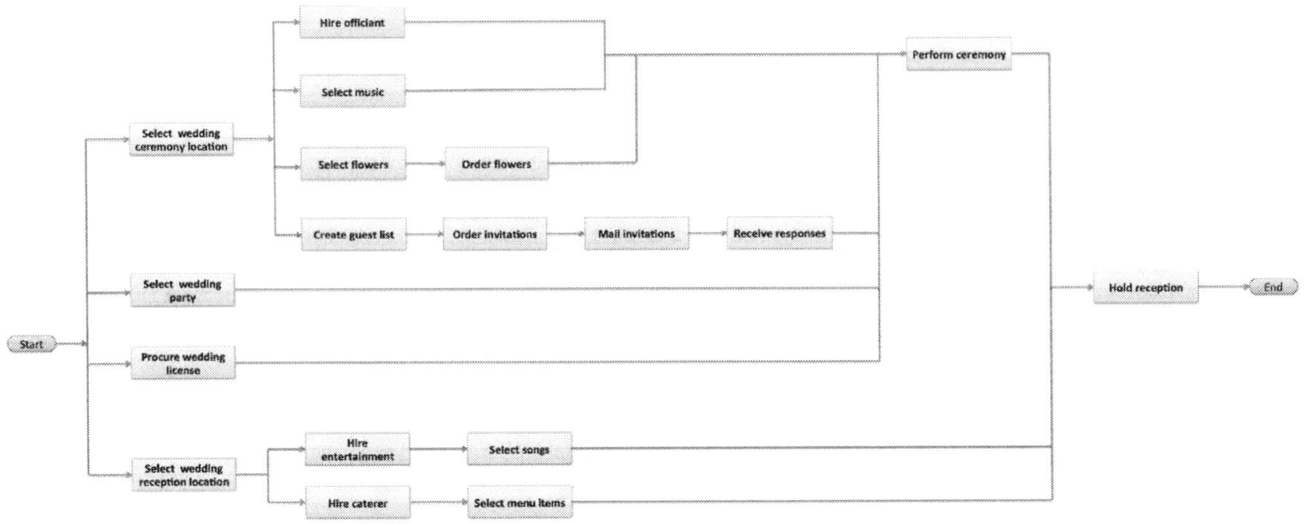

Figure 53: Activities and their relationships shown as an *activity network*

As you can see from the network in Figure 53, our wedding project includes many activities. (Note: like the WBS, the network seen here is for the purpose of providing an example and does not necessarily reflect all practical activities required for managing a wedding). Let us take a look at some of these activities in more detail to understand activities and their relationships. First, an activity (as explained above) is a step in completing the project and involves a type of work that needs to be performed. As you can see, there are four activities which are independent of each other and can be started as soon as the project begins (*Select a Location for the ceremony*, *Select wedding party*, *Procure a wedding license*, and *Select a Location for the reception*). There are no activities that need to be completed prior to these four and they do not have any dependency on each other. Thus when the project starts, these activities can be performed independently, and can run concurrently if needed.

If we look at the activity, *Perform Ceremony*, we clearly see several other activities that must be completed directly prior to performing the ceremony. These activities include: *Hire an Officiant*, *Select music*, *Order flowers*, *Receive responses*, *Select wedding party* and *Procure a wedding license*. The arrows connecting these activities to *Perform Ceremony* define the relationship between them. From a project perspective, this means the ceremony cannot be performed until these activities have been completed. You also notice that some of these activities have prior activities upon which they depend. This dependency helps form the network structure. Furthermore, in this example, the wedding project would be complete once the reception ends.

This might lead you to wonder why we need WBS Elements if we have Activities, or why we need a Network of Activities if we have WBS Elements in a WBS? Keep in mind, the WBS is a hierarchical representation of the project while the Network describes the relationships (dependencies) between the activities, and the order in which they must be completed. However, this does not mean WBS Elements and Activities are independent of one another. In fact, when managing projects, activities are assigned to WBS Elements. Doing so facilitates planning, managing, and closing out projects. Figure 54 shows the assignment of activities to WBS Elements for our wedding example. It is important to note that an activity may only be assigned to a single WBS Element, while a WBS element may have none, one, or many activities assigned to it.

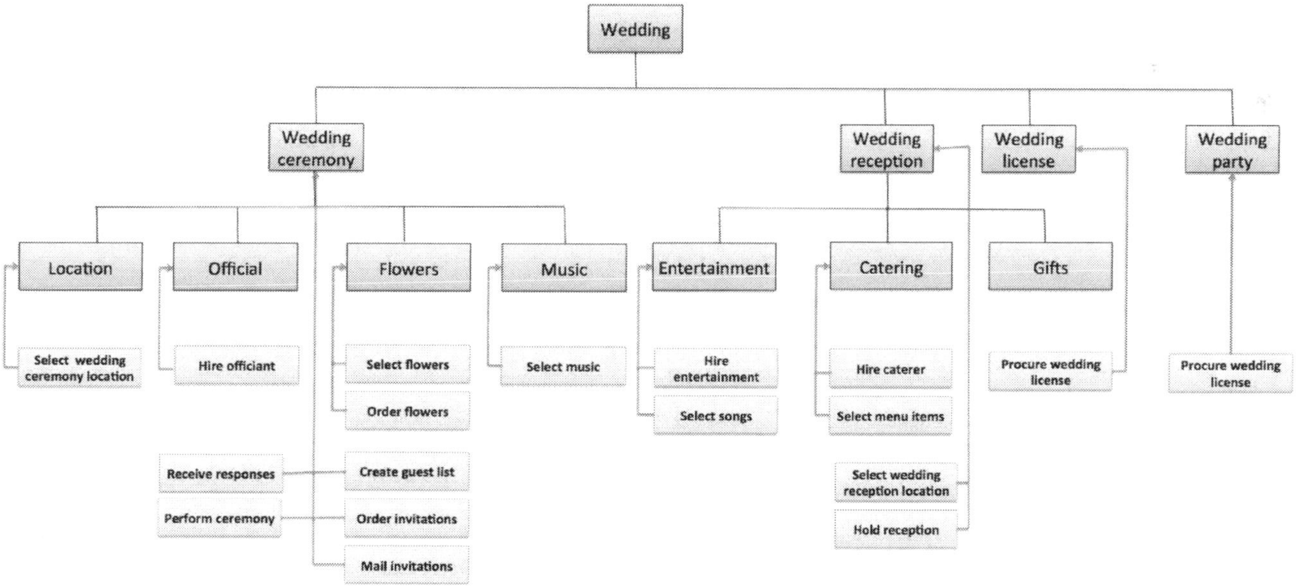

Figure 54: Activities on the activity network connected to WBS elements

Work Breakdown Structures (WBS) Elements and Activities – A More Detailed View

To fully gauge how WBS and Network tools help with project management, we will look at WBS Elements and Activities more closely. SAP provides project teams with some basic functionality surrounding WBS Elements and Activities. Understanding the functionality of each will help make sense of the project as a whole.

To begin, SAP designates one or more *Operative Indicators* for each WBS Element in a project. The *operative indicators* tell project team members whether the WBS Element is used to *plan costs*, *collect costs*, and/or *collect revenue*. Figure 55 shows the list of *Operative Indicators* as well as a symbols we will use to demonstrate how they are associated with each WBS Element.

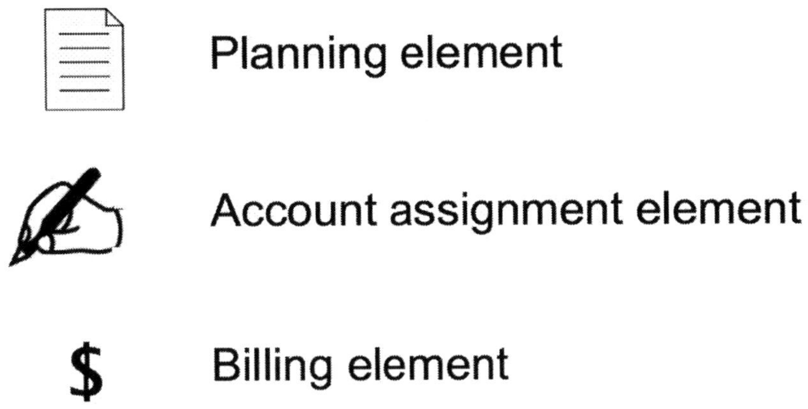

Figure 55: Operative indicators

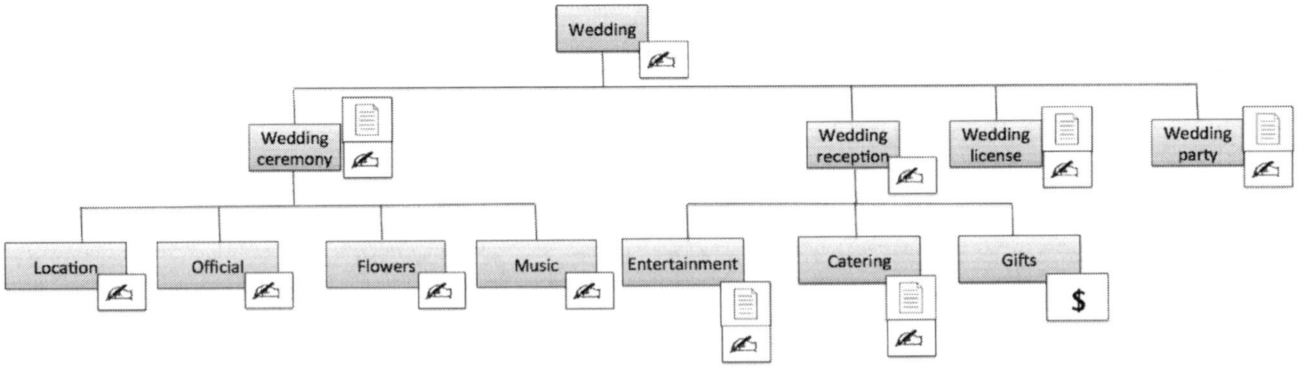

Figure 56: WBS with operative indicators

Figure 56 gives us insight into how SAP can help project team members plan, manage, and close a project. Let us begin with planning. If we look closely at this example, we can see that costs are planned at various WBS levels. What should be obvious to you is that the *Wedding License* and *Wedding Party* WBS Elements are planned at their own levels. However, the *Wedding Ceremony* and *Wedding Reception* WBS Elements are planned at different levels. The *Wedding Ceremony* WBS Element is planned at a high level, meaning costs associated with the Location, Official, Flowers, and Music are not planned individually, but rather collectively at the *Wedding Ceremony* level. On the other hand, the *Wedding Reception* costs are planned on a more detailed level. The costs of Entertainment and Catering are planned individually at that level, not at the *Wedding Reception* level. This exemplifies the flexibility that SAP Project Systems provides for planning projects.

The actual posting of costs to the WBS Elements is represented with the ✍ symbol. Each WBS Element containing that symbol is a cost collector (discussed in CO), meaning costs associated with that WBS Element are posted directly to it. The only Billing Element in our example is *Gifts*, which we can use to record any monetary or other gifts. These two operative indicators are used to help manage projects as they are progressing. Typically, at period-end closing, those costs and revenues that were posted are settled. We will discuss settlement a little later in this chapter.

In addition to Operative Indicators, WBS Elements serve several other functions:

- Dates
- Budgets
- Commitments
- Costs and revenues
- Payment information
- Period end closing

WBS Elements are used to help plan and manage dates in the project. For rough-cut planning, the project leaders may want to enter some basic dates for each WBS Element to provide an overview of when and how long it will take for starting and completing all aspects of each WBS Element. Other dates will also include dates that get scheduled in the project as well as the actual dates recorded for the WBS Elements. We now know that WBS Elements can be used for planning costs, which is generally a method for requesting a budget for the project. As costs are planned at the *Planning Element* levels, these costs can be rolled up to the Project Definition to request a budget. Funds can be made available to WBS Elements according to the budget using *Availability Control* in SAP, which we discuss later in this chapter. While discussing budgeting as one of the functions of WBS Elements, it makes sense to also address the concept of *Commitments* as a function of WBS Elements. We have seen commitments before in the chapter on Management Accounting (CO). Recall that a commitment can occur when we have a planned expense against budgeted funds, usually in the form of a purchase requisition (PR) or purchase order (PO). For a *commitment* to take place, the purchasing document (PR or PO), must include the WBS Element as the account assignment object in the line item. When that happens, the user can see committed costs against assigned budgeted funds for a WBS Element.

While WBS Elements with the *Planning* operative indicator allow for the planning of costs, we know that WBS Elements with the *Account Assignment* indicator are used for posting actual costs. Additionally, WBS Elements with the *Billing* operative indicator are used for posting revenue. Thus the planning and posting of costs, and the posting of revenue are also functions of WBS Elements.

Payment information can also be seen in a WBS Element. From a business perspective, payments are outgoing for costs and incoming for revenue. Any incoming or outgoing payments, planned or posted, can also be managed in the WBS Element.

Finally, project team members will want to periodically evaluate the progress of a project and ensure that all costs and revenues are accurately posted and settled accordingly. These actions are generally performed at period-end closing. *Settlement* is among a number of action items performed at period-end closing.

Similarly to WBS Elements, there are functions associated with *Activities*:

- Internally processed
- Externally processed
- Materials
- Costs
- Milestones
- Period-end closing

Activities can be either *internally* processed or *externally* processed. To help make sense of the difference, we will look at two different activities in our wedding example. We have identified the mailing of invitations as an activity. This is an activity that would be considered internally processed, because we will use internal resources to perform it. Each invitation needs to be addressed, stamped, and placed in the mail to the invitees. Assuming that these steps are not outsourced as a service, members of the wedding party, family, and/or friends will perform these tasks. Their ability to successfully complete these steps depends on their availability to do so. We refer to this availability as *capacity*. Recall from the Manufacturing Execution chapter that work performed internally requires a *work center* and *available capacity*. That same concept applies to internally processed activities. In a business sense, internally processed activities could include production orders, maintenance orders, service orders or even internal orders. These are all typically performed internally by the enterprise.

An *externally processed activity* is procured externally. This generally requires a purchase order for services performed. Using our wedding example, we can identify *catering* as externally processed. We might hire a caterer to perform this activity. In other words, that service is a purchased activity for the project. In the purchase order, it would make sense then to include the *Catering* WBS Element as the account assignment object, so the costs can be posted to it when the services activity is completed.

Materials are another function of activities and can only be planned for activities, not WBS Elements. For example, the physical invitations had to be purchased before they could be mailed to invitees. The invitations would be considered materials used in the project. Those materials are required for the activity *Mail Invitations*. When purchased, the materials are listed in a purchase order, again with an account assignment object. Before they are received for the project, a commitment can be seen for the costs associated with these materials. Once received, the committed costs will become actual costs. Thus, the tracking of costs is also a function of Activities.

The completion of an activity can also be used as a *milestone* for billing in projects. Our wedding example is not a very good representation of this, but if we were to associate billing with our wedding example, the activity, *Mail invitations* could serve as a milestone. Once invitations are placed in the mail, it generally triggers invitees to send gifts to the wedding couple. Although the gifts may or may not arrive until the wedding reception, the mailing of the invitations can be identified as a milestone from which revenue will soon be posted.

Finally, as with WBS Elements, project team members will want to periodically evaluate the progress of a project from an activity viewpoint. All costs need to be accounted for and settled. Again, these actions are generally performed at period-end closing.

Phases of a Project

Now that we have a pretty good understanding of WBS Elements and Activities, we can once again look into the various phases associated with a project. Projects can differ, but generally speaking, the different phases for each project are relatively unchanged and can be seen in Figure 57.

Let us apply Figure 57 to what we know about WBS and Activities. Using the wedding example, the *Concept phase* occurs when the wedding couple begins discussing the wedding. That phase is represented in Figure 58.

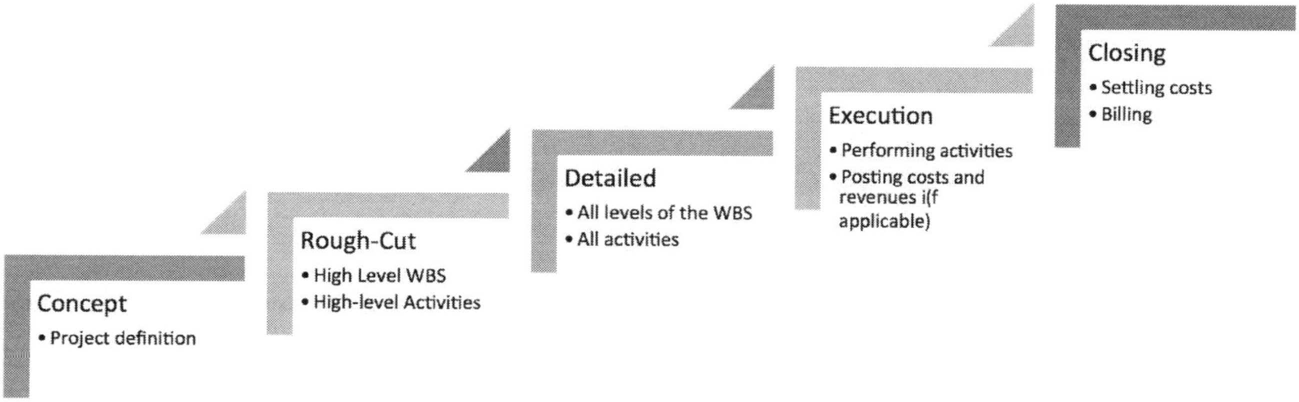

Figure 57: Phases in projects

The concept phase can be used to initiate the planning of the project at a very high level. No detail at all is included. The Project Definition is clearly identified and then a basic idea of other things to be considered is also included. The project then moves to the *Rough-Cut* phase. Here, WBS Elements are added to the Project Definition and are organized in a hierarchy as Figure 59 shows.

Wedding
- Wedding Ceremony?
- Wedding Reception?
- Wedding License?
- Who will be in the Wedding Party?

Figure 58: Concept phase of the wedding project

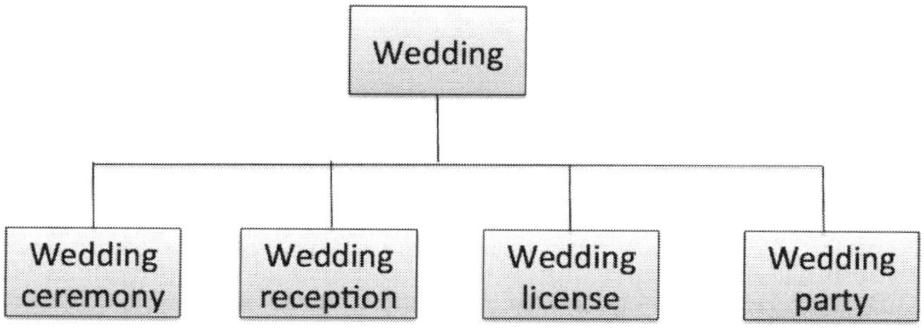

Figure 59: Rough-cut phase of the wedding project

Notice the absence of activities in the rough-cut phase of our example. As a matter of fact, the project is still shown at a high level, with no detail included. In our example, we haven't included activities. It is possible to include activities during the rough-cut phase. However, any activities included here would also be at a high level, with no detail.

It is at the next phase of the project where all of the Activities and WBS Elements are included. This is the *Detail* phase shown in Figure 60.

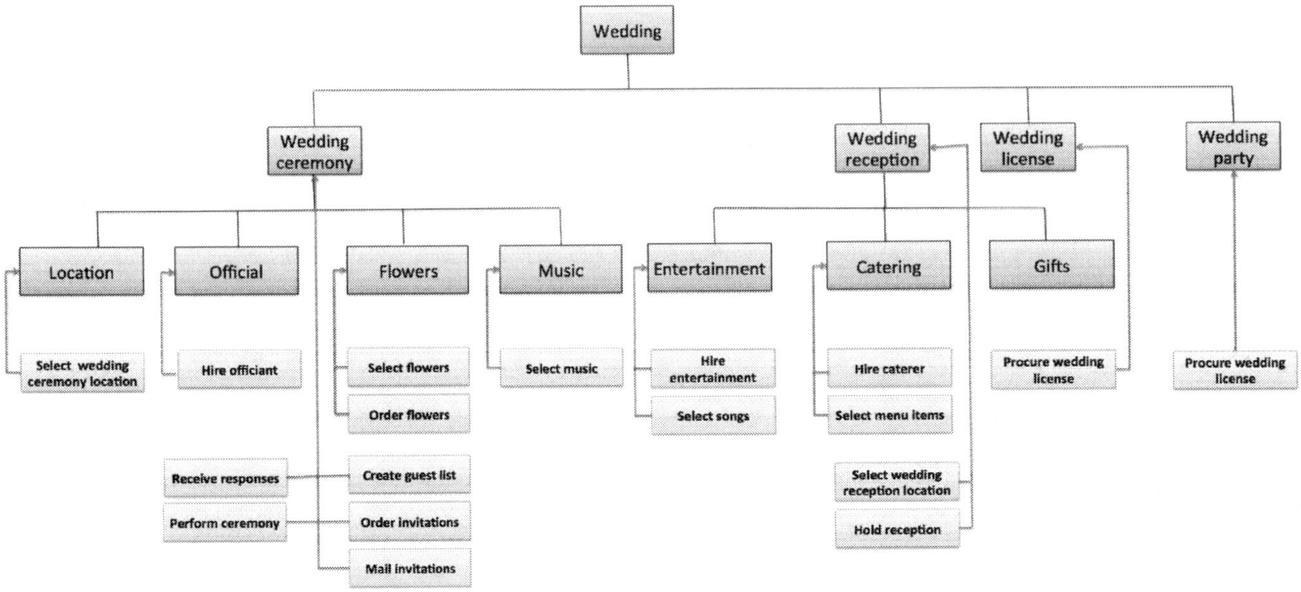

Figure 60: Detail phase of the wedding project

The discussion about the WBS Elements and Activities helps put the project phases into perspective. Though we discussed them to a small degree earlier in this chapter, only now can we start piecing all of this together. The remaining phases in the project are the *Execution* and *Closing* phases. Figure 61 shows the functions of both WBS elements and Activities, and includes those functions which support the execution and closing phases of a project.

Figure 61: WBS elements and Activities support the *Execution* and *Closing* phases of a project

SAP Tools in Project Systems

SAP provides project team members with an assortment of tools to work with projects. There are many similarities between them, which allow users to work with the tools with which they are most familiar and comfortable. One of the primary objectives of this text is to provide you with business context to increase your knowledge and to facilitate your learning of the SAP TERP10 materials. However, it is necessary at times to deviate somewhat and provide you with more in-depth insight into SAP. This is one of those times.

There are two primary tools that SAP provides for working with projects. They are the *Project Builder* and the *Project Planning Board*. Both provide users with the capability of achieving the same results. Users can create, save, release, and edit projects using either or both of these tools. For simplicity, we will focus on the similarities and differences between these two tools. Figure 62 demonstrates these.

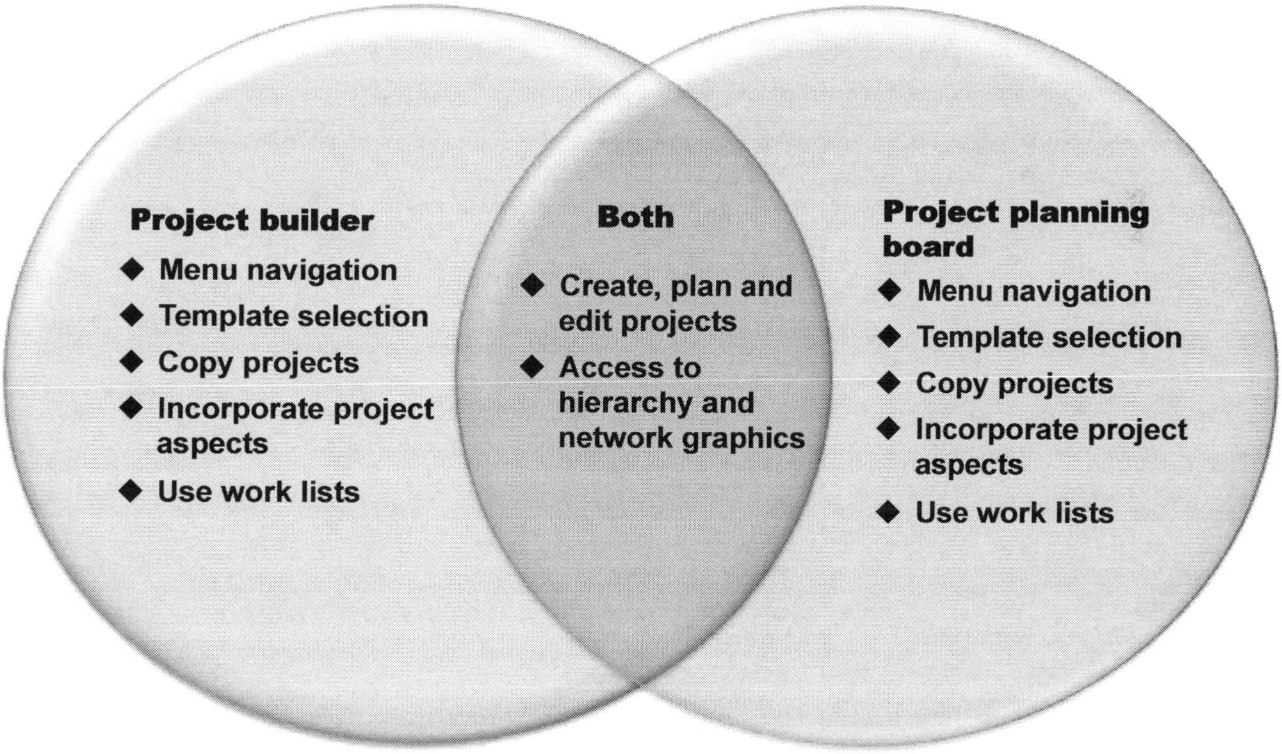

Figure 62: Features of Project Builder and Project Planning Board

As you can see, the major differences between the Project Builder and the Project Planning Board are mostly navigational. Having both of these tools available allows users to work comfortably in an environment they are used to. The Project Builder offers a menu tree navigational feature and also takes advantage of the use of project templates. A user can call up a template of a project, or portion of a project and create a new project by copying it. In addition to this, users can also call up a worklist of recently accessed projects to simplify navigation. The Project Planning Board offers a more graphical experience for the user. The key interface is an interactive Gantt chart where users can call up and work with both WBS Elements and Activities. The Project Planning Board also offers users access to graphical overviews of materials, capacities, and cost/revenue information in the project.

While there are differences between these two tools, there are several similarities. Regardless of the tool employed, the user has the capability to manage similar aspects of the project. Both tools allow the user to create a project complete with a WBS and Network of Activities. As we have seen with WBS, dates are an important function. In the Project Builder, the user can plan and post actual dates in fields located in each WBS Element screen. The Project Planning Board allows users to use mouse functionality, like right-clicking on a WBS Element to plan dates and post actual dates. If the project includes a network, both tools also offer the ability to carry out scheduling functions which will automatically plan dates on activities and WBS Elements. Finally, the Project Builder and the Project Planning Board have links to viewing and working with the project using additional graphical tools. Users can view the WBS in a Hierarchy Graphic, and the Activities in a Network Graphic. The user can also edit both WBS Elements and Activities from these two additional views.

Cost Planning and Budgets in Project Systems

Perhaps one of the most important aspects of projects is the planning of costs. There are a number of different methods for planning costs, but we will focus on just a few of them. To assist us in understanding cost planning, let us again refer to our wedding example. Recall that not all of the WBS Elements received the Planning operative indicator. Only those WBS Elements with the Planning Operative indicator will be used for planning of costs. Let us again take a look at the operative indicators shown in Figure 63.

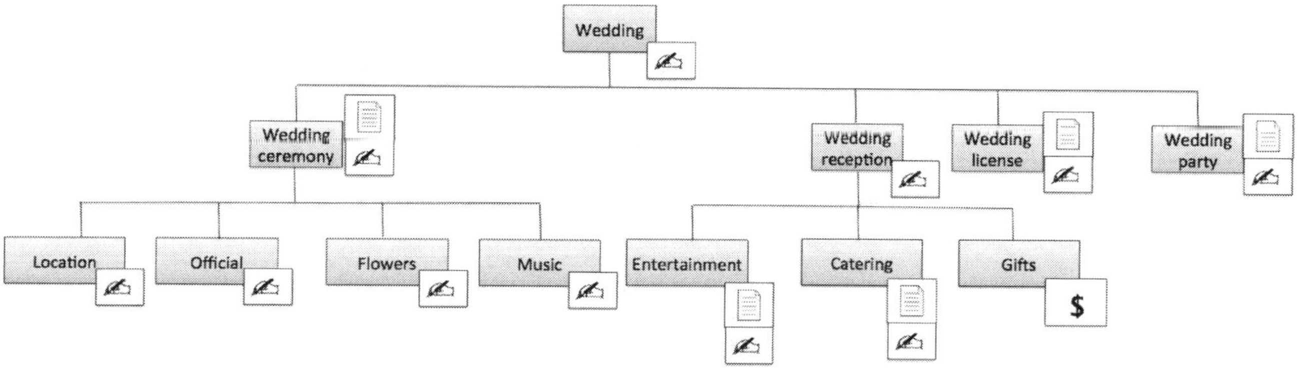

Figure 63: Wedding project WBS with Operative Indicators

As noted earlier, the costs associated with the *Wedding Ceremony* WBS Element are planned at its own level. While costs associated with the *Wedding Reception* WBS Element are planned at the WBS level beneath it. Let us first consider the planning of costs for *Wedding Reception*. Since these costs are planned at the lower-level WBS Elements, we need to take those into consideration. We would then have to plan costs for *Entertainment* and *Catering* individually. To plan these costs, we could use the activities associated with each of them as shown in Figure 64.

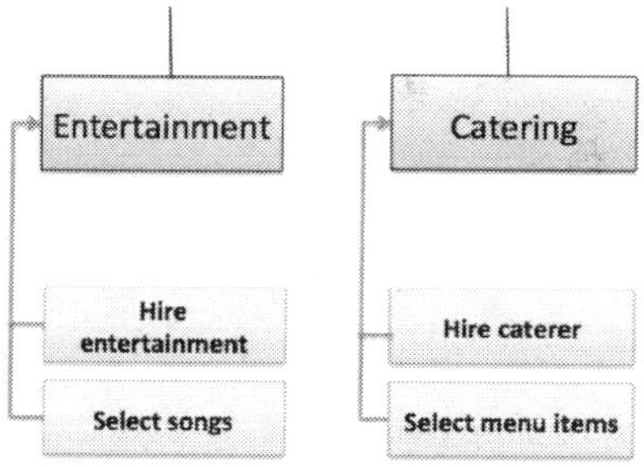

Figure 64: WBS elements and activities help in cost planning

Since there are costs associated with the activities assigned to these WBS Elements, one could plan the costs on these activities and use those costs to plan the cost at the WBS level. While planning these costs for the wedding, suppose a band provided a cost quotation to the wedding couple. Should the wedding couple decide to hire that band, they could plan the costs for this externally processed activity of hiring entertainment, which is then used to plan the cost at its respective WBS Element *Entertainment*. Likewise, as we discussed earlier, the hiring of a caterer is also an externally processed activity. Similarly, costs for catering could be planned in the external activity, and those costs used to plan the costs at the *Catering* WBS

Element. Once we have the planned costs for these two WBS Elements, they can be used to determine the planned costs for *Wedding Reception*.

In the case of the *Wedding Ceremony* WBS Element, those planned costs are not derived from lower-level WBS Elements or Activities. The planning of these costs will have to be done differently. One potential method for planning these costs is something called, *Overall Planning*. In this case, the wedding couple could simply research and get some insight into what a wedding ceremony normally costs and use that overall value as the planned cost for the *Wedding Ceremony* WBS Element.

There is not a single method that can be labeled as being the best. Which method is best is the method that is most appropriate for the situation. Cost planning is not only one of the most important aspects of working with projects; it can also be one of the most challenging. SAP offers an alternative tool called *SAP Easy Cost Planning*. *SAP Easy Cost Planning* offers the use of planning templates and simple data entry fields to help with complex cost calculations.

One of the reasons cost planning is so important is because it provides the basis for budget requests. To see how this works, consider our wedding example again. Looking at Figure 65, we can see that costs are planned for WBS Elements labeled with the Planning operative indicator. Those planned costs can then be rolled up to higher WBS Elements, and ultimately to the Project Definition (upward arrows). This method forms the basis of the budget request. Once a budget request is made, an approved budget is created and released top-down in the WBS.

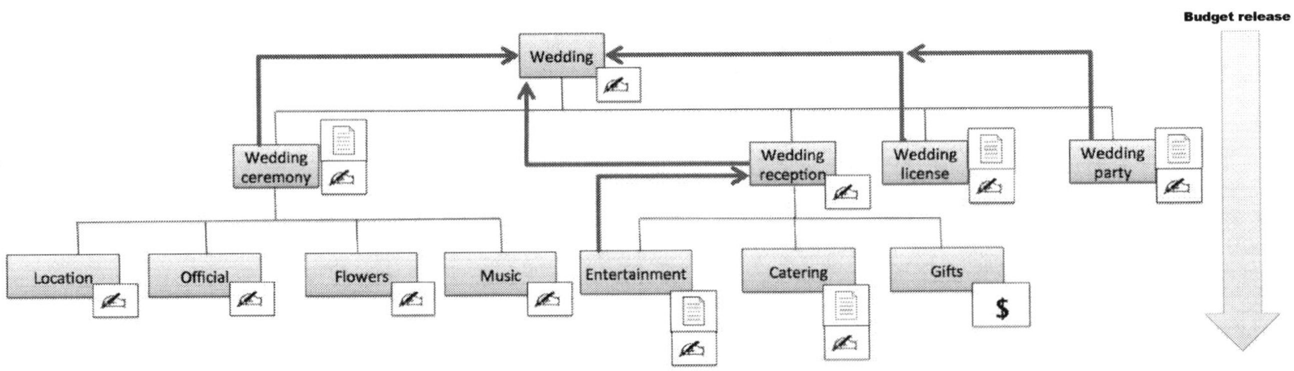

Figure 65: SAP cost planning, budgeting and budget release

In SAP, the budget release is managed with *Availability Control. Availability Control* provides flexibility in managing the project budget. *Availability Control* manages changes to the budget which may include changes in budgeted values as well as reallocation of budgeted funds. It also offers flexibility regarding how much and when to release budgeted funds. Funds can be released and allocated to all levels of the WBS at one time or the budget can be released in increments at different WBS levels.

Project team members will also want to have visibility into the budgeted funds, planned costs, actual costs, and committed costs for WBS Elements. SAP provides two options to help manage this visibility. Users can take advantage of *Passive Availability Control* or *Active Availability Control. Passive Availability Control* gives project team members the capability of running cost and budget reports on WBS Elements. From these reports, the user can see budgeted funds, planned costs, actual costs, and committed costs. In doing so, the project team members can manage their costs against the budgeted funds and see where they are at risk of exceeding the budget. There are times when project team members may want the system to generate a warning message when planned, actual, or committed costs are close to exceeding the budgeted funds for a WBS Element. For such cases, SAP also offers *Active Availability Control.*

Posting Actual Costs and Dates in Project Systems

After having spent significant time discussing the planning and budgeting of projects, we now move on to the execution phase. While we spend time on this phase, you should be reminded of the functions of WBS Elements and Activities, as well as their relationship to one another.

Remember that actual dates, costs, and payments are posted to WBS Elements. Functions of Activities include the association with materials, actual costs, and milestones for billing. Let us take a look at one of the activities and WBS Elements in our wedding example (Figure 66).

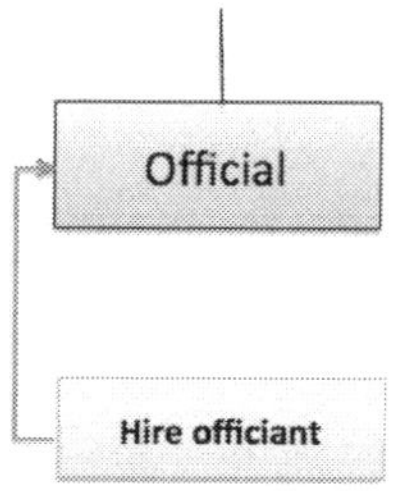

Figure 66: Activity we will consider for discussing the *Execution* phase for externally procured activity

We can identify the activity, *Hire an Officiant* as an externally processed activity. This means, it will require the use of the purchase process for consumption in MM Procurement which we discussed in an earlier chapter. If we were using SAP to procure the services of an officiant, we would create a purchase order and include the WBS Element, *Official* as the account assignment object. We can use that WBS Element as an account assignment object because in our example, we gave it the operative indicator, *Account Assignment*, which means it is used to collect costs. When the purchase process is completed, dates associated with the purchase as well as actual costs are collected in the WBS Element, *Official*.

Now let us look at another example, except this time we will demonstrate how this works with an internally processed activity. Since we are familiar with the activity, *Mail invitations*, let us use that example (Figure 67).

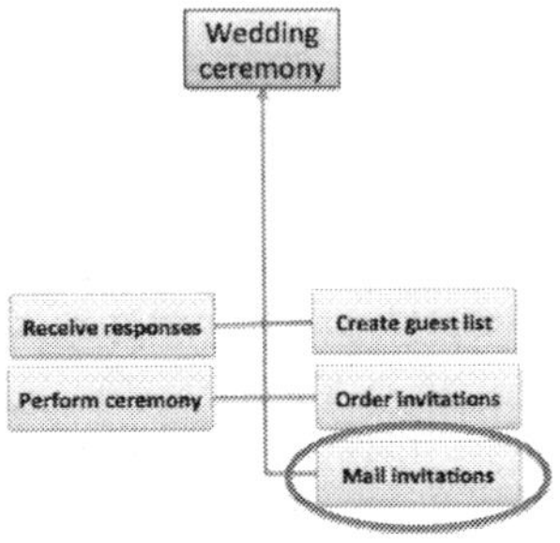

Figure 67: Activity we will consider for discussing the *Execution* phase for internally processed activity

Again, we will look at this example from the perspective of using SAP. In this example, we have a lot of things to consider. First off, we need to create an order in SAP for this activity so that it can be managed as an internally processed activity. A viable option is to create an internal order. (We discussed internal orders in the Order-related Cost Object Controlling section of the Management Accounting chapter. Now might be a good time to review that if you need to.)

By doing this, the internal order manages the activity. The second need is to acquire the materials for this activity (Internal Order). In order to perform this activity, let us assume that we need invitations and stamps. A purchase order would need to be created and we would include the Internal Order as the account assignment object. Again, we are leveraging the use of the purchase process for consumption in MM Procurement. (Interestingly, you are now seeing a lot of integration across many things we have already learned.)

When the purchased materials are received, we must ensure that the internal order has been released, so that costs can be posted directly to the activity (internal order). This again reinforces that materials are only associated with activities in a project, not WBS Elements. Now that the materials are available for the activity (internal order), the wedding couple, friends, family, etc., can begin mailing the invitations. As we discussed earlier, in SAP the people performing this work would be considered work centers and they would need available capacity to start this work. Thus, the activity (internal order) will get scheduled when the workers are available. (Recall from our discussion of Order-related Cost Object Controlling, that scheduling occurs when the order is created.) Once work is completed, the workers will *confirm* that the activity has been done. At this step, any labor-related costs can be posted to the internal order. Using our wedding example, let us assume that the wedding couple offered gifts as compensation for assisting with the mailing of invitations. Such compensation would be considered a cost of this activity.

At this stage for the internally processed activity, notice that the actual costs have only been posted to the Activity and not the WBS Element, again reinforcing what we already know. That is, functions of Activities include materials and actual costs. That may lead you to ask, when and how does the cost of the Activity, *Mail invitations* get posted to the WBS Element *Wedding Ceremony*? That is a very good and insightful question, and the answer to that is: At period-end closing when we perform settlement. That is the next topic of discussion.

Settlement in Project Systems

At period-end closing, project team leaders will want to evaluate the progress of the project, but equally important, they will want to properly allocate costs and revenues. The further allocation of costs and revenues is referred to as *settlement*. *Settlement* is not foreign to us as we have discussed it in earlier chapters, notably during the discussion on *Order-Related Cost Object Controlling*. *Settlement* occurs using a *Settlement Rule*. A *Settlement Rule* defines who the receiver(s) will be for the allocation of costs or revenues. SAP offers two options for settlement in Project Systems. One of these options is *Direct Settlement*. During *Direct Settlement*, the sending cost object (WBS Element or Activity) will settle directly to one or more receivers as defined in the *Settlement Rule*. To demonstrate how this works we will again refer to our wedding example. Suppose the bride-to-be's family has agreed to pay for the entire wedding. In SAP we would create a cost center for the family.

At the end of the period (typically at month end), all costs will be settled to that family (Settlement Rule). Using the examples from the previous section, the WBS Element, *Official* and the activity, *Mail invitations* would settle their costs directly to the family cost center. This form of Direct Settlement can be seen in Figure 68.

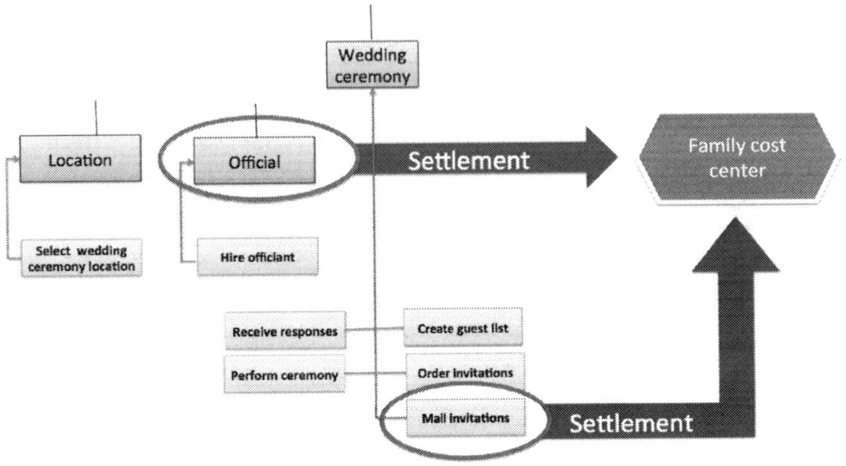

Figure 68: Direct Settlement

The second option for settlement is called *Multi-level Settlement*. In Multi-level Settlement, the Activities are settled upwards in the project to their respective WBS Elements, and WBS Elements are settled upwards in the project to the next level WBS Element. This continues until all costs are eventually settled to the Project Definition. The Project Definition then settles to a predefined settlement receiver according the Settlement Rule. Using the same example as above we will perform settlement again, only this time we will demonstrate Multi-level Settlement.

Once again, assume the bride-to-be's family has agreed to pay for the entire wedding, except this time we are not going to settle WBS Elements and Activities directly to the *Family* cost center. This time we will use *Multi-level Settlement* and settle the costs of the Internal Activity, *Mail invitations* to its respective WBS Element, *Wedding Reception*. We will also settle the *Official* WBS Element up to the *Wedding Ceremony* WBS Element since that is the WBS Element at the next level. Since *Wedding Ceremony* is assigned to the Project Definition *Wedding*, it must then be settled there as seen in Figure 69.

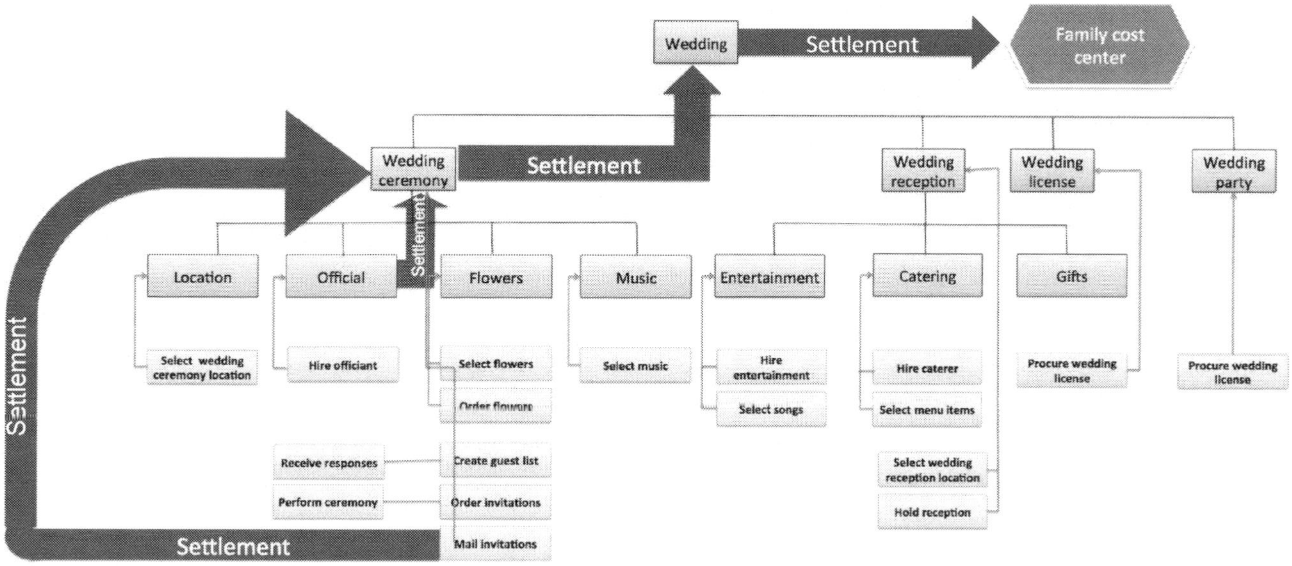

Figure 69: Multi-level Settlement

Summary of Project Systems

By now you should have noticed that SAP Project Systems involves a great deal of integration across various SAP modules. Keep in mind that this chapter – like the unit on Project Systems in the TERP10 certification course – is not designed to teach one how to manage a project. Its intent is simply to provide you with information on the tools available to project managers and project team members.

Chapter-end questions

You can find suggested answers to these questions starting on page 275

To answer questions marked with ★, you will need to have read the official SAP TERP10 course material.

1. Which of the following represent the organizational levels specific to project management? (one)

   A Company code
   B Plant
   C Storage location
   D Project management in SAP has no organizational levels to itself

2. Define the characteristics of projects.

3. Figure 70 represents which of the following? (one)

   A Project builder
   B Project planning board
   C Work breakdown structure
   D Network

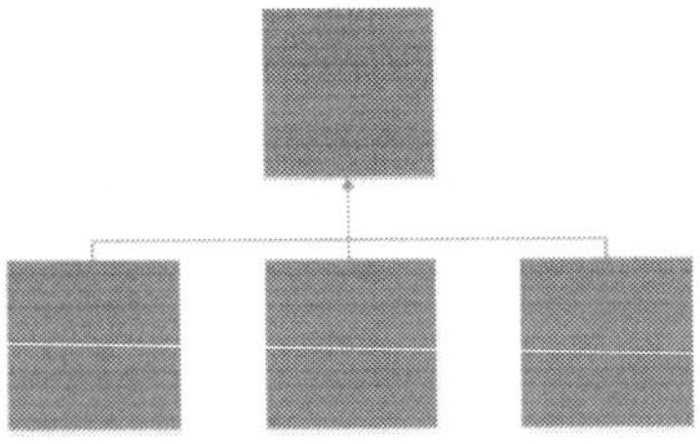

Figure 70: Figure for question

4. Figure 71 represents which of the following? (one)

   A Project builder
   B Project planning board
   C Work breakdown structure
   D Network

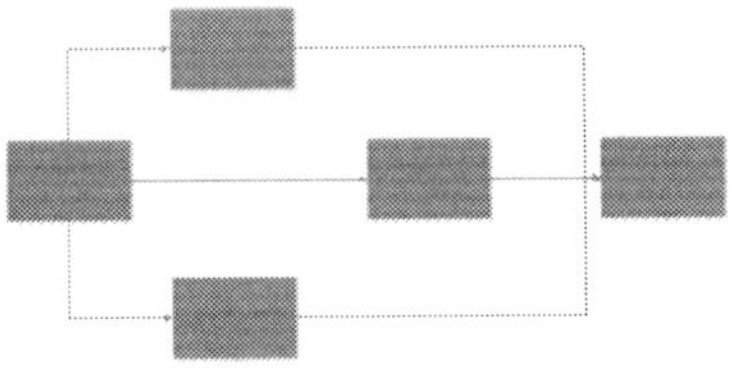

Figure 71: Figure for question

5. Define a Work Breakdown Structure.

6. Define Activities.

7. Define Networks.

8. Describe the relationship between WBS Elements and Activities.

9. List the operative indicators for WBS Elements.

10. A WBS element that has the operative indicator, "Planning Element", is an element for which ________________. (one)

    A costs are planned
    B materials are planned
    C MRP will create planned orders
    D a G/L account is assigned

11. A WBS element that has the operative indicator "Account Assignment", is an element for which ________________. (one)

    A costs are planned
    B costs are posted
    C revenues are posted
    D a G/L account is assigned

12. A WBS element that has the operative indicator, "Billing Element", is an element for which ________________. (one)

    A costs are planned

B costs are posted
C revenues are posted
D a G/L account is assigned

13. List the functions of WBS Elements.
14. List the functions of Activities.
15. List the five phases of a project.
16. Describe the concept phase of a project.
17. Describe the rough-cut phase of a project.
18. Describe the detailed phase of a project.
19. Describe the execution phase of a project.
20. Describe the closing phase of a project.
21. Which of the following are functions of the Project Builder? (three)

    A Menu navigation
    B Create projects
    C Edit projects
    D Gantt chart navigation

22. Which of the following are functions of the Project Planning Board? (three)

    A Menu navigation
    B Create projects
    C Edit projects
    D Gantt chart navigation

23. Which of the following are additional graphical tools that are available in SAP Project Systems? (two)

    A Activity graphic
    B Network graphic
    C WBS graphic
    D Hierarchy graphic

24. The Hierarchy graphic can be accessed from both the Project Builder and Project Planning Board (T/F)
25. Which of the following are graphical overviews available in the Project Planning Board? (three)

A Activity overview
B Capacity overview
C Material overview
D Cost overview

26. In order to plan costs on a WBS Element, that WBS Element must be assigned the Account Assignment operative indicator. (T/F)

27. For planning costs for WBS Elements with one or more activities, costs can be planned at the activity level and rolled up to the WBS Element level. (T/F)

28. List two different methods for planning costs on projects in SAP.

29. Cost planning in projects is important because it provides the basis for _______________? (one)

   A the budget request
   B the budget release
   C Easy Cost Planning
   D settlement

30. Which of the following controls how the budget on a project is released? (one)

   A Budget balance
   B Availability control
   C Activity control
   D Easy Cost Planning

31. List two different versions of Availability Control for projects in SAP.

32. Describe the difference between Active Availability Control and Passive Availability Control.

33. Explain how costs are posted to the project using the MM Procurement process.

34. Explain how costs are posted to the project using activities.

35. Which of the following are settlement options in projects? (two)

   A Single-level settlement

B Multi-level settlement

C Direct settlement

D Indirect settlement

36. Explain the difference between direct settlement and multi-level settlement.

Answers to review questions

This section contains answers to all the review questions in the book.

Big Picture: Inline review questions

Review 1: Look around you and select an object. Make up a BOM for it.

Answer: Obviously, since you could have picked any object whatsoever, we do not provide *the answer* You should have identified an object and listed the components that might have been assembled to make the object.

Review 2: If TRUS has to make 50 tables and already has 100 legs, 12 tops, 60 liters of primer and 80 liters of paint in inventory, how much of each material would it need to buy or *procure*?

Answer: Not considering the materials already in stock, to make 50 tables TRUS would need 200 legs, 50 tops, 100 liters of primer and 100 liters of paint. Subtracting what is already in stock we get: 100 legs, 38 tops, 40 liters of primer and 20 liters of paint.

Review 3: Refer to tables 2 and 3. If we have to make 10 pieces of material A and have no stock of materials B, C, D and E, how much of each of these materials would we need to *procure*?

Answer: From Table 2 we can see that making 10 units of A requires 30 units of B and 10 units of C. However, B itself has a BOM. Referring to Table 3 we see that to make 30 units of B we will need 60 units of D and 150 units of E. Putting all this together, to make 10 units of A, we will need 10 units of C, 60 units of D and 150 units of E.

Review 4: Answer the following:

1. What information does a BOM contain?

   Answer: The BOM for a material A tells us what other materials and how much of each we need in order to make one unit of A.
2. What information does a routing contain?

   Answer: The steps or operations needed to make a material. The routing also shows the work center where each operation needs to be performed and the time required to perform each operation.
3. What is purchasing lead time? **Answer:** The time between the placement of the purchase order and the receipt of goods.
4. What is lot size? **Answer:** A number such that the material to which the lot size applies can only be purchased in multiples of that number. For example, if a material has a purchasing lot size of 50, then the organization can only order multiples of 50 units of that material.
5. How many different lot sizes have been mentioned in this document? What are they?

   Answer: Four lot sizes have been mentioned – one for each of the raw materials.
6. What is the name of the document that indicates to a vendor what materials and in what quantities we want to buy them?

   Answer: Purchase Order
7. Where is information about a particular material stored?

   Answer: Material Master Record
8. What is the name given to the entity that keeps information about all materials?

   Answer: Material Master

9. What contains information about a particular vendor?

   Answer: Vendor Master Record

10. Which term names the entity that stores information about all vendors?

    Answer: Vendor Master

11. To store information about the vendors mentioned in Table 5, how many vendor master records would we need? Explain.

    Answer: Two. One for each vendor.

12. To store information about the materials mentioned in Table 1 as well as information about a TRUS table itself, how many material master records would we need? Explain.

    Answer: Five. Four for the raw materials (legs, top, primer and paint) and one for the finished good (the table).

13. What *type* of material is a TRUS table?

    Answer: Finished good

14. What *type* of material is paint in the context of TRUS?

    Answer: Raw material

15. List the different types of materials discussed in this chapter.

    Answer: Raw Materials, Finished Goods and Trading goods.

16. What is a Trading Good?

    Answer: A material that the company just buys and resells without further processing.

Review 5: Answer the following:

1. How many tables are to be made on March 31?

   Answer: 140

2. How many legs are needed?

   Answer: 140*4 = 560

3. How many tops are needed? **Answer:** 140

4. How many liters of primer are needed?

   Answer: 140 tables * two liters per table = 280 liters

5. How many liters of paint are needed?

   Answer: 140 tables * 2 liters per table = 280 liters of paint.

6. At the latest, when should the purchase order for legs go out?

   Answer: Legs have a lead time of 1 month. So the order has to go out on or before the last day of Feb.

7. How many legs should they order?

   Answer: Legs have a lead time of 1 month. So the order has to go out on or before the last day of Feb.

8. At the latest when should the purchase order for tops go out?

   Answer: Tops have a lead time of 2 months and so the order should go out latest by Jan 31.

9. How many tops should they order?

   Answer: They need 140 tops. The lot size is 25 and so they should order 150.

10. At the latest when should the purchase order for primer go out?

    Answer: Primer has a lead time of 2 weeks and so the order should go out by March 15.

11. How many liters of primer should we order?

    Answer: They need 280 liters and the lot size is 100 liters. So they should order 300.

12. At the latest when should the purchase order for paint go out?

    Answer: Paint has a lead time of three weeks and so they should send the order out by March 7

Review 6: Answer the following. Try to give concrete examples wherever possible:

1. What is BOM explosion?

   Answer: Given a material, say X, with its BOM, BOM explosion is the process of computing the raw materials and the quantities needed to make a certain quantity of X.

   For example if we have to make 50 cars, what materials and in what quantities would be needed? We will need 200 tires, 50 steering wheels, 50 accelerator pedals, 50 brake pedals, and so on.

2. What is MRP? Don't just expand the acronym. Instead give a concrete example of your own.

Answer: Given a plan to sell certain quantities of materials (say finished goods), MRP is the process of determining how much of each of the many materials are needed at what times and also adjusting this to reflect what the company already has on hand and the shipments it expects to receive for Purchase Orders already placed.

3. In the TRUS case, what information should be considered when determining when a purchase order should be sent out?

   Answer: The purchasing lead time as well as the date on which the material is needed.

4. What information determines the quantity of an item to be ordered?

   Answer: BOM explosion to determine the quantity needed for making the items, quantity already on hand and the lot size.

5. In the TRUS case, all materials needed to produce a table are purchased from outside and therefore MRP only has to produce purchase documents. Suppose some of the parts to assemble a final table are themselves assembled in our own factory using raw materials procured from outside, what other considerations enter the MRP process?

   Answer: In this case MRP will also have to account for the time needed to produce these intermediate products.

Review 7: Explain in your own words the terms *Configuration* and *Customization*.

Answer: In the context of computer packages, *Configuration* occurs when organizations use the features provided by a product to select the specific options that they need. For example, what fields should appear on a particular screen.

Customization occurs when an organization *adds new programming language code* to change how a product works.

Review 8: Find two reasons why *Customization* might require more time and resources than *Configuration*.

Answer: Customization requires time and resources for determining the functionality needed and for the whole process of specifying, coding and implementing the new functionality. Developing new functionality through programing requires many people and takes up a lot of time. In addition, there is the risk of the new code not working correctly under new versions of the product.

Configuration does not require any new software development and the process of determining the necessary functionality is a lot less complex.

Financial Accounting: In-Chapter questions

Review 1: For each of the following items, indicate whether it is an Asset, Liability, Owners' Equity or none of those:

1. New shares worth $450,000 that the company issued.

   Answer: Owners' Equity

2. Shares worth $100,000 that this company purchases in other companies as a way of investing some of its earnings.

   Answer: Asset

3. $26,500 that the company is yet to pay its suppliers for goods already supplied.

   Answer: Liability

4. The value of goods supplied in the above item (lying in inventory and not yet used).

   Answer: Liability

5. Money in a checking account maintained by the company

   Answer: Asset

6. Money that the company has paid as salary to its employees in the current month.

   Answer: None of these

7. Value of a power generation plant that the company maintains to supply power to one of its factories.

   Answer: Asset

8. Bank loans amounting to a total of $700,000 that the company has taken out to finance its business operations.

   Answer: Liability

Review 2: Explain, in your own words, the logic behind the accounting equation.

Answer: It represents the common sense point that any asset that a company has ought to have been acquired only through money obtained from one of the following: liabilities (loans, accounts payable, etc.,), owners' equity (shares and retained earnings).

Review 3: Draw up a balance sheet from the following information about John, a kid who operates a lemonade stand:

- John borrowed $15 from his parents and put $7 from his profits back into his business
- John has equipment (glass jugs, drinking glasses, mixing spoons, etc.,) worth $10.
- John has borrowed 10 lemons from mom and will pay them back after the next weekend. These lemons cost $5.
- John has stocks of sugar worth $5
- Some of John's friends bought lemonade worth a total of $7 during the past weekend and have promised to pay him back soon.
- John has $5 in his cash box.

Answer:

- **Assets: $27**
  1. Equipment worth $10
  2. Sugar stocks worth $5
  3. $7 that friends owe
  4. $5 cash
- **Liabilities: $20**
  1. $15 borrowed from mother
  2. $5 of borrowed lemons
- **Owners' equity: $7**
  1. $7 of profits invested back into business

Review 4: For each of the following business transactions, explain whether the total of assets (and therefore liabilities and owners' equity) will have a different value at the end of the transaction than it had at the beginning. If there will be a change, explain which components on the two sides of the accounting equation change. If the total does not change, explain whether there will be any redistribution among the components within a particular side of the equation. We have given two examples:

1. **Example:** Company uses cash to buy raw materials worth $500.

   Answer: No change to total assets. Redistribution occurs only within the assets side. Cash decreases by $500 and inventory increases (the company now has additional raw material worth $500).

2. **Example:** Company takes out a new long term loan for $100,000

   Answer: Total assets increase because the company now has $100,000 more in cash (on the left hand side of the equation). To compensate, there is now also an additional long-term liability (the new bank loan that the company now has to pay back) of $100,000 on the right hand side. The two balancing entries therefore ensure that the accounting equation balances.

3. The company receives raw material worth $50,000 and has been invoiced by the vendor in full. The company has not yet paid for this purchase.

   Answer: Since the company now has an additional $50,000 worth of raw material, assets have increased by $50,000. The company owes the supplier $50,000 and hence its accounts payable – a liability – has increased by $50,000.

4. The company uses $200,000 of its cash to buy back (repurchase) some of its own stock.

   Answer: Assets decreased by $200,000 because the company now has that much less cash. Owners' Equity decreased by $200,000 because the value of outstanding shares with shareholders went down as well.

5. The company pays back $100,000 of its outstanding loan.

   Answer: Cash decreased by $100,000. At the same time, loans – a liability – also decreased.

6. The company pays $50,000 to the vendor mentioned above.

   Answer: Cash decreased by $50,000. Accounts payable – a liability – also decreased on $50,000.

7. The company places a new purchase order with a vendor to supply goods worth $35,000

   Answer: No formal financial impact. Impact only starts when the company receives the good ordered as that will change the value of material stock.

8. The company sells some of its land for $1,000,000

   Answer: Value of land – an asset – decreases by $1,000,000. Cash – also an asset – increases by $1,000,000. Thus this transaction only impacts the assets side of the balance sheet.

Review 5: For each account mentioned in the Chart of Accounts in Table 9, identify the category to which it belongs (asset, liability, etc). Do you see any pattern?

Answer:

- 1000, 1100 and 1200 are all assets.
- 2000 and 2100 are liabilities
- 3000 and 3200 are owners' equity
- 4000 and 4100 are revenue accounts
- 5000, 5200, 5300 and 5400 are all expense accounts

Pattern is obvious – all accounts of the same type have the same first digit.

Review 7: What is the relationship between the Chart of Accounts and the General Ledger?

Answer: The Chart of Accounts specifies the various accounts that a company wants to use and assigns a number to each. It represents the structure that a company uses or wants to use for its financial accounting. We could say that it represents the design of a company's accounting structure.

Specifically, the Chart of Accounts does not have any details of actual transactions. The General ledger on the other hand represents the actual accounts and holds the various transactions posted to each account. The general ledger (GL) is based on a Chart of Accounts. All the accounts with their account numbers specified in the Chart of Accounts exist in the G/L and we can see the various postings as well in the G/L.

Carrying the design analogy further, the G/L represents a product based on the design that a Chart of Account represents.

Review 8: If two different company codes use the same Chart of Accounts for their General Ledger, does this mean that they will always have identical transactions posted for each account? Explain.

Answer: No. The Chart of Accounts is just the structure. Each company will post its transactions to its own general ledger. For example, suppose the account number for the expense Account rents in the shared Chart of accounts is 5400. Each company posts rent expenses to this account number **in its own general ledger**. Obviously therefore the actual transaction amounts posted will differ for the two companies.

Review 9: What is impact on profits if a company charges less depreciation than it should?

Answer: If we look at the computation of profits in the income statement, we see that various costs as well as depreciation are subtracted from the sales revenues to arrive at the profit. If a company charges a lower depreciation than it should, then it will clearly end up with higher profits.

Financial Accounting: Chapter-end questions

1. What are reconciliation accounts?

   Answer: Accounts that accumulate the postings made in subledger accounts. Example: Accounts Receivable account at the Balance Sheet level. This account accumulates all the postings made to individual customer accounts.

2. What level is the G/L managed at?

   Answer: Company code

3. What is the organization level corresponding to a legal entity in SAP?

   Answer: Company code

4. Which is the smallest SAP entity that supports a full set of books?

   Answer: Company code

5. Which organization element supports the creation of Balance Sheet and income statements that cut across company codes?

   Answer: Business area or Segment

6. Which organization element is concerned with tracking of profits within a component of a company code?

   Answer: Profit center

7. Which organization element is concerned with tracking the performance of external market segments?

   Answer: Operating concern

8. How many company codes can be in a client?

   Answer: Many

9. How many company codes can a business area be associated with?

   Answer: Many

10. How many business areas can a company code be associated with?

    Answer: Many

11. Where does controlling area fit into the organizational elements of SAP?

    Answer: It exists within the *Client* and has one or more *Company Codes* assigned to it.

12. How many company codes can be allocated to a controlling area?

    Answer: Many

13. What restriction applies to a company code when we consider its assignment to a controlling area?

    Answer: All company codes associated with the same Controlling Area must use the same Operative Chart of Accounts

14. At what level are charts of accounts maintained?

    Answer: Client

15. How many charts of accounts can a company code use?

    Answer: One

16. How many company codes within a client can use the same Chart of Accounts?

    Answer: Many

17. From where do G/L accounts get their definition?

    Answer: Chart of accounts

18. What are the segments in a G/L master record?

    Answer: Chart of Accounts segment and company code segment

19. Which segment of the G/L master contains general information about an account?

    Answer: Chart of Accounts segment

20. Which segment of the G/L master contains specific information about how a company chooses to use an account?

    Answer: Company code segment

21. _______________ allows for "real-time integration" of G/L accounts with sub-ledger accounts.

    Answer: Reconciliation accounts

22. The account for an individual vendor or customer would be found in the _______________ ledger.

    Answer: Sub

23. The Accounts Receivable G/L balance sheet account used to consolidate individual customer receivables is a _______________ account.

    Answer: Reconciliation

24. The feature of the G/L that allows for postings within a document to be categorized into different areas, such as profit centers and segments is called ______________.

    Answer: Document splitting

25. SAP customers can take advantage of light-weight management accounting functionality by using ______________ within FI.

    Answer: Profit center

26. In SAP FI, there is a single ledger at the client level called, the ______________.

    Answer: Leading Ledger

27. It is always possible to drill down into the line item list of an account from the balance display for a G/L account T/F?

    Answer: F: Drilling down into the details of an account is possible only if it is enabled for that account.

28. The vendor master is defined at the following three levels: ______________, ______________ and ______________.

    Answer: Client, Company code, Purchasing organization

29. The reconciliation account number for Accounts Payable in the G/L is stored in the ______________ level of the vendor master.

    Answer: Company code

30. Information about the payment terms for a vendor can be found in the ______________ level of the vendor master.

    Answer: Company Code or Purchasing Organization

31. When a purchase order is created, the ______________ account is credited and the ______________ account is debited.

    Answer: Trick question! Creating a purchase order has no accounting impact and so no account is debited and none is credited either.

32. When goods are received against a PO, the ______________ account is credited and the ______________ account is debited.

    Answer: GR/IR is credited , Stock or inventory is debited

33. When a vendor invoice is saved, the _______________ account is credited and the _______________ account is debited.

    Answer: Vendor sub-ledger account is credited (results in the A/P reconciliation being credited) and GR/IR is debited.

34. When the vendor is paid, the _______________ account is credited and the _______________ account is debited.

    Answer: Cash is credited and vendor sub-ledger account is debited (results in the A/P reconciliation being debited)

35. The customer master has information at the following three levels: _______________, _______________ and _______________.

    Answer: Client, company code, sales organization

36. The credit control master record is stored as an extension of the _______________ master record.

    Answer: Customer

37. The two levels of the credit control master are: _______________ and _______________.

    Answer: Credit profile and credit segment

38. Information about the total credit limit for a customer across all credit control areas is stored in the _______________ level of the credit control master record.

    Answer: Credit profile

39. When a customer payment is posted, the _______________ account is credited and the _______________ account is debited.

    Answer: Customer sub ledger is credited and cash is debited

Management Accounting: In-Chapter questions

> **Review 1:** Explain in your own words why the information gathered for financial accounting might not be readily usable for decision-making.

Answer: Financial accounting gathers information needed for accurate external financial reporting. This might not always have the level of detail needed for decision-making.

Review 2: Explain why financial accounting might not be well-equipped for the profitability computations mentioned in the previous paragraph.

Answer: Financial accounting does not necessarily have to disaggregate the information to the extent needed. It only has to do what is necessary for external reporting.

Review 3: Explain how you might go about calculating the profit margin separately for the two products. Just mention the approach – you do not have enough information to come up with a number.

Answer: Get the direct costs for each product. Get the fair share of the indirect costs for each product. This will give the total costs for each product. Divide the cost for each product by the number of units produced to get the unit cost. Subtract this from the price to get the margin.

Review 4: From the above description, which costs can we directly attribute to the individual products?

Answer: Direct labor, cost of dedicated machinery and raw materials

Review 5: Choose any one of the indirect costs mentioned above (costs of the foremen, supervisors, top management, marketing and sales) and explain one way by which you can allocate the cost to the two products. We cannot specify a single correct answer, but thinking about it can aid understanding.

Answer: Foreman and supervisors: Time spent on each product or even an estimate of the level of difficulty of managing the production of each product.

Review 6: Identify at least one indirect cost that the above narrative has not explicitly mentioned.

Answer: Rent/space cost, electricity and other utilities, other overheads like cost of accounting department. Cost of IT infrastructure ...

Review 7: Identify at least two decisions that might be influenced by your calculation of the profit margins of the two products.

Answer: Discounts to offer Pricing Distribution channel choices Salesperson commissions Distribution channel commissions :.

Review 8: Suppose we allocate a third of the foreman's cost to product A and two thirds to product B. If it actually turns out that the foreman actually spends an equal amount of time on both products. How would this affect our cost estimates for products A and B?

Answer: We will then under allocate the cost to Product A and over allocate to product B. We will under estimate product A's cost and overestimate product B's cost.

Review 9: Explain how under or over-allocating indirect costs to a particular product might affect the quality of the decisions you identified in an earlier question.

Answer: We could price a product incorrectly based on an inaccurate cost estimate.

We could make poor decisions on commissions

Review 10: Suppose our company uses machine X only for product A. The company produced 10,000 units of product A during the previous year. How can we compute cost per unit of machine X per unit of product A for the previous year?

Answer: Take the depreciation for the machine for the previous year – say it is $20,000. Divide this across 10,000 units to get $2 per unit of product A.

Review 11: Would it make sense to treat the accounting department of a company as a profit center? Why or why not?.

Answer: Usually not. Accounting departments do not generate revenues and hence cannot be seen to generate profits.

However, it is possible for a company to actually charge user departments for the use of the services of the accounting department and also allow the accounting department to use its skills and resources to provide services to external clients in addition to their own company. In this situation, it is conceivable, although very unlikely, for an accounting department to be treated as a profit center (as well as a cost center)

Review 12: We know that in SAP a *client* represents a conglomerate company and can have several company codes within it. Given this scenario, can management accounting cut across company code boundaries? Support your answer with examples.

Answer: If the various company codes share common resources – like a purchasing department, manufacturing facilities, buildings, power generation, etc, then these shared costs will need to be allocated across company code boundaries.

Review 13: List three utility costs that might be assigned to the "Administration" cost center.

Answer:

1. Electric
2. Water/sewer
3. Telephone
4. Internet services

Review 14: Name three other possible cost centers in a typical organization. Do not take the easy path and go off the same theme as utilities and name other utilities. Try harder!

Answer:

1. Marketing department
2. IT department
3. Production department (etc.,)

Review 15: Having a cost center called "Administration" helps the company keep track of utility costs and manage them. Suppose a company found that it spent $1,200,000 on utilities during a specific quarter. How might this impact the profit margin that the company calculates for a particular product?

Answer: The fair share of this cost has to be allocated to each of the products that the company makes and hence this plays a role in computing the profit margin.

Review 16: Through an example, bring out the difference between a *cost element* and an *occurrence* of a cost element.

Answer: Cost element is a category of cost. It does not have an actual monetary value associated with it. When an instance of the cost element occurs, that instance has the monetary value.

For example, from a personal viewpoint, "food expense" could be a cost element. When we go out and spend $25 at a restaurant, that becomes an instance of the cost element "food expense."

For a company, "Rent" could be a cost element and the rent of $3,000 that it pays this month would be an occurrence of the "rent" cost element.

Review 17: A company has created a cost center called *CEO's Office* to track the expenses of the CEO's office. At the end of each settlement period, it allocates these costs to ten different cost centers corresponding to the overhead expense for various divisions. When settlement occurs, what will be the sending and receiving cost centers?

Answer: Sender cost center: CEO Office. **Receiver cost centers**: All the cost centers that share the cost incurred by the CEO's office.

The *Sender cost center* represents the cost center that is holding the cost – before *settlement* – on behalf of other cost centers. Receiver cost centers are those that will, at the time of *settlement*, share the cost held in the sender cost center.

Management Accounting: Chapter-end questions

1. Which of the following questions might the Overhead Cost Controlling module of CO deal with? (two)

   A What is the unit cost of Product A?

   B **How much did we spend on utilities in July 2011?**

   C **How should we allocate the costs of our IT department?**

   D Did Profit Center X meet its target profit?

2. Which of the following questions might the Product Cost Accounting module of CO deal with? (two)

   A **What is the unit cost of Product A?**

   B How much did we spend on utilities in July 2011?

   C **How much did production order Y cost as a whole?**

   D Did Profit Center X meet its target profit?

3. Which of the following questions might the Profitability Analysis module of CO deal with? (one)

   A Did Profit Center X meet its target profit?

   B How profitable was company code 1000 in the Northern Region?

   C How much did we spend on utilities in July 2011?

   D How much did production order Y cost as a whole?

   E How much did project X cost?

4. Name one cost that might flow from each of the following modules to CO. Also indicate one sub-module within CO where it might be used.

A FI (general): **utility payment – overhead cost controlling**

B FI-AA (Asset Accounting): **depreciation – product cost accounting**

C HCM (Human Capital Management): **payroll – overhead cost controlling**

D MM (Materials Management): **purchasing of materials for consumption – overhead cost controlling**

E PP (Production planning and execution): product cost – profit center accounting

F SD (Sales and distribution): **discount – profit center accounting**

5. Indicate one way in which CO might have an impact on FI.

   Answer: Product costing, which is an aspect of management accounting (CO), impacts valuation of finished goods.

6. Which organization element is concerned with Profitability analysis CO-PA?

   Answer: Operating concern

7. Which organizational element is the top level for Overhead cost controlling?

   Answer: Controlling area

8. Which organizational element is the top level for Product Cost Accounting CO-PCA?

   Answer: Controlling area

9. Which organizational element is the top level for Profit Center Accounting EC-PCA?

   Answer: Controlling area

10. A Business Area should be totally contained within one controlling area T/**F?**

11. One controlling area can have multiple company codes **T**/F?

12. One company code can belong to multiple controlling areas T/**F**?

13. A controlling area can have only one standard hierarchy (**True**/False).

14. A Client (in the SAP sense) has many controlling areas with each containing multiple cost centers. What restriction applies to the movement of costs across cost centers in this context?

    Answer: Cost movements can occur only between cost centers belonging to the same controlling area.

15. Two company codes (1000 and 2000) in a given SAP client belong to the same controlling area. Account 100000 in company code 1000 is an expense account and account 200000 in company code 2000 is an asset account. What other facts can you infer from these two facts?

    Answer: Because these two company codes must use the same Chart of Accounts, the same account numbers must reflect the same type of account in each company code.

16. Explain the mechanism used to transfer information from FI to CO.

    Answer: Every expense account is connected to a primary cost element. Whenever an expense is posted in FI, a corresponding primary cost element instance is created in CO and posted to an appropriate CO object.

17. What type of cost elements can be posted to directly from FI and what type cannot?

    Answer: Primary cost elements can be posted directly. Secondary cost elements cannot.

18. Which Master Data Group is mandatory for a controlling area (not in SAP notes)?

    Answer: Cost center standard hierarchy

19. What does the above contain?

    Answer: Hierarchy of how cost centers are organized in a controlling area. Controls how costs roll up.

20. What does the above group enable?

    Answer: Rolling up of actual costs, and also rolling up of costs for cost planning and budgeting

21. Unit price of an activity in Activity Based Costing is determined by ________________ and ________________.

Answer: cost center, activity type

22. A company has determined that rents will be allocated based on square footage used by various departments. The square footage is fixed across time periods. This is an example of a Type ______________ Statistical Key Figure.

    Answer: 01 or "Fixed"

23. You are preparing an assessment in SAP ERP Management Accounting. Which type of cost element is used to perform an assessment? (one)

    A Primary
    B **Secondary**
    C Revenue
    D Cost object

24. What must be created for every expense account in FI, which needs to be managed as a cost in CO. (one)

    A **Primary cost element**
    B Secondary cost element
    C Activity type
    D Activity price

25. A company accumulates the cost of its cafeteria and allocates this cost to other cost centers at the end of each month. What is this process broadly called?

    Answer: Settlement

26. What is the difference between CO postings to primary cost elements and to secondary cost elements in CO?

    Answer: Primary cost elements represent the flows from FI. Secondary cost elements represent how that cost is divided across many cost objects.

27. What are the four main elements of a controlling document apart from the document number?

    Answer: Sending object, receiving object, cost element and amount.

28. What three conditions must be met for a journal entry posted to an expense account in FI to flow to a primary cost element in CO?

Answer: It requires a primary cost element, an account assignment category, and an account assignment object for CO.

29. What is periodic allocation used for?

    Answer: To accumulate costs in a bucket and then allocate to other CO objects periodically.

30. Which of the following cannot an example of periodic allocation? (select one)

    A **Direct activity allocation**
    B Assessment
    C Distribution
    D Periodic reposting
    E Template allocation

31. What is the purpose of using template allocation to allocate costs?

    Answer: It allows complex posting logic.

32. Which of the following might be a good use for an Internal Order? (three)

    A The company is going to produce finished goods and wants to have a mechanism to accumulate production costs.
    B **The company is organizing a promotional seminar and needs to track all costs incurred for this purpose.**
    C **The company is buying a new machine and wants an object to which to charge the cost of the machine as well as future costs incurred on the machine.**
    D **The company is constructing a new parking lot and wants to accumulate the costs incurred.**

33. A client in SAP has two different company codes 1000 and 2000 (among others). Company 1000 wants to track commitments but company 2000 does not want to do this. What should company 1000 do that company 2000 does not have to do?

    Answer: It should turn on commitment management.

34. What are the two different occasions at which an internal order can be settled?

    Answer: End of each settlement period, or at end of order.

35. Which of the following cannot be a receiver when the costs of an internal order are settled? (One)

A **Profit center**
B Cost center
C Project
D Asset
E Profitability segment

36. What mechanism does SAP use to relate various controlling objects to profit centers?

Answer: Master records of controlling objects contain a profit center field.

37. What is the difference between a true cost object and a statistical object?

Answer: True costs can be reallocated. Statistical costs are only for information purposes and cannot be reallocated.

38. What is the purpose of a statistical object?

Answer: Sometimes we want to just compute certain cost statistics for information without such numbers having any scope to be reallocated. We then create statistical cost objects

39. Which of the following are examples of characteristics used in profitability segments? (three)

A **Sales region**
B Cost of goods sold
C Sales revenue
D **Product**
E **Customer**

40. What is the effect on the material master of marking a material standard cost estimate?

Answer: The new cost estimate becomes the "future" standard price.

41. What is the effect on the material master of releasing a material standard cost estimate?

Answer: The "future" standard price becomes the "current" standard price and the "current" price becomes the "previous" price.

42. What does the price control field on the material master determine?

    Answer: The price used for material valuation.

43. What two things is the material price in the material master used for?

    Answer: Stock valuation and target costs for determining calculation of variances.

44. Which of the following is used in profitability analysis? (one)

    A Standard price in the material master
    B **Standard cost estimate from product costing**

Procurement: In-chapter review questions

Review 1: Which of the above is the first step that has an accounting implication? Why?

Answer: *Goods receipt.* Until the vendor actually delivers goods the company has no legal financial obligations.

Of course from a practical viewpoint, once the company places a purchase order, it can assume that the vendor will deliver and invoice the company. Hence the company will most likely have to pay the vendor – however, the amount only represents a commitment and has no place yet in the financial books.

When goods are received, the value of the company's material stocks increases and this increases the company's assets and hence impacts the financial statements.

Review 2: What is the difference between a Purchase Requisition and a Purchase Order? Which of these do you think commits the company to something?

Answer: A *Purchase Requisition* is an internal document to a company. It only represents a need for some material that some entity in the company has. A *Purchase Order* has legal implications and commits the company to receive goods sent by the vendor and then pay for the goods. Of course if the vendor supplies the wrong items or if the items are not of acceptable quality, then the company need not accept or pay for the goods.

Review 3: Based on the above discussion, which other SAP modules might integrate with Procurement? (Procurement is part of Materials Management or MM.)

Financial accounting, (FI), Management accounting, (CO), Inventory Management and possibly *Warehouse management*

Procurement: Chapter-end questions

1. Which of the following represent organization levels at which stock can be tracked? (three)

   A **Storage location**
   B **Client**
   C Business area
   D **Company code**
   E Controlling area

2. Which of the following represent valid options for purchasing organizations? (three)

   A Cross client
   B **Cross company code**
   C **Cross plant**
   D **Dedicated to a single plant**
   E For a single storage location

3. How many plants can a storage location be attached to?

   Answer: One

4. How many storage locations can a plant have?

   Answer: Many

5. How many plants can a company code have?

   Answer: Many

6. How many company codes can a plant belong to?

   Answer: One

7. What information is needed to uniquely identify a plant within an SAP client?

   Answer: Plant number

8. What information is needed to uniquely identify a storage location within an SAP client?

   Answer: Plant number and storage location number

9. What is the difference in customizing when creating a centralized purchasing organization and when creating a decentralized purchasing organization?

   Answer: When creating a centralized purchasing organization, we cannot assign a company code to it during customization. The company code will have to be specified each time a Purchase Order is created for this purchasing organization.

10. Which of the following represent levels at which material master data is defined? (three)

    A **Plant**
    B **Client**
    C Company code
    D Purchasing organization
    E **Storage location**

11. Which of the following represent levels at which vendor master data is defined? (three)

    A Plant
    B **Client**
    C **Company code**
    D **Purchasing organization**
    E Storage location

12. Which master data contains information about the combination of a material and a vendor?

    Answer: Purchasing Info Record

13. Describe the condition under which the price of a material on a purchase order might come from the Purchasing Info Record.

    Answer: When there exists a Purchasing Info Record whose material and vendor match the purchase order in question.

14. Which of the following processes is not part of SAP procurement? (one)

    A Supply source determination
    B **Goods issue**
    C Purchase order monitoring
    D Invoice verification
    E Goods receipt

15. Which of the following is not a feasible option in SAP procurement? One **cannot** create a purchase order for: (one)

    A Procuring a stock item with a material master record
    B Procuring an item without a material master record for consumption
    C Procuring an item with a material master record for consumption
    D **Procuring a stock item without a material master record**

16. Which of the following represent ways by which a purchase requisition might be created? (four)

    A **By SAP SRM**
    B By SAP CRM
    C **By SAP SCM**
    D **Manually**
    E **By MRP**
    F From a purchase order

17. A purchase requisition can be created in one of many ways. What in the purchase requisition enables us to find out how a purchase requisition was created?

    Answer: Creation indicator in the purchase order

18. What could be one reason for maintaining a material master record for which we intend to perform no inventory management whatsoever?

    Answer: To keep information that can be conveniently pulled up while creating purchase orders. This will be useful when we order the item often. A non-stock item is a good example.

19. What could be one reason for maintaining a material master record for a material for which we intend to perform inventory management only for quantity, but not value?

Answer: As above, and also for storing information like units of measure and storage location specific information. A consumable, such as office supplies (pens, markers, post-it notes) is an example.

20. When purchasing material for which there is no material master, how does the material description get populated on the purchase requisition?

    Answer: Manually entered

21. Which of the following purchasing situations require us to provide an account assignment object? An account assignment object is mandatory for procuring: (pick two)

    A Any material that is subject to value based inventory management

    B **Any material that is not subject to value based inventory management**

    C **Any material without a material master record**

    D Any material for stock which will later be consumed for production of finished goods

22. Which of the following represent valid account assignment categories? (four)

    A **Cost center**

    B Profit center

    C Vendor

    D **Project**

    E **Asset**

    F **Order**

23. What is the difference between an account assignment category and an account assignment object?

    Answer: Account assignment category: Represents the general types of things that can be used in account assignments while purchasing for consumption. Object: The actual object that is serving as the cost collector. For example, "Cost center" is an account assignment category. The specific Cost center 1000 might be an account assignment object. Similarly "Asset" is a category. A particular asset (say cutting machine with serial number 30202) might be an account assignment object.

24. In terms of immediate financial accounting impact, how do purchasing to stock and for consumption differ?

    Answer: Purchasing for consumption: an expense is incurred as soon as the goods receipt is posted. This posts to an expense in FI and a primary cost element linked to that expense account will be use to debit the account assignment object in CO.

    Purchasing for stock: no immediate expense impact. All that happens is that our current assets increase. Expense will be incurred only when the material is later issued (say, against a production order).

25. What name is given to an internal purchase order that is used to move stock?

    Answer: Stock Transport Order

26. While checking the status of a purchase order, SAP supports status checking for the order as a whole and for individual items **T**/F?

27. Which of the following is not part of a purchase order? (one)

    A Header
    B Items
    C **Schedule lines**

28. Which item category represents vendor-owned material kept in a company's storage, and will be billed based on actual usage only? (one)

    A Standard
    B Subcontracting
    C **Consignment**
    D Third party
    E Stock transfer

29. Which item category represents material that a company provides to a vendor to incorporate in a product that we are buying from the vendor? (one)

    A Standard
    B **Subcontracting**
    C Consignment
    D Third party

E Stock transfer

30. Which item category represents material that a company asks the vendor to ship directly to an entity different from the company placing the order? (one)

   A Standard
   B Subcontracting
   C Consignment
   D **Third party**
   E Stock transfer

31. Which of the following does not represent a consequence of a goods receipt from a vendor against a purchase order? (one)

   A Creation of a material document
   B **Posting to a vendor account**
   C Creation of an accounting document
   D Update of the purchase order

32. A company wants to ensure that all goods receipts of a specific material from all vendors are first inspected before use. Where can this be set?

   Answer: In the material master on the "Post to QI stock" in the Purchasing tab.

33. A company wants to ensure that all goods receipts of a specific material produced in-house are first inspected before use. Where can this be set?

   Answer: In the material master on the "QI stock" in the Work scheduling tab.

34. In general, what are the four different places within SAP where one can specify that particular material should first be inspected before use?

   Answer: Two as above, plus while creating a purchase order and also while goods receipt is performed.

35. When material is received into stock in quality inspection, will the value of stock increase before it clears inspection?

   Answer: Yes, it is increased.

36. Stock overview is said to be a static view. What does this mean?

    Answer: This means this overview shows only the current stock situation and does not automatically update or refresh should there be any goods movements.

37. A material was in a storage location and awaiting quality inspection. It was inspected in place and cleared for unrestricted use. What type of goods movement occurred – stock transfer or transfer posting?

    Answer: Transfer posting

38. A company has activated inspection processing in its quality management system. What implications does this have for inventory management?

    Answer: Under these conditions, inventory management cannot post any stock movements for stock that is in Quality Inspection. Only Quality Management can do that – after all, they have to determine if the stock is acceptable or not first.

39. Will a stock transfer of a material from one storage location to another in the same plant have any financial impact?

    Answer: No. Unless there is split valuation between the two storage locations

40. All goods movements result in material documents **T**/F?

41. If warehouse management is active, how might a goods receipt impact warehouse management?

    Answer: If the storage location/plant combination that is assigned for the goods being received is linked to a warehouse then the goods receipt creates a Transfer Request for Warehouse management and the materials are booked into an interim storage area.

42. What impact might a goods receipt have on the material master?

    Answer: It could change the moving average price in the material master. At goods receipt, the material master also shows an increase in stock levels and value.

43. What is the impact of a goods receipt if QM is active?

    Answer: An inspection lot is created.

44. What step completes the logistics steps in the procurement process?

    Answer: Posting of the vendor's invoice (invoice verification)

45. What is the difference between purchase order based invoice verification and delivery based invoice verification?

    Answer: In purchase order based invoice verification, the invoice is verified against the purchase order. In the latter, the invoice is only verified against what was delivered.

46. Under what conditions would an invoice posting need to update the moving average price in the materials master?

    Answer: If, for whatever reason, the price on the invoice differs from the price on the PO. This is because when the goods receipt was performed, the moving average price would have been calculated per the price on the PO. If the subsequent invoice mentions a different price, then a correction needs to be applied to the moving average price.

47. Which of the following could represent characteristics used in reporting structures for procurement? (two)

    A **Purchasing organization**
    B Order quantity
    C PO value
    D **Vendor**
    E Delivery quantity

48. Which of the following could represent Key Figures used in reporting structures for procurement? (three)

    A Purchasing organization
    B **Order quantity**
    C **PO value**
    D Vendor
    E **Delivery quantity**

Material Planning

1. At which organizational level is material planning generally performed? (one)

    A Client

B Company code
C **Plant**
D Storage location

2. Which of the following represent master data required in Materials Planning? (three)

A **Materials**
B Work centers
C **Routings**
D **Bill of materials**

3. Which of the following represent plant-specific views in the material master record? (three)

A **MRP**
B **Work scheduling**
C **Accounting**
D Forecasting
E Quality management

4. Explain how each of the following fields in the material master is used:

a MRP Type: **To determine how MRP will plan materials**
b Procurement type: **Whether material is internally produced or externally procured**
c Strategy group: **How independent requirements behave – that is, if a sale occurs, is it treated as forecast sales materializing or as new sales. This has an impact on how material requirement is calculated.**

5. When creating a material master record, you have to assign it a material type. What does the material type determine? (three)

A In house production
B **Raw material**
C **Finished good**
D Externally procured
E **Operating supplies**

6. Which of the following can the material type specified in the material master determine? (two)

A **What screens are displayed for maintaining the material**

B **How the material number is assigned**
C The strategy group assigned to the material
D The MRP Type for the material

7. BOMs in SAP can be multi-level T/**F**?

Answer: False, not because SAP cannot handle multi-level BOMs, but because each individual BOM master record is single level. A component in a BOM may also contain its own BOM master record, allowing the user to see a multi-level BOM.

8. What is the difference between the quantity in the header and those in the item level of a BOM?

Answer: Header quantity says how many or how much of the material will be produced. That is, it specifies the quantity of the header product which that BOM represents. Item quantities indicate how many or how much of each of the input materials are needed to make the quantity specified in the header.

9. In SAP it is possible for a material to have multiple BOMs. Explain why this might be necessary.

Answer: We can have many BOMs for the same material. This could be because the list of materials might be different for producing different output batches of the same material. Also, different plants might use different sets of materials to produce the same output.

10. What does the BOM usage field in the BOM header determine?

Answer: It determines the purpose for which the BOM is used. Thus far we have seen BOMs for manufacturing. Later we will see that BOMs are also used in *Enterprise Asset Management*, The usage field in the BOM tells us what business process it is intended for. For example, manufacturing or maintenance.

11. Which of the following represent valid item categories in BOM? (three)

A In house production
B External procurement
C **Stock item**
D **Non-stock item**
E **Variable-size item**

12. Can a consumable material be included as a component in a BOM?

    Answer: Yes – that component would require an item category of "non-stock item".

13. SAP provides a planning table for Sales and Operations Planning. There is a planning table for each ______________.

    Answer: product or product group.

    Several versions of a planning tables can exist for one product or product group.

14. When we create a product group, SAP creates a material with type ______________

    Answer: PROD

15. The lowest level of a product group hierarchy contains ______________.

    Answer: materials

16. The proportion factors in a product group definition can be created ______________ or be ______________.

    Answer: manually or be calculated.

17. Which of the following values are calculated by the system when using a planning table? (one)

    A Sales
    B Production
    C **Stock level**
    D Target stock
    E Days supply
    F Target days supply

18. Sales data in the planning table can be created: (three)

    A **Manually**
    B By calculating backwards from prior yearsâĂŹ consumption of raw materials
    C **By transferring from CO-PA**
    D By calculating from production and stock level
    E **By running forecast models in the system.**

19. Disaggregation of product group level plans is not automatic T/**F**?

    Answer: It is not automatic. We determine how to disaggregate.

20. While disaggregating data for a product group which of the following options are valid? (two)

    A We can disaggregate the stock of the higher level group
    B **We can disaggregate the sales plan of the higher level group**
    C **We can disaggregate the production plan of the higher level group**
    D We can disaggregate the production or sales plans of the lowest level elements in the hierarchy

21. With respect to requirements in MRP, which of the following statements are true? (two)

    A Planned independent requirements represent customer orders
    B Customer independent requirements are based on forecasts and plans
    C **Planned independent requirements can be based on forecasts and plans**
    D **Customer independent requirements are sales orders**
    E Dependent requirements can be based directly on forecasts and plans

22. Demand management results in the creation of independent requirements. What does MRP create for these independent requirements? (one)

    A **Planned orders**
    B Purchase requisitions
    C Production orders
    D Schedule lines

23. Which of the following is considered demand when MRP runs the net requirements calculation? (one)

    A Purchase orders
    B **Safety stock**
    C Firmed planned orders
    D Firmed purchase requisitions

24. What is the goal of Master Production Scheduling?

    Answer: To ensure that capacities and materials are available for critical items

25. MRP type _______________ is based on independent requirements and type _______________ is based on past consumption.

Answer: PD, VB

26. For what kinds of materials is reorder point planning suitable?

Answer: Items with stable demand

27. Which of the following can represent procurement proposals generated by MRP? (three)

A Sales orders
B **Planned orders**
C **Purchase requisitions**
D **Schedule lines**
E Purchase orders

Answer: You should understand b and c well. As for d, Schedule lines are delivery orders against existing contracts. For example, if a company uses a material in large quantities and on a regular basis, then there is no point in going through an elaborate procurement process each time the material is needed. In fact that approach could be risky. So companies often enter into long term contracts with vendors to supply materials as needed for a certain length of time at certain rates with agreed delivery conditions like lead times, quality, etc,. Then once this agreement is in place, as and when needed, the company simply tells the vendor to supply certain quantities by certain dates against the contract. Thus the whole purchase process is not invoked again.

28. Which of the following is not part of net requirements calculations in MRP take into account: (one)

A **Planned sales**
B Firmed purchase requisitions
C Current stock
D Safety stock
E Lot size

29. Which of the following does not represent MRP relevant changes to a material? (one)

A Change in BOM

B **Goods receipts against existing purchase orders**
C Unplanned goods issues
D New sales orders

30. What is the main difference between the stock/requirements list and the MRP list?

Answer: The MRP list is valid ONLY for the current MRP run. If MRP is run again, the original MRP list becomes obsolete. The stock requirements list is dynamic and can be refreshed after additional MRP runs.

Manufacturing

1. At which organizational level are costs managed in a production order? (one)

A Client
B **Controlling area**
C Company Code
D Plant

Answer: All cost objects are managed within a controlling area.

2. During the manufacturing execution process, which steps include a material availability check?

Answer: An availability check can be performed manually at the time of the creation of the production order. It is automatically performed when the order is released.

3. When a production order is created, costs are planned and the order is scheduled. Which master data is responsible for the scheduling of the order? (two)

A Material
B **BOM**
C **Routing**
D Work center

4. When a production order is created, materials are reserved. Which master data is responsible for these reservations? (one)

A Material

B **BOM**
C Routing
D Work center

5. A production order can be confirmed before the release of the order. (T/**F**)

   Answer: False: The order must be released before any goods movements or confirmation can occur.

6. What is the procurement type in the material master for finished goods that we only make?

   Answer: In-house production

7. What are task lists and what are the different types of task lists in SAP?

   Answer: Task lists indicate the steps used in making an item. *Routing* is one type of task list used for discrete manufacturing. For process manufacturing, the set of steps needed to make a product is called a *master recipe*. For repetitive manufacturing (assembly line) it is called a *rate routing*.

8. What are PRTs?

   Answer: Production resources and tools

9. What field in a work center master record controls the types of activities in which it could be used?

   Answer: Task list types (that is, what kinds of task lists can this work center be used in?

10. Data stored in the work center master can be used for which of the following: (three)

    A Actual cost determination
    B **Scheduling**
    C **Costing**
    D **Capacity planning**

11. What mechanism enables connecting a work center to CO?

    Answer: Work center is associated with a cost center and thus all its costs go to that cost center.

12. What name is given to a task list in:

    a Discrete manufacturing: **Routing**

b Assembly line manufacturing: **Rate routing**
c Process manufacturing: **Master recipe**

13. What is the analog of Production order in process manufacturing?

    Answer: Process order

14. Give an example of a fixed time element in a routing operation.

    Answer: Setup time. This is the time to set up the work center. This is fixed irrespective of how many units are them produced at the work center.

15. Give an example of a variable time element in a routing operation.

    Answer: Time per piece – that is, how much time does it take to do the operation for a single piece?. Thus if the order has n pieces, we can calculate the total time for that operation for that order.

16. BOM components not assigned to an operation in a routing are assumed by the system to be required when?

    Answer: For the first operation

17. In addition to BOM components, name one other thing that can be assigned to an operation.

    Answer: PRT

18. Which of the following things do Formula Keys in work centers help with? (three)

    A **Calculation of costs**
    B **Calculation of capacities**
    C Activity based costing
    D **Scheduling**
    E Determining the task lists in which a work center can be used

19. When a work center is assigned to an operation in a routing, what part (view) of the information from the work center master might be used to determine the operation time?

    Answer: Scheduling

20. Production Resources Tools might be needed to produce a finished product. In which master data pertaining to the product are they included?

Answer: BOM

21. Which of the following steps in the manufacturing process can be automated? (two)

    A Order creation
    B **Order release**
    C Material staging
    D **Material withdrawal posting**
    E Order archiving

22. Is it possible to create a production order directly without a planned order? If so, mention a few variations.

    Answer: Yes. Without routing and BOM, with both, with routing alone

23. Which of the following can be assigned to operations on a production order? (three)

    A **Materials**
    B Cost center
    C **PRT**
    D **Trigger points**
    E Profit center

24. Under what controlling scenario would we assign a settlement rule and calculate planned costs and track actual costs for a production order?

    Answer: Order-Related cost object controlling

25. At what level are costs for an order determined and at what level are they managed?

    Answer: Costs are determined at operation level and managed at order header level.

26. What has to take place before one can issue goods for a Production Order?

    Answer: It must have been released.

27. At what two time points can availability checks be performed for a production order?

    Answer: Order creation and order release

28. Availability checks for production orders can check for availability of: (select three)

A Spare parts
B **Material**
C **PRT**
D **Machines**
E Warehouse resources

29. What impact can goods issue for production have on material reservations?

Answer: Reduce reservations. Because earlier we had made reservations for the order. Now that we have issued the material the reserved quantity can now be reduced by the amount issued. To be concrete, suppose an order has reserved 200 units of a material. Now suppose 50 units were issued. Clearly we need to reduce the reservations down to 150 now.

30. Which of the following accounts are affected when goods issue occurs against a production order? (two)

A **Stock**
B Product
C Overhead
D **Consumption**

31. The production order is updated when goods are issued against a released production order **T**/F?

32. Can goods issue against a production order generate a controlling document? Why or why not?

Answer: Yes they can. Because when goods are issued against a production order an expense is incurred in FI and the cost of the issued materials will now be allocated to the production order.

33. What two main possibilities exist for order confirmation?

Answer: Order based and operation based

34. Which of the following represent possible detailed options for production order confirmation? (two)

A **Time at which setup was initiated for an operation**
B Work center related
C **Reaching a milestone**
D Material related

35. Explain how automated goods receipt postings against a production order might work – at what point will this occur?

Answer: When an order is confirmed we can automatically post a goods receipt. What we are saying here is – suppose someone posts an order confirmation saying that 50 units of finished goods were made. Now the manual process of posting goods receipt will wait till the goods are actually received in inventory and post a receipt at that time. In the automated process we can assume that these goods will be put into finished goods stock and can thus make that posting along with the confirmation itself. There is no right or wrong way. It all depends on what approach makes sense for an organization.

36. Explain how automated goods issue postings against a production order might work – at what point will this occur and what is this mechanism called?

Answer: This is called *backflush* posting. Suppose we are making cars and we manually post a good issue of 4 tires for a car. That is the manual approach. The alternative approach is to simply keep the tires on the shop floor. When a confirmation is posted for 20 cars, then we can assume that 80 tires were used and post a goods issue for 20 tires at this point. This could improve efficiency because we avoid the step of posting goods issue separately.

37. What linkage to the warehouse management system might exist with goods receipts from a production order?

Answer: Clearly the finished goods that have been taken into stock have to be put away within the warehouse. Thus the goods receipt will trigger a warehouse operation. We will see more of this in the unit on inventory and warehouse management.

38. Which accounts are updated when goods are received against a production order?

Answer: Stock account and plant activity account

39. When a production order is settled, it is credited/debited?

Answer: Credited

40. Which of the following scenarios might be well suited to use order-related cost object controlling? (two)

A Production of large quantities

B **Flexible production environment**
C **Manufacture of co-products**
D When quality is very important
E When the cost variance across orders is low

Sales order processing

1. Which of the following are used to define a sales area? (three)

   A **Division**
   B **Sales organization**
   C Sales Group
   D **Distribution channel**
   E Plant

2. Which of the following organization levels are dedicated to SD? (two)

   A **Shipping point**
   B Sales Order
   C **Sales organization**
   D Sales location
   E Product Group

3. How many sales organizations can a company code have?

   Answer: Many

4. How many company codes can a sales organization belong to?

   Answer: One

5. Which of the following can represent a distribution channel? (two)

   A **Internet sales**
   B **Wholesale sales**
   C Distribution center
   D Shipping point
   E Loading dock

6. What does a division represent?

   Answer: It represents a product line. For example, in the Dell computer company, Desktops, laptops, tablets and severs may all represent different product lines and hence different divisions.

7. Which of the following statements are true about sales areas? (two)

   A One division can be part of only one sales area
   B **A single sales organization could exist in several different sales areas**
   C **A division can be used in defining several different sales areas**
   D The same combination of sales organization, distribution channel and division can occur in multiple sales areas

8. How many sales areas can a plant be associated with?

   Answer: Many – because a plant can be linked with one or more sales organizations.

9. How many plants can a sales area serve?

   Answer: Many

10. What is the role of the plant in SD?

    Answer: The location from which products are distributed or services or rendered.

11. Give an example of a plant for a service organization.

    Answer: A local office of a consulting organization.

12. Regarding the relationship of shipping points and plants, is the assignment of shipping points to plants one-to-one, one-to-many, or many-to-many?

    Answer: Many to many. One plant can have many shipping points. One shipping point can serve many plants.

13. Which component in SAP determines a customer's credit-worthiness when a sales order is created? (one)

    A Quality Management
    B Management Accounting
    C Financial Accounting
    D **Financial Supply Chain Management**

14. In which step of the standard sales order process will the first financial posting occur? (one)

    A Creation of the sales order
    B Creation of the outbound delivery
    C **Goods Issue**

D Billing

15. Which of the following represent master data used in a sales order? (three)

    A Plant master

    B **Customer master**

    C **Output master**

    D **Condition master**

    E Price master

16. Which of the following represent mandatory partner functions in the customer master? (two)

    A **Sold to party**

    B Contact persons

    C **Ship to party**

    D Billing party

    E Forwarding agent

    Answer: Although some of these items are valid partner functions, they are not valid choices here because they are not **mandatory**.

    Contact person and forwarding agent are not mandatory. Billing party is not a proper choice because *bill-to party* would have been a valid choice here.

17. At least two different partner functions appear in a sales order. **T**/F?

18. Which of the following pieces of information might appear on the customer-material info record? (two)

    A Moving average price

    B **Customer material number**

    C **Delivery tolerances**

    D Average monthly sales

19. What master data determines how documents are communicated or sent to various parties?

    Answer: Output master

20. The _______________ master is used to define material prices for various complex combinations of criteria.

    Answer: Condition master

21. Which of the following represents the standard sequence of steps in the sales order process? (one)

   A Sales order> Inquiry> Billing> Payment
   B **Inquiry> Sales order>Delivery> Billing> Payment**
   C Inquiry> Sales order> Billing> Delivery>Payment
   D Sales order> Delivery> Payment> Inquiry

22. Which of the following documents can a sales order reference? (two)

   A **Sales Inquiry**
   B Purchase order
   C **Quotation**
   D RFQ
   E RFI

23. Which of the following represent benefits of using pre-sales features? (two)

   A **Ability to track lost sales**
   B Enables better tracking of billing
   C **Advantage when doing business with customers who want to document the whole sales process**
   D Speedier delivery times

24. Which of the following must be specified in order to create a sales order? (three)

   A Sales group
   B **Sales area**
   C **Customer**
   D **Required delivery date**
   E Customer material number

25. Which of the following represent possible ways in which a sales order can be created? (two)

   A A purchase order can be the reference document for a sales order
   B **Can be created independently of any other sales document**
   C **Multiple pre sales documents can be combined into one sales order**
   D Can be based on prior scheduling agreements

26. Which of the following represent item types on a sales order? (two)

A **Material item**

B In house production

C **Free of charge item**

D Externally procured

27. Which of the following scenarios would require separate schedule lines for a single line item in a single sales order? (one)

 A **Customer orders 500 units of a material and wants them to be delivered in two different sets of 250 units on two different dates**

 B Customer orders two materials in one order and specifies a different delivery date for each material

 C Customer places two separate sales orders with separate delivery dates, and one item on each order. Customer wants all the pieces of the materials on each order to be delivered on the date specified in the respective orders.

28. While placing a sales order, the system determined that the requested date for a material could not be met. What kind of scheduling did the system use to determine this?

 Answer: Backward

29. In the above scenario, what kind of scheduling might the system use to propose a delivery date?

 Answer: Forward

30. The ________________ can be used to find out required fields that have not been supplied in creating a sales order.

 Answer: Incompletion log

31. Sales orders can become ________________ requirements in MRP.

 Answer: Customer independent

32. Under which of the following conditions can an availability check be triggered for a sales order? (two)

 A It has been set in *customizing* for the specific customer

 B It has been set in *customizing* for the specific material

 C It has been set in *customizing* for the specific user

 D **It has been set in *customizing* for the transaction**

 E **It is specified in the material master for the item**

33. Which of the following documents can have schedule lines? (one)

    A Billing documents
    B Invoices
    C **Sales orders**
    D Outbound deliveries
    E Inbound deliveries

34. Picking lists can be created from which of the following documents? (one)

    A **Transfer orders**
    B Transfer requirements
    C Sales orders
    D Outbound deliveries
    E Billing documents

35. Under what conditions would a transfer requirement be created for an outbound delivery?

    Answer: If the plant/storage location combination in the delivery has a warehouse. number assigned.

36. You are in the process shipping an item against a sales order. You have created an outbound delivery and look at the stock/requirements list. In a different session, you go ahead and post goods issue for the outbound delivery. You then go back and refresh the stock/requirements list. What changes would you see on it?

    Answer:

    a Stock quantity will be reduced
    b The requirement for the material for this order – which was present earlier – has been satisfied and no longer appears.

37. Which accounts are affected when a goods issue occurs against a sales order?

    Answer: Stock, stock change or (COGS)

38. Which accounts are affected when a billing document is generated against a delivery?

    Answer: The Revenue account and the customer sub-ledger account. When the posting to the customer sub-ledger occurs, this posting automatically gets updated in the accounts receivable reconciliation account in the G/L.

39. Which feature of SAP supports seeing all related SD documents on one screen and allows the user to navigate to any one of these documents?

    Answer: Document flow

40. Which of the following modules has an integration with SD? (three)

    A **Materials management**
    B **Warehouse management**
    C Manufacturing execution
    D **Material planning**

41. How can ad-hoc reporting requirements be met?

    Answer: Using ABAP queries.

42. When a valid sales order is saved, it affects which of the following worklists? (one)

    A Picking worklist
    B Billing worklist
    C **Shipping worklist**
    D Goods issue posting worklist

Inventory and Warehouse Management

1. Which of the following can result in a goods receipt posting in our company? (two)

   A **Receipt of shipments against purchase orders raised by us**
   B Receipt of raw material by an employee against a production order
   C **Receipt of goods returned by customers to us**
   D Receipt of our shipment by a customer of ours
   E An outbound delivery document

2. Which of the following can result in goods issue postings in our company? (two)

   A **Issue of raw material by an employee against a production order**
   B Deposit into stock of finished products from production
   C Issue of goods by a vendor to fulfill our purchase order
   D **An outbound delivery for a sales order**

E Receipt at our plant of a Stock Transport Order from another plant

3. Which of the following could represent a transfer posting? (two)

   A The warehouse confirms a transfer order for an inbound delivery
   B **We take some materials from consignment stock into our possession**
   C We move stock from one plant to another within the same company code
   D **Some material to be inspected in a storage location clears quality inspection**

4. Which of the following are true about one and two step stock transfers? (two)

   A One step stock transfer creates two material documents
   B **One step transfer creates one material document with two items**
   C Two step stock transfer creates two material documents with two items on each
   D **Two step stock transfer creates two material documents each with one item**

5. What is an advantage of the two-step stock transfer process over the one-step process?

   Answer: It can be managed with authorization. If you disallow users to post goods movements in more than one plant, then a two step procedure must be used. In a two step procedure, you can also see the material in-transfer at the receiving plant.

6. In two-step stock transfer where is the stock shown on the stock overview between the time it leaves the first location and is checked into the second?

   Answer: The material appears *in-transfer* in the receiving plantâĂŹs inventory.

7. If there is valuation involved in a two-step transfer process, at which step does valuation take place?

   Answer: Valuation always occurs at the time of goods issue.

8. Under what conditions is an accounting document created for a stock transfer?

Answer: An accounting document will be created any time there is a change in valuation. This is true for all plant-to-plant and company code-to-company code stock transfers.

9. What impact does the two step process have on physical inventory?

   Answer: During the time of physical inventory, there should be no materials in-transfer.

10. Under what conditions can an accounting document be created for goods movements across two plants of a single company code?

    Answer: There will always be an accounting document created whenever there is a stock transfer between plants within the same company code.

11. Under what conditions can an accounting document be created for goods movements between two storage locations within a single plant?

    Answer: An accounting document will be created in this case only when the material is split-valuated. This means the value for the same material is different in each storage location.

12. If a stock movement happens across two storage locations in one plant and simultaneously changes stock type from goods in quality inspection to unrestricted use, this involves stock transfer and a transfer posting. T/**F**?

    Answer: This is false. A one step stock transfer between two storage locations within the same plant can take be issued and received from any stock type into any stock type. Therefore, there is no need for a second transaction.

13. Which of the following is required in two step stock transfers across storage locations in a single plant? (one)

    A Unrestricted stock from the origin can be moved to stock in QI at the destination

    B Unrestricted stock from the origin can be moved to blocked stock at the destination

    C **Unrestricted stock from the origin can be moved to unrestricted stock at the destination**

    D Stock in QI at the origin can be moved into stock in QI at the destination

14. Suppose stock is transferred from one company code to another. Which two G/L accounts will be affected in the sending company code?

    Answer: At the time of goods issue, the sending company code will have its inventory account credited and an income statement account debited.

15. Suppose you are planning to move stock from one plant to another and would like to include additional costs such as freight charges associated with this move. What mechanism would be best? What other benefits does this approach provide over the alternative approach available?

    Answer: In this case, it would be best to use a stock transport order (STO). An STO acts as an internal purchase order. In this special case of a purchase order, conditions can be entered into the STO, the STO is MRP relevant, the material can be received into any stock type, and inspection can be planned.

16. If MRP creates a Purchase Requisition it can be converted into a purchasing document. Which two options exist for this conversion to a purchasing document?

    Answer: The purchase requisition can be converted to a purchase order (PO) or a stock transport order (STO).

17. How is inventory management connected with warehouse management?

    Answer: A warehouse number is assigned to a plant/storage location combination. Goods movements which are subject to a warehouse number, would then require additional logistic execution steps in warehouse management.

18. Is posting a goods issue a part of inventory management or warehouse management?

    Answer: It is part of inventory management.

19. Is the execution of a transfer order part of inventory management or warehouse management?

    Answer: It is part of warehouse management.

20. For what reason might a stock transfer not involve warehouse operations?

Answer: Warehouse management would not be necessary if a warehouse number is not assigned to the plant/storage location combination in the stock transfer.

21. Your company has received a sales order and has created an outbound delivery for it. In what order will the inventory and warehouse operations be performed?

    Answer: When a goods movement is managed with a delivery, the warehouse management activities are performed prior to the inventory management postings. Therefore, a transfer order and confirmation will occur before the goods issue.

22. Your vendor has given you advance notification of a shipment and you have created an inbound delivery in anticipation. In what order will the inventory and warehouse operations be performed?

    Answer: When a goods movement is managed with a delivery, the warehouse management activities are performed prior to the inventory management postings. Therefore, a transfer order and confirmation will occur before the goods receipt.

23. With respect to warehouse management which of the following statements is valid? (one)

    A **Multiple storage locations from multiple plants can all be assigned to a single warehouse number**

    B All the storage locations assigned to a warehouse number must belong to the same plant

    C Different storage locations of a given plant cannot be allocated to different warehouse numbers

    D If one storage location of a plant is allocated to a warehouse number, then all have to be allocated to warehouse numbers, but not necessarily the same one

24. Transportation planning points are allocated at which organization level?

    Answer: They are linked to a company code.

25. Under what conditions would a goods receipt generate a transfer requirement?

    Answer: If a warehouse number is assigned to a plant/storage location combination a transfer requirement would be generated. Goods movements which are subject to a warehouse number, would then require additional logistic execution steps in warehouse management.

26. What three things determine a specific location in a warehouse?

    Answer: A warehouse number is composed of a storage type; storage section; and bin.

27. When a goods receipt results in the creation of a transfer requirement, where will the material appear in the warehouse?

    Answer: The material is booked into an interim storage area for putaway.

28. Explain the hierarchical sub structure of a warehouse.

    Answer: A warehouse number is composed of a storage type; storage section; and bin.

Enterprise Asset Management

1. When creating a maintenance order, which of the following represent two examples of master data that might require maintenance? (two)

    A Structure
    B **Functional location**
    C Planner group
    D **Equipment**

2. Prior to creating a maintenance order, which of the following documents might be created to support the maintenance process? (one)

    A Purchase requisition
    B Transfer order
    C **Maintenance notification**
    D Maintenance requisition

3. Which of the following is considered master data in *Enterprise Asset Management*? (two)

    A Maintenance plant
    B **Work center**
    C **Technical object**

D Maintenance planning plant

4. Which of the following are examples of technical objects? (three)

   A Work centers
   B **BOMs**
   C **Functional locations**
   D **Equipment**

5. What is the role of a functional location?

   Answer: A functional location refers to a physical place where we may have equipment installed. It helps us keep track of various locations in our plant that may require maintenance or has equipment installed that may require maintenance.

6. What is the role of equipment?

   Answer: Equipment are items that need to be managed individually from a maintenance perspective. A material that has been assigned a serial number is also managed as a piece of equipment. Examples of equipment are vehicles, machines, etc. Equipment can be kept in inventory or installed in functional locations.

7. What is the role of assemblies?

   Answer: Assemblies is another term for bill of materials. For *Enterprise Asset Management*, assemblies are used by planners to plan materials needed for maintenance purposes. Assemblies exist for functional locations, equipment, and materials. If a material BOM is being used to manage a piece of equipment, it is assigned in the master record for that piece of equipment.

8. What is the role of a planner group?

   Answer: Planner groups are individuals or groups of individuals and they are assigned to a maintenance planning plant. The planner group is responsible for creating notifications of maintenance items and planning the maintenance in the maintenance order.

9. What is the role of a maintenance planning plant?

   Answer: A maintenance planning plant is the plant designated for planning maintenance requirements. When a maintenance item is identified, the maintenance plant is where the planning will take place. Planner groups assigned to the maintenance planning plant perform the planning tasks.

10. What is the role of a notification?

    Answer: A notification is generally the first step in the maintenance process. When a maintenance need occurs, the planner groups are contacted. The planner groups gather as much information as possible in order to be able to plan the maintenance. The notification may contains one or more technical objects (it may also contain no objects), items to be maintained, tasks, an activities. The maintenance notification is managed in parallel with the maintenance order.

11. What is the role of a maintenance order?

    Answer: The main planning and execution aspects of maintenance are contained in the maintenance order. The order also collects all of the costs associated with the maintenance process. Planner groups create the order and can plan work to be performed as well as materials required.

12. What is the significance of releasing a maintenance order?

    Answer: A maintenance order must be released in order for work to be performed. The maintenance order cannot collect any costs associated with the maintenance until it is released. Thus, the release sets the order as a cost object.

13. What is the difference between *Enterprise Asset Management* and *Asset Accounting*?

    Answer: Enterprise asset management deals with the physical maintenance of assets. Asset accounting deals with managing these assets from an accounting point of view.

14. Which of the following are examples of equipment? (three)

    A Cafeteria
    B **Oven**
    C **Steamer**
    D **Cooler**

    Answer: Cafeteria would be an example of a functional location and not equipment.

15. When the maintenance order is created, the maintenance notification is deleted. (T/**F**)

    Answer: False, the maintenance notification is managed in parallel with the maintenance order.

16. Which of the following are different types of maintenance described in this chapter? (two)

    A **Preventive maintenance**

    B Overall maintenance

    C **Breakdown maintenance**

    D Material maintenance

17. Explain the main differences between centralized and decentralized maintenance planning.

    Answer: Centralized maintenance planning occurs when a single maintenance planning plant is used to plan the maintenance at other maintenance plants. Decentralized maintenance planning occurs when each maintenance plant is also its own maintenance planning plant.

18. A maintenance plant is an example of master data. (T/**F**)

    Answer: False, maintenance plants are considered organizational levels.

19. Which of the following is considered master data that is responsible for performing maintenance activities? (one)

    A Maintenance plant

    B **Work center**

    C Technical object

    D Maintenance planning plant

20. Which of the following is considered master data that is used by planner groups to plan materials on a maintenance order? (one)

    A Functional location

    B Work center

    C Equipment

    D **Assembly**

21. A maintenance order is managed using order-related cost object controlling. (**T**/F)

    Answer: True, the maintenance order must be released to become a cost object. It will collect costs from goods movement and confirmation. At period end, the order is settled to one or more receivers. It is managed using order-related cost object controlling.

Human Capital Management

1. Which of the following is not part of the HCM cycle? (one)

   A Recruitment
   B Performance appraisals
   C Time management
   D **Work center planning**

2. Define the beginning and end to the HCM cycle.

   Answer: There is no definitive beginning and end to the HCM cycle. Each of the process steps in the cycle is dependent on one another.

3. When a person is promoted into a new position, a vacancy occurs. Planning to have that vacancy filled efficiently and effectively is part of. (one)

   A Recruitment
   B Hiring
   C **Succession planning**
   D Performance appraisals

4. Keeping track of how much vacation an employee currently has is part of which process in the HCM cycle? (one)

   A **Time management**
   B Compensation
   C Organizational structuring
   D Planning

5. The Profile Matchup compares which two things?

   A CandidateâĂŹs requirements
   B **CandidateâĂŹs qualifications**
   C **Position requirements**
   D Position qualifications

6. Which processes in the HCM cycle use the Profile Matchup? (two)

   A **Personnel development**
   B Compensation
   C **Recruitment**
   D Planning

7. Explain how SAP supports the keeping track of costs for various organizational units in SAP HCM.

   Answer: An organizational unit in HCM is similar to a department where people work. In order to keep track of costs for these departments, a cost center is often used.

8. Explain the use of Jobs in SAP HCM.

   Answer: Jobs are generic descriptions of work that people will do. They are used to describe one or more positions as well as evaluating pay rates for people who hold those positions. Jobs should be created to be as general as possible, but as specific as necessary.

9. Explain the use of Positions in SAP HCM.

   Answer: Positions are described by Jobs. Several positions could be described by the same Job. People are hired into a position in SAP HCM. A person can hold only one position, but a position can be occupied by more than one person. Positions can be entirely vacant, completely filled, or partially filled.

10. The Hiring component in the HCM cycle supports the internal postings of positions for internal candidates. (T/**F**)

    Answer: False – the Recruitment component supports this.

11. Explain how the SAP ERP system supports the integration of data between the Recruitment and Hiring components in the HCM cycle.

    Answer: Data can be transferred from the Recruitment component to the Hiring component in SAP HCM. When an applicant is hired, their application information can be transferred to an Info Type to facilitate the hiring process.

12. When someone is hired into a position, explain how this new employee is associated with a cost center.

    Answer: When someone is hired into a position, this position is assigned to an organizational unit (department). Typically, this department is assigned a cost center and the employee will inherit that cost center from their position.

13. Which transaction in HCM will result in the posting of a cost to a cost center? (one)

    A Hiring

B **Payroll**
C Recruitment
D Planning

14. Which of the following best describes an Info Type? (two)

A **A collection of related data about an employee**
B A collection of related data about a cost center
C Organizational data
D **Master data**

15. Explain a personnel file.

Answer: A personnel file is a record of an employee's personal information as well as other information relating that employee to the enterprise. The personnel file contains information that assist the Humans Resource department in managing various aspects associated with an employee. Some examples include, but are not necessarily limited: to address information; employee banking information; pay rate information; and organizational structuring information. Thus, a personnel file is a collection of various info types for an employee.

16. Which of the following are possible examples of Info Types? (three)

A **Personal information**
B Banking information
C **Work center information**
D **Pay rate information**

17. Which of the following are methods for maintaining Info Types? (three)

A Multiple screen
B **Single screen**
C **Fast entry**
D **Personnel actions**

18. Explain personnel actions info type maintenance.

Answer: In personnel actions, many info types will be maintained at one time for one personnel number. The info types appear and are maintained in sequential order.

19. Explain single screen info type maintenance.

Answer: In single screen info type maintenance, only one info type can be maintained at one time for one personnel number.

20. Explain fast entry info type maintenance.

Answer: In fast entry info type maintenance, only one info type can be maintained at one time, but can be maintained for more than one personnel number. Each personnel number will appear sequentially one after the other.

21. It is not possible for an employee to maintain any of their own info type information. (T/**F**)

Answer: False – through Employee Self-Services (ESS), an employee may have access to change information in an info type as long as they have authorization to do so. For example, using ESS an employee could update their address information which in turn will update their info type.

22. Training and development in HCM also takes advantage of the Profile Matchup. (**T**/F)

Answer: True – in training and development, an existing employee may be interested in a promotion. Because of this, they will need to know what the requirements are for being eligible for this promotion. The Profile Matchup will compare their current qualification to the desired position to find shortfalls that can be used for a development plan.

23. A company is preparing an employee to fill a future vacancy. As a result, they also need to prepare for the vacancy left behind by this employee. This is an example of _______________. (one)

   A **Succession planning**
   B Development
   C Training
   D Appraisals

24. A current employee is interested in being promoted to a higher position. The employee works closely with his/her manager to create a plan for achieving this. This is an example of _______________. (one)

   A Succession planning
   B **Development**
   C Training
   D Appraisals

25. A manager meets with an employee on an annual basis to discuss their performance. This is an example of _______________. (one)

    A Succession planning
    B Development
    C Training
    D **Appraisals**

26. Wages, salaries, benefits, and insurance are all examples of _______________ (one)

    A Pay scale
    B Job pricing
    C **Compensation**
    D Promotion

27. Explain CATS.

    Answer: CATS is Cross-Application Time Sheet. It is used by employees and third party business partners for time entry. Those times can be transferred to various business applications, one being HCM. As an example, an employee can enter their working times using CATS and have those times transfer to HCM for payroll processing.

28. List various types of times that are used in HCM.

    Answer: Sick time; vacation time; overtime; leave time; maternity time; paternity time; time on sabbatical; and travel time.

29. Explain the concept of Job Pricing in HCM.

    Answer: Job pricing is used to determine if the pay compensation offered to employees is competitive in the market place. The location where an employee works can greatly influence their rate of pay.

30. Planning is the last phase of the HCM cycle and therefore ends the HCM process. (T/**F**)

    Answer: False – There is no definitive beginning and end to the HCM cycle. Each of the process steps in the cycle is dependent on one another.

31. Which of the following is available to assist managers in making planning decisions in HCM? (one)

    A Employee desktop
    B **Manager's desktop**

C Planning table
D Sales and operations plan

Project Management

1. Which of the following represent the organizational levels specific to project management? (one)

   A Company code
   B Plant
   C Storage location
   D **Project management in SAP has no organizational levels to itself**

2. Define the characteristics of projects. **Answer:**

   Projects are unique in purpose, generally capital intensive and time intensive. They are usually complex in nature and involve many different functional areas.

3. Figure 72 represents which of the following? (one)

   A Project builder
   B Project planning board
   C **Work breakdown structure**
   D Network

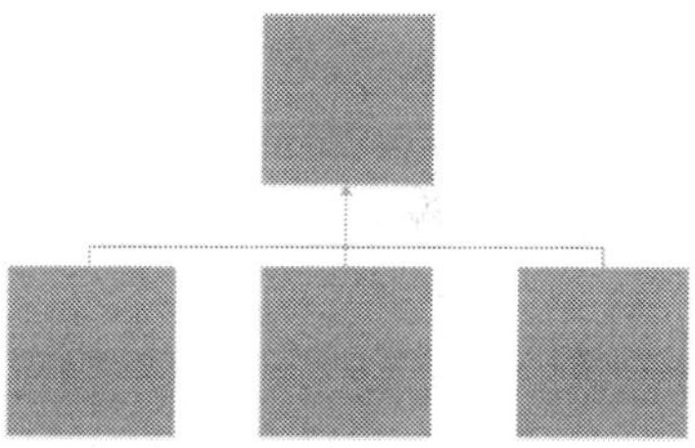

Figure 72: Figure for question

4. Figure 73 represents which of the following? (one)

   A Project builder
   B Project planning board
   C Work breakdown structure
   D **Network**

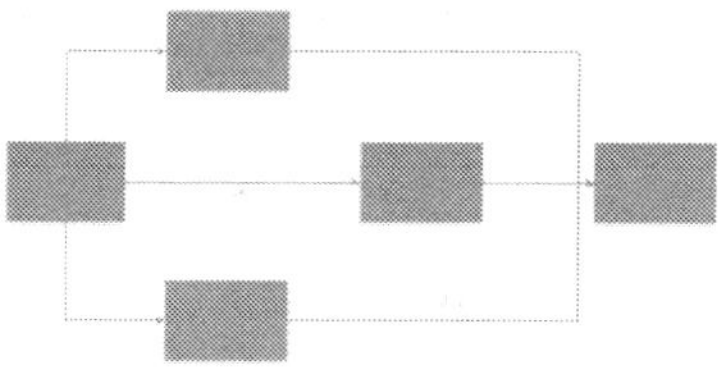

Figure 73: Figure for question

5. Define a Work Breakdown Structure.

   Answer: A WBS contains WBS Elements arranged as a hierarchical representation of a project.

6. Define Activities.

   Answer: Activities represent the work or steps that need to be accomplished to complete the project.

7. Define Networks.

   Answer: The activities of a project can be linked to one another in a precedence diagram. The precedence diagram describes the relationships (dependencies) between the activities, and the order in which they must be completed. The precedence diagram is called a Network.

8. Describe the relationship between WBS Elements and Activities.

   Answer: Activities are assigned to WBS Elements. A WBS Element may have many activities assigned to it, but an activity may only be assigned to a single WBS Element.

9. List the operative indicators for WBS Elements.

   Answer: The operative indicators include: Planning element; Account assignment element; Billing element.

10. A WBS element that has the operative indicator "Planning Element", is an element for which _______________. (one)

    A **costs are planned**
    B materials are planned
    C MRP will create planned orders
    D a G/L account is assigned

11. A WBS element that has the operative indicator, "Account Assignment", is an element for which _______________. (one)

    A costs are planned
    B **costs are posted**
    C revenues are posted
    D a G/L account is assigned

12. A WBS element that has the operative indicator, "Billing Element", is an element for which _______________. (one)

    A costs are planned
    B costs are posted
    C **revenues are posted**
    D a G/L account is assigned

13. List the functions of WBS Elements.

    Answer: WBS Elements are associated with the following functions:

    - Dates
    - Budgets

- Commitments
- Costs and revenues
- Payment information
- Period end closing

14. List the functions of Activities.

    Answer: Activities are associated with the following functions:

    - Internally processed
    - Externally processed
    - Materials
    - Costs
    - Milestones
    - Period-end closing

15. List the five phases of a project.

    The five phases of a project include:

    (a) Concept
    (b) Rough-cut
    (c) Detailed
    (d) Execution
    (e) Closing

16. Describe the concept phase of a project.

    Answer: During the concept phase of a project, the project definition is created an discussion of the project is at a very high level. No detail is present in this phase.

17. Describe the rough-cut phase of a project.

    Answer: During the rough-cut phase of a project, WBS Elements are defined at a high level. It does not include all WBS Elements that will be required for the project. Activities are not essential at the rough-cut phase, but may also be present at a high level.

18. Describe the detailed phase of a project.

    Answer: During the detailed phase of a project, all of the WBS Elements are created and included in the Work Breakdown Structure. In addition, all Activities are created, assigned to WBS Elements, and included in a Network.

19. Describe the execution phase of a project.

Answer: During the execution phase of a project, the project must be placed in released status. At that time, work on the project can be performed and the functions of WBS Elements and Activities are activated. Actual dates, costs, and revenues can be posted to the project.

20. Describe the closing phase of a project.

    Answer: During the closing phase of a project, period-end activities occur. Billing can take place and aspects of the project are settled.

21. Which of the following are functions of the Project Builder? (three)

    A **Menu navigation**
    B **Create projects**
    C **Edit projects**
    D Gantt chart navigation

22. Which of the following are functions of the Project Planning Board? (three)

    A Menu navigation
    B **Create projects**
    C **Edit projects**
    D **Gantt chart navigation**

23. Which of the following are additional graphical tools that are available in SAP Project Systems? (two)

    A Activity graphic
    B **Network graphic**
    C WBS graphic
    D **Hierarchy graphic**

24. The Hierarchy graphic can be accessed from both the Project Builder and Project Planning Board (**T**/F)

25. Which of the following are graphical overviews available in the Project Planning Board? (three)

    A Activity overview
    B **Capacity overview**
    C **Material overview**
    D **Cost overview**

26. In order to plan costs on a WBS Element, that WBS Element must be assigned the Account Assignment operative indicator. (T/F)

    Answer: False, in order to plan costs on a WBS Element, that WBS Element must be assigned the Planning operative indicator.

27. For planning costs for WBS Elements with one or more activities, costs can be planned at the activity level and rolled up to the WBS Element level. (**T**/F)

28. List two different methods for planning costs on projects in SAP.

    Answer: Overall Planning and SAP Easy Cost Planning.

29. Cost planning in projects is important because it provides the basis for _______________? (one)

    A **the budget request**
    B the budget release
    C Easy Cost Planning
    D settlement

30. Which of the following controls how the budget on a project is released? (one)

    A Budget balance
    B **Availability control**
    C Activity control
    D Easy Cost Planning

31. List two different versions of Availability Control for projects in SAP.

    Answer: Active Availability Control; Passive Availability Control

32. Describe the difference between Active Availability Control and Passive Availability Control.

    Answer: When Active Availability Control is in use, the system will generate a message when the budget has or will be exceeded. Passive Availability Control allows users to evaluate costs on the project to see if the budget has been exceeded, but it does not generate any messages.

33. Explain how costs are posted to the project using the MM Procurement process.

Answer: In MM procurement, consumable items needed for the project require an account assignment category. The user could select account assignment category "Project" or "Network". As a result, an account assignment object will be required pending the account assignment category selected. At the time of the goods receipt posting, the cost will post to the appropriate account assignment object in the project.

34. Explain how costs are posted to the project using activities.

    Answer: Activities could be internally processed or externally processed. Externally processed activities will post costs to the project using the MM Procurement process. Internally processed activities can be managed with Orders, such as Internal Order, Production Orders, or Maintenance Orders. When materials are issued to the order and/or when the order is confirmed, those costs post to the order. Since the activity can be managed with such an order, the order collects the costs which can later be settled to its WBS Element.

35. Which of the following are settlement options in projects? (two)

    A Single-level settlement
    B **Multi-level settlement**
    C **Direct settlement**
    D Indirect settlement

36. Explain the difference between direct settlement and multi-level settlement.

    Answer: If direct settlement is used in the project, all WBS Elements and Activities that need to be settled are settled directly to the receiver of the project. If multi-level settlement is used, all activities are settled to their respective WBS Elements, and the WBS Elements are settled upward in the hierarchy until everything is settled to the Project Definition. Once settlement reaches the Project Definition, it is then settled to the receiver for the project.

42980357R00156

Made in the USA
Lexington, KY
13 July 2015